School Choice Policies and Outcomes

School Choice Policies and Outcomes

Empirical and Philosophical Perspectives

Edited by

Walter Feinberg

and

Christopher Lubienski

SUNY
PRESS

Published by
State University of New York Press, Albany

For information, contact State University of New York Press, Albany, NY
www.sunypress.edu

Production by Eileen Meehan
Marketing by Anne M. Valentine

Library of Congress Cataloging-in-Publication Data

School choice and outcomes : empirical and philosophical perspectives /
    edited by Walter Feinberg and Christopher Lubienski.
        p. cm.
    Includes bibliographical references and index.
    ISBN 978-0-7914-7571-3 (hardcover : alk. paper)
    ISBN 978-0-7914-7572-0 (paperback : alk. paper)
    1. School choice—United States.   2. Education and state—United
States.   3. Educational equalization—United States.   I. Feinberg,
Walter, 1937–   II. Lubienski, Christopher.

LB1027.9.S356 2008
379.1'110973—dc22   2007050730

10 9 8 7 6 5 4 3 2 1

Contents

Acknowledgments   vii

Introduction   1
Walter Feinberg and Christopher Lubienski

1 Common Schooling and Educational Choice as a
Response to Pluralism   21
Rob Reich

2 Educational Equality and Varieties of School Choice   41
Harry Brighouse

3 Evidence, the Conservative Paradigm, and School Choice   61
Kenneth R. Howe

4 Intergenerational Justice and School Choice   79
Kathleen Knight Abowitz

5 The Politics of Parental Choice: Theory and Evidence
on Quality Information   99
Christopher Lubienski

6 Social Class Differences in School Choice: The Role of
Preferences   121
Courtney A. Bell

7 Managers of Choice: Race, Gender, and the Philosophies
of the New Urban School Leadership   149
Janelle T. Scott

8 Where Does the Power Lie Now? Devolution, Choice,
and Democracy in Schooling   177
Liz Gordon

9 Parental Choice: The Liberty Principle in Education Finance
    in Postapartheid South Africa   197
    Bekisizwe S. Ndimande

10 The Dialectic of Parent Rights and Societal Obligation:
    Constraining Educational Choice   219
    Walter Feinberg

List of Contributors   237

Index   241

Acknowledgments

This volume draws on papers presented at a conference on school choice held at the University of Illinois in Urbana in March of 2006. The conference organizers, who went on to edit this book, would like to gratefully acknowledge the generous support from the Hewlett International Conference Grants Program at the University of Illinois, as well as a grant from the Spencer Foundation. Additional support was also provided by the Agora Program, and the Departments of Education Policy Studies, Educational Organization and Leadership, and Philosophy at the University. Additional University of Illinois support was offered through the program in Arms Control, Disarmament, and International Security, the Center for Advanced Study, the Center for Global Studies, the program for Religious Studies, and the Program in Jewish Culture and Society. Colleen Vojak provided invaluable assistance in organizing the event. Jeffrey Thibert and Andrew Race assisted in preparing the papers for publication. Peter Weitzel provided editing and indexing assistance.

Introduction

Walter Feinberg and Christopher Lubienski

School Choice and Traditional School Schemes

Perhaps no school reform has generated as much interest and controversy in recent years as the simple proposal to have parents select their
children's school. On the one hand, school choice advocates believe that
state provision, oversight, and regulation stifle the creativity that they
see evident in the business world and wherever markets are to be found.
They believe that choice will create more educational innovation, reduce
inequality, and lead to a general improvement in the overall quality of
education. On the other hand, many opponents of school choice fear
that such programs will put profits before children, further advantage
the already advantaged, and reduce the unique potential of schools in
creating democratic citizens. Furthermore, they fear that scaling back
the government's role in schooling will lead to profit-driven financial
scandals as well as societal ills such as sectarianism and increased class
and racial isolation.[1]

    Why such a seemingly innocuous, commonsense idea would ig-
nite such passionate debate is a question that can best be addressed
by understanding the specific details and implications of school choice
proposals, policies, and program implementation. Since Milton Friedman
first put forward the idea of school vouchers in an otherwise obscure
essay in the 1950s, the idea has rapidly gained ground, accelerating
particularly since it was embraced by odd coalitions of liberals and
conservatives in open-enrollment plans, charter school legislation, and
voucher programs in the 1990s.[2] As of this writing, four out of every
five states have endorsed charter schools that now educate well over a
million children; a growing number of states are considering joining the

1

handful of places that already subsidize attendance in private schools through vouchers and tax credits; an estimated two million children are educated at home; and countless children enjoy access to schools that are chosen through open-enrollment schemes or by their parents' selection of a home near a desirable school. The school choice movement is quickly maturing. However, the exponential growth of the movement gives pause to critics concerned about the effects of racial and ethnic sorting, the implications for costs and achievement, and the integrity of the public school system.

The severity of opposition to school choice is proportional to the centrality that the market takes in specific proposals and programs. Unlike traditional public schooling arrangements that are based almost exclusively on residency, school choice essentially positions parents as consumers empowered to select from different options—thereby injecting a degree of consumer-driven, market-style competition into the system as schools seek to attract those families. This is a direct challenge to the public education paradigm fashioned by Horace Mann and other common school reformers in the nineteenth century. They argued that the plethora of choices at the time—church schools, private and quasi-public academies, charity schools, town schools, et cetera—was undermining the common civic values of the young republic.[3] While this thinking formed the basis of the locally-controlled district system in the United States, it has more recently been faulted by those who favor choice as a remedy to the government monopoly at the root of the educational malady, trapping disadvantaged families even while the more affluent still have the option of choosing a private school or moving to a better district. Although by no means a pure market innovation, school choice introduces essential market mechanisms, such as consumer choice and competition between schools, into the education sector. The debate around various choice plans then centers on the degree to which a particular program should be situated in the state-run regulatory apparatus. This range includes open-enrollment plans that allow selection, but only between different public schools in a district, or options set in more market-based environments, as when families are given tax funds in the form of vouchers to expand their range of options across the public and private sectors. However, it is important to note that all of the various programs and proposals evince market forces in varying manifestations. Yet, debates about the role of markets and governments no longer exist only in the abstract world of theory as was the case when Friedman first proposed the idea. Choice-based school reforms in the United States and elsewhere have established a track record with which to examine the various claims for and against school choice in its different forms.

School Choice Policies and Outcomes brings together both empirical and philosophical research on the issues, examining both the philosophical justifications for choice and the evidence on its track record as its various manifestations have evolved over the last decade. While examining choice of schools, this book focuses on what we might call formal choice programs—things such as charter schools and vouchers that represent explicit efforts by policymakers to create or expand options and opportunities in education by introducing market-style mechanisms into the education sector. This means that other forms of educational choice in the broader but more informal sense—course selection, purchasing a home in a particular school district, or even the popular homeschooling movement—fall largely outside the scope of this book. The decision to assume this focus reflects our interest in the forms of choice that have risen to the top of the political and policy agendas in the United States. Consequently, we solicited contributions from authors who represent a range of philosophical perspectives on the different varieties of formal school choice reforms, including advocates who see choice as a promising development that has the potential to improve education for all and skeptics who are more concerned about the possibility of negative ramifications of school choice programs. Furthermore, we sought scholars representing a range of disciplinary perspectives on choice, from ethicists to theorists to empiricists who could offer insights in their interpretations of the growing body of knowledge on the many choice programs in the United States and elsewhere. However, before summarizing the state of knowledge on school choice, it makes sense to review some of the main justifications for these reforms. This will allow us to understand how choice has assumed different forms in various programs and to understand the basis on which these policies are to be assessed.

School Choice and Liberty

Advocates of choice emphasize the importance of individual freedom. School choice is advanced as a form of freedom best accessed in a free marketplace.[4] In this line of thinking, public provision of education is rejected as a coercive government monopoly, often equated with the old Soviet Bloc, or illustrated by comparisons to the Berlin Wall.[5] Since markets represent free, voluntary action, market mechanisms bring freedom to the education sector. This is a particularly appealing argument when applied to disadvantaged families trapped in failing public schools. Choice is thought to offer an alternate route to education, between the inherent inequalities of local district control and the coercive constraints of centralized bureaucracies. This justification has two distinct strands:

(1) an institutional element that champions moving tax-supported schools into the private sector (what some call privatization, but what might be better termed marketization), and (2) an individualist-libertarian element best reflected in the homeschooling movement.

While some criticize choice as antidemocratic because it removes public education from direct control of elected entities, proponents argue that it is simply an alternate form of democracy.[6] That is, instead of relying on a public composed of often disinterested voters whose wishes are manifest through elected representatives and entrenched bureaucracies, choice appeals directly to a public composed of consumers—those immediately using the services. This view is advanced by a number of prominent scholars and has now received considerable traction. It is also supported by the activities of important organizations such as the Brookings Institute, and the Olin, Bradley, and Walton family foundations (see Janelle Scott, chapter 7).

Yet, imbedded in this view are some very critical assumptions that need to be examined carefully. Consider the terminology as an example: Is a school whose students raise their average test scores by fifteen points in a given year, but still do not meet a given cutoff point, a failing school? And if the students who attend the school are in a crime-ridden area, with rampant poverty and unemployment, is it the school that is failing? Possibly, but other factors are involved as well. Or, bear in mind the idea of a government monopoly in education. Is a system where thousands of different public school districts exist together competing for teachers and families the same kind of monopoly the post office once was?

In examining the merits of different choice schemes, it is critical to consider some of the intricacies buried in the assumptions behind this thinking. Indeed, the rhetoric of freedom, which classical liberals from Mill to Freidman promote, can ignore the trade-offs inherent in a complex, pluralistic society of multiple constituencies and competing claims. If a choice scheme offers more opportunities for parents to control the education of their children, does that necessarily entail the rollback of the responsibilities and prerogatives of the broader public interest in education? What about the rights and freedoms of children whose parents fail to choose, or fail to choose wisely? Or the voice of those childless individuals and couples who pay taxes and support schools but are themselves no longer direct consumers of schooling. Even the most committed libertarian might want to place limits on parental choice in order to insure that children have an opportunity to become autonomous adults.[7] Given that the liberal state has an interest in fostering autonomy, schools may sometimes need to loosen the bonds between parent and child, not to destroy the family, but to challenge generational cycles of inherited privilege, resources, and other less tangible factors that contribute to the autonomy of an individual.[8] This notion would put the idea of parental choice in a more negative light, and emphasizes the fact that government has a special role to play in the education of children and to see to it that their future autonomy is nurtured and protected. Finally, critics have argued that this consumer-driven view is a very thin conception of democracy.[9] For example, some parents complain that forced choice really destroys the neighborhood school and with it the opportunity for children to learn alongside neighbors. It is possible that this may actually have the effect of reducing the collective influence of parents on their schools, and thereby reducing the coherence of neighborhoods. While we do not know of any studies that have tested this possibility, the advocates of choice seem not to have considered it.

School Choice and Academic Achievement

Another prominent perspective holds that school choice engenders the market forces necessary to increase school efficiency and effectiveness. This view, based in neoliberal economic theory, sees a general malaise in the government-run public education sector. As articulated by public choice theorists, it is not only public funding, but subsequent government administration of schools, reflecting direct democratic control, that leads to a startling uniformity of curriculum and organization.[10] According to this line of thinking, the monopoly claim that government schools make on public funding also deprives public education of the competitive incentives needed to encourage efficient use of funds, as well as organizational effectiveness. In using school choice to animate competitive incentives, schools would be forced to improve their performance or risk losing students and funding (or go out of business) as consumers choose higher performing alternatives. As advocates often observe, these dynamics work in many consumer-oriented markets, where choices drive innovation and quality improvements.[11] In education, such improvements would appear in increased efficiency and academic achievement.

While many see such competitive forces as integral for getting schools to focus on the basic core academic function, one potential problem is that such competition around a narrowly defined role, measurable academic achievement, largely negates the many other, less tangible responsibilities we place on schools (building social cohesion, teaching marketable or critical skills, environmentally conscious citizens, health conscious consumers, etc.). Furthermore, although this view is set firmly only one of me and I didn't die in the Varner Clinic or anywhere else last Sunday. I was an aeronautical software engineer and I had never been to Columbus or heard of Center Financial Advisors much less been its President. Still, when somebody points a .45 automatic at your chest, it is hard to argue the fine points.

But I'm getting ahead of myself.

That day began normally enough. For the past two months, I had been settling into a new job as a systems designer and software engineer with Symbiotic Software in Waltham, Massachusetts. It was one of a hundred programming shops in those big, mirror-glass office buildings that dot the Route 128 Beltway around Boston. You know the kind: no hard walls, no doors, just dozens of low, pastel-colored cubicles filled with a mixed bag of grungy 20-somethings in every size, shape, color, orientation, and gender. My cubicle was like all the others, except for the cheap plastic nameplate that said "Peter E. Talbott, Senior Systems Engineer" hanging at the entrance. Inside, the wall behind my chair featured a framed poster of Eric Clapton, signed by The Man himself, ripped-off from a LA record store back in my younger and much crazier days. On the wall across from my desk hung a beautiful Air Mexico travel poster: a color shot of a beach at sunset near San Jose down on the Baja, with a thin, solitary young woman in a bikini walking away down the sand. That was where Terri and I were supposed to go that last fall, but she got sick and we never made it. Other than the simple 8" x 10" photograph of her sitting on my desk smiling up at me, the Baja beach poster was easily my most prized possession.

It was already 5:30 PM. Headset on, I stared at my big, flat-screen computer, pounding away at the keyboard, dressed in my treasured, but badly faded, Rolling Stones 1995 Voodoo Lounge World Tour T-shirt, blue jeans, and a worn-out pair of Nikes. Like the shoes, I was a tad older and more scuffed than the rest of the hired help, so clothes helped me fit in during those first awkward weeks after I moved there from LA. Anyway, I had just finished a crash project and was slowly coming back down as I listened to the last tracks of a two CD set of *Clapton's Greatest Hits.* When I really get into a problem, the building could go up in flames, and I'd never notice unless my monitor went blank.

I leaned back in my chair, eyes closed, playing air guitar riffs along with "Tears in Heaven," when a cold hand lifted one of the earpieces and whispered in my ear. "Earth to Petey, you are going to have the sub-routines done by tomorrow, aren't you?"

in a strong empirical tradition, the claims made in this regard must still be viewed largely as hypothetical. Even after well over a decade of voucher and charter programs, compelling evidence of significant achievement gains is lacking. Studies of voucher programs in Milwaukee, Cleveland, and other cities have found little or no (or even negative) effects for children using vouchers to attend private schools, or have found larger gains, but have been fiercely contested on methodological grounds.[12] Research on the more prolific charter school movement has indicated relative academic benefits from these types of schools in some states, but detriments in others; studies of national samples have not been too promising.[13] In fact, early optimism regarding the potential advantageous effects of competitive forces on academic achievement have more recently been tempered by the argument that they at least do not appear to do much harm,[14] a far cry from the panacea that was claimed earlier.[15] Moreover, on the question of efficiency, charter school advocates are now asking for additional money on par with other public schools, despite early promises of doing more with less.[16]

The lack of clear evidence for the academic benefits of choice should be surprising because up to now choice schemes like those in Milwaukee and Cleveland have operated under certain advantages. This is because choice should work best where all choosers are voluntary as they are in most choice situations in operation today. Voluntary choosers are parents who decide to choose and who might be expected to be more concerned about education. They may be perceived to be better judges of quality than similar parents who do not take advantage of choice schemes. Given this difference, we should expect students who move to choice schools to do significantly better than students who remain behind. Even though randomized field trials have attempted to control for these unobservable factors, it is far from clear that this is the case. Under the expanded choice schemes that some reformers and foundations would like, in schemes where everyone must choose, every parent would be compelled to choose. Thus, while some parents, who would have chosen even without compulsion, can be seen as voluntary choosers, those who exercise their right to choose (only because compelled to do so) can be seen as involuntary choosers. It would seem reasonable to expect that involuntary choosers will be less concerned or less knowledgeable than voluntary choosers. Given the differences between voluntary and involuntary choosers, we need to pause when considering the fact that the benefits of the present systems of voluntary choosers are unclear, when we consider claims that more choice will automatically make things better.

School Choice and Equality

A third view advocating school choice sees choice as an effective mechanism for leveling the playing field and providing more opportunities for minorities and disadvantaged children. This perspective has been embraced over the years by some prominent liberals as an innovative way to promote equality of educational opportunity and outcomes—and is a position for which we here acknowledge some affinity. Going back to the earlier writings of scholars like James Coleman, Christopher Jencks, and John Coons and Stephen Sugarman, policy analysts concerned about equity have often seen choice as a way to offer some opportunities to children who were otherwise disadvantaged in their school or home situations. More recently, this argument has been embraced by what Frank calls market populists seeking to use market forces to solve social problems.[17] This thinking is illustrated in new Democrat or third way groups (see chapter 7) such as the Progressive Policy Institute, Brookings Institute, and Education Sector.

Essentially, in this thinking, disadvantaged students are trapped in failing public schools, while more affluent families enjoy access to a wider variety of quality options. Therefore, by lowering political barriers or subsidizing costs, policies can grant disadvantaged students access to the same high quality options that others enjoy. Particularly in a context characterized by chronic racial, ethnic, and economic segregation, as in the United States or South Africa, such policies could negate the advantages that have been institutionalized in favor of the more affluent, and are thus often popular with some community activists. Furthermore, even if research raises questions as to whether or not these alternatives are necessarily superior,[18] allowing poor children to have exposure to a more academically ambitious peer group would probably be enough to justify such arrangements.

This view combines economic logic on the freedom of the marketplace with moral concerns for the least advantaged. Although we share this concern, it is important to acknowledge problems with this perspective, particularly in terms of how the economic logic tends to play out in the real world as well as in the politicized world of education policy. While some see markets as a solution, others argue that markets, as systems of individual choice, are part of the problem, so that choice may represent a more effective, less visible "sorting machine."[19] Instances of market failure in areas such as public safety, pollution control, and public health, demonstrate that the market is not always best suited for addressing certain issues that, like education, involve a strong equity concern.[20]

Moreover, the peculiar nature of public education may confound efforts to apply market models in what may fundamentally be a nonmarket enterprise.[21] For instance, as Christopher Lubienski notes in chapter 5, asymmetries of information between schools and parents can put families at a relative disadvantage, giving schools in competitive climates opportunities to select more affluent students. As in other mixed sectors, such as health care, this can encourage adverse selection where private providers avoid more costly clients, leaving them to public institutions that then risk falling into spirals of decline. Indeed, while advocates have argued that competitive incentives would force the supply side to open up additional quality opportunities for disadvantaged students, it may be that the opposite is happening instead.[22] In addition, there is the possibility that the equity concern will be hijacked, as equity-driven efforts around school choice may be co-opted by other interests pushing a more complete, profit-driven privatization agenda. In this regard, equity-driven school choice may simply represent a wedge necessary to marginalize opposition to choice in order to advance more universal, market-driven choice plans. Finally, the distinction between voluntary and compulsory choosers may have a bearing on whether choice leads to greater equity or whether it leads to complacency and acceptance of one's social and economic situation, and reduces collective scrutiny of the economic conditions of poor and working-class children

Communities and School Choice

School choice appeals to some because of the communitarian elements it exhibits. Schools can and do represent forms of communal association, and can serve as a focal point for building communities of learners, educators, and families. This is perhaps best illustrated by the charter school movement. Groups of like-minded teachers seeking to pursue a particular vision of schooling, for instance, can benefit from the charter school model.[23] Similarly, a comprehensive system of charter schools would represent small communities of preference clusters—families and teachers grouped together around particular views of education.[24] Essentially, such a system allows for diversity of preferences overall, but encourages sorting based on commonalities of preferences. This emphasizes communities of interest and worldview rather than communities based on housing and neighborhood. Indeed, research suggests that shared visions of schooling can be more effective in pursuing academic outcomes, and may help foster valuable social capital.[25] In subsidizing such a system to expand participation, according to this thinking, policymakers could realize efficiencies by reducing political conflict over the curriculum, and minimizing the bureaucratic apparatus necessary to mediate such conflict.

On the other hand, communities are defined not only by their internal focus, but also by their boundaries. That is, even an inclusive community has a degree of exclusivity in identifying who is a member and who is not. Community membership under such a model is typically self-selected, which fosters free choice, but also undercuts efforts at integration intended to counteract racial and socioeconomic sorting. This dynamic raises the question of the role of education in a democracy. If policymakers are looking simply to reduce conflict, then it might make sense to divide people up into homogenous clusters so each individual may better pursue a particular, private version of their educational preferences. However, we hold not only private goals for education, such as academic attainment and economic advancement, but also public goals, such as increased tolerance and civic cohesion.[26] Many political theorists have argued, therefore, that education is inherently a public endeavor. As Aristotle notes:

> the system of education in a state must be one and the same for all, and the provision of this system must be a matter of public action. It cannot be left, as it is at present, to private enterprise, with each parent making provision privately for his own children, and having them privately instructed as he himself thinks fit. Training for an end which is common should also itself be common.[27]

Education necessarily involves individual conceptions of possible worlds. Since such individual visions will come into conflict, those conflicts will carry over into conflicts about education.[28] But retreating from discussions due to potential conflicts does not diminish the fact that education is a public issue,[29] and providing parents with the opportunity to choose schools for their children does not erase the influence of their choice on the lives of others.

Rothstein

Choice Reconsidered

While we often hear that public education is failing, in fact, instances of school failure are concentrated largely in inner-city urban and rural areas with high concentrations of poverty. In such cases, it is not just the schools that are failing the children; instead, failure is evident across many social, economic and political institutions. Indeed, sometimes the school may be the only safe haven.[30] Although many have called for universal systems of school choice, a number of the papers in this volume indicate that such programs, if not thought through carefully, could be detrimental to some of the basic ideas of public education. For instance, universal choice would create not only voluntary choosers, but force unwilling choosers into a marketplace that they would not otherwise engage. Those most likely to benefit are those already in positions of advantage, who can use their resources and rules to protect such positions. Universal choice could also largely undercut the possibility of neighborhood schools serving geographic neighborhoods (although, admittedly, that can be a good thing in cases of residential segregation). However, even universal choice does not guarantee the availability of integrated options. In order for an integrated school to be available, people have to choose it, and there is evidence from many areas that suggest this is not always the case.

Instead, if we are to encourage choice as a policy, and if choice is actually an effective policy mechanism in creating opportunities and closing achievement gaps, many of the papers in this volume suggest that choice programs must be targeted to serve primarily disadvantaged populations. However, two important concerns need to be considered. First, many choice advocates and opponents see targeted choice as a strategic precedent for broadening acceptance of and demand for choice—a preliminary step to broader programs such as universal vouchers. As noted above, we believe such moves would have detrimental effects far outpacing claimed advantages. Therefore, policymakers embracing choice should take this possibility into account when fashioning targeted choice programs that remain targeted. Second, by virtue of being choice programs, even programs tailored to disadvantaged populations may very well fail to serve those most in need of new options, but least likely to utilize them. Past experience shows that it is the most educated and motivated who enroll in choice programs, while parents of the poorest students often forgo the opportunities offered.[31] Choice programs would have to be structured and supported in ways that do not concentrate benefits only for those who are relatively better off.

The Meaning of Choice

As Rob Reich reminds us in chapter 1, choice is more than just a term describing a recent set of educational innovations. It is a fundamental principle of democratic society and a critical component of liberal pluralism. We need choice (with a small "c") because we need diversity, and we need diversity because we value liberty. This does not settle the question, whether Choice (with a capital "C"), that is choice as a policy in which public funds are used to support private educational preferences, is ultimately a worthwhile policy. For some, we have always had choice—in the form of private and religious schools—as well as the selection of more expensive housing in better-funded neighborhood public school districts. What we have not had, and what Choice now introduces, is government support for parental preferences outside of the traditional neighborhood public school system.

While Reich does not take a stand on this issue, he argues persuasively that common ends can be served by private schools and that any school supported by public funds must have the future autonomy of the child as a primary goal. Hence, he concludes that the common school ideal can be compatible with contemporary conceptions of choice as long as common educational purposes are served and student autonomy is respected and developed. Thus, for Reich, the common school ideal can survive in either public or private schools.

Equality

Whereas Reich develops an argument for choice, broadly understood on grounds of plurality and liberty, Harry Brighouse (chapter 2) narrows the focus, arguing that the special character of educational markets requires that government support for parental choice can only be adequately justified in the service of equality. Drawing on a distinction made by Kenneth Howe (chapter 3) between equality-led reforms (i.e., reforms that view choice as a possible strategy to improve equality), and choice-led reforms (or reforms that views choice as a good in itself), Brighouse, argues that choice is good only if it functions to serve equality. Yet, unlike many who reject choice on equalitarian grounds, Brighouse points out that even neighborhood schools employ choice for those who can afford the right neighborhood. The goal then is not to oppose choice but to tame it towards equality. In the process of developing his argument, Brighouse provides a useful measure of the equity levels of different kinds of voucher plans.

While Brighouse and Howe share the same concern for equality, they differ significantly in their view that choice is likely to be an effective vehicle for achieving it. Howe's chapter is important because it documents the array of conservative foundations and think tanks that are aligned to promote choice for its own sake rather than choice for the sake of equality. He suggests that many states and the federal government are following their lead. While there is some rhetorical congruence about goals, including reducing the achievement gap, stemming de facto segregation, and the like, the conservative lens though which the data is examined has been so powerful that evidence showing no discernable effect in some areas and harm in others has been ignored. Yet, in spite of the evidence, these programs continue to grow without significant adjustments in the direction of equality.

While there are strong differences in tone between Brighouse and Howe, they both agree that if choice of any kind is to be justified, then it must serve equality, and serving equality means lowering the achievement gap, providing more opportunities, and decreasing class and racial segregation in real, not just rhetorical ways.

Choice and the Common Good

Education must take into account not only parents' right to educate their own children, and a child's right to a future of hope and opportunities, but also the rights of children not yet born onto a planet that can sustain their lives and promote hope and happiness. Kathleen Knight Abowitz (chapter 4) explores the role of school choice in promoting a sustainable environmental agenda. Abowitz is concerned that unless school choice policies and the rhetoric that supports them are modified substantially, future generations and planetary life will be harmed. She examines the choice policy in Ohio and uses it to argue that there must be constraints on the rights of families to choose an education for their children. She then explores ways in which choice systems can further environmental goals. Intergenerational needs and planetary well-being, while clearly a part of the common good, may not coincide with the desire of individual parents to maximize the good for their own children. Indeed, the commons may well be seriously hurt as a result of each of us striving to maximize the individual good or our own child without regard for the good of others.

Markets, Information and Preferences

Markets vary regarding the quality of information, its distribution and the ability of consumers to assess the information they receive. Note, for example, the difficulty many highly educated people have in choosing a health care plan. The issue of school choice then is not just a question about who cares the most, or who is the most knowledgeable about the needs of an individual child. It is also a question of information. As Christopher Lubienski notes in chapter 5, we need to consider what kinds of information may be needed, how it is distributed, who gets it, and how is it used. Chapters 6 and 7 explore these issues, taking into account the concerns of equity raised in the first section.

Lubienski explores the claim that parents are in the best position to evaluate the quality of education their child is receiving by looking at the special characteristics of information flow in educational markets. He examines both philosophical and empirical grounds for positioning parents as the exclusive authority over educational decisions, finding that the best arguments, which are largely hypothetical, break down in the real-world context of schools. Lubienski highlights evidence, from choice advocates themselves, that parents are often mistaken about the quality of schools in their areas, and that they often judge schools independently of their academic quality. He analyzes these concerns and traces them to characteristics of the educational market itself, suggesting that the issue is not whether or not parents are able to make the best decisions on behalf of their children, but whether education markets generate and distribute essential information in an equitable and effective manner. The essay concludes by providing a summary of the kind of information readily available to parents and its limitations.

Whereas Lubienski considers the flow of information and the characteristics of markets, Courtney Bell's essay (chapter 6), looks at the way in which social class factors influence the preferences that motivate parents. She raises an important challenge to simplistic theories of choice that make no distinction between the preference formed by a suburban house parent with enough time to scout out the schools in the area, for instance, and an inner-city working parent with little time to spare.

Taken together, these two essays point to serious flaws in the market analogy when used to guide educational policy, both in terms of the information generated and in information consumed. The typical market theorist has the consumer come to the market with a set of preferences that the producer attempts to satisfy in competition with other producers. Information is a mediating factor used by the consumer to decide which competitor's product will best service her need.

In contrast to this model, where preferences are formed prior to and independent of the producer, Bell shows that, in education markets, preferences are shaped by the producer as well as the consumer, and social economic class influences this formation. She shows how, in response to the input of the school, a parent's preferences undergo changes, and how this influence varies depending, in part, on social class factors. Middle-class parents, whose children fell behind, were likely to use their resources to challenge and redirect the school's expectations of their children, while poor and working-class parents found it more difficult to do so. The expectations of these parents were more frequently lowered by their interaction with the school.

Knowledge, time, skills, and confidence can make a big difference in the way parents shape their preferences in conformity or response to the school's definition of their child. As Bell writes, "parents had different resources for mediating school interaction." Educational markets are unlikely to work in an equitable way unless these different resources are taken into account, and parents who accept the school's definition of their failing child are likely to respond by blaming themselves or their child. Of course, failure need not be an inevitable consequence of lower economic and social status, but Bell's essay is a warning for simplistic advocates of educational markets. If children are to do well under choice schemes, schools will need to understand their role in the formation of parental preferences and find ways to help parents be effective advocates for their children.

Educational Leadership and Minorities

Janelle Scott shows that the move toward privatization is altering advances made by women and minorities in the 1960s and reasserting the leadership role of white males. At the same time, an educational philosophy that focuses on democracy, inclusiveness, social justice, and critical thinking has been in retreat, with the new leadership emphasizing efficiency, competition, and test scores. One of Scott's important findings is that, while the rhetoric of equality can still be found in these private initiatives, the rhetoric is not always matched by the reality. For example, to improve performance, schools may discourage more difficult students from returning. While research is needed to understand just how widespread this practice is, it should not be surprising if, in the absence of strong regulation, privately-run, publicly-financed schools behave like other enterprises in market-like settings and eliminate poor investments.

Power

One of the promises that school choice advocates make is that choice will increase the power of parents and local communities, and will thereby provide an education best tailored to meet the needs of individual children. Scott's essay raises questions about the effects of choice on school leadership and the tendency to replace women and minorities with White men. In chapter 8, Liz Gordon expands on this theme, exploring the relationship between choice and power. Gordon reminds us that school choice is a multinational movement that is expressed differently in different countries, and she draws on research in these countries—with special emphasis on New Zealand and the United States—to assess its effect. She appropriates recent philosophical and sociological works to show that power resides in more than just the political sphere. Gordon's analysis illuminates how power relations work within choice policies, and how choice alters the distribution of power by, among other things, increasing segregation between population types, maintaining hierarchies of rich and poor schools, even when resource gaps are reduced, and by rewarding desirable school communities rather than good schools. The most important factor is the ability of a group to shape the educational landscape, and, Gordon argues, middle-class families hold onto this advantage whether or not they are operating under a choice regime. Gordon makes clear other effects, including less innovation, more conformity, a reduction in regional authority, and a strengthening of the central steering mechanism.

Similarly, Bekisizwe Ndimande looks outside the United States for insights on the role of choice in power relationships. He underscores the emerging patterns surrounding opportunities for poor and Black students to attend better-resourced schools in South Africa. Ndimande juxtaposes the individual freedom to choose with the institutional autonomy of wealthier public schools to adopt policies that essentially exclude poorer students. He suggests that demands for options are insufficient when expressed in the context of power relations of social class. If those seeking expanded options are poor, then more desirable educational organizations may seek to exclude, rather than accommodate them. In fact, institutions do not simply respond to accommodate consumer demand. Ndimande situates issues of resources and access within the larger neoliberal emphasis on privatization, and within the neoconservative effort to undermine diversity and multiculturalism.

Rights and Obligations

In chapter 8, Liz Gordon observes that advocates of choice have been successful because they associate choice policies with private initiatives and contrast them to more public forms of schooling—which are then associated with bureaucratic lethargy. She questions this by reminding us of the dynamic role schools often play in the life of a community, a role choice tends to eviscerate by disempowering teachers and directing attention away from the social and economic causes of success and failure.

In chapter 10, Walter Feinberg examines the normative side of choice, and explores the basic principle—that parents have a right to determine the education of their children—that makes the idea appealing to many different groups. He argues that this principle needs to be reconciled with another, seemingly competing one—the obligation of society to provide a level educational playing field for all children. Feinberg believes these principles can be reconciled if we begin to unpack the public and private distinctions they entail.

Feinberg distinguishes between choice on the retail level and choice on the wholesale level and shows the problems that arise from confusing the two. He argues education cannot be reduced to market considerations alone, and that choice on the wholesale level must be evaluated with the ideals of a fair and equitable social system in mind. He explains how the presence of private schools create problems for proposals that want to use choice to advance equality, and suggests ways in which these two principles can be reconciled by reconceptualizing the idea of public and private schools. Feinberg argues that a fair, sound policy must consider the multiple interests involved in the education of the young. These include interests of advantaged parents to advantage their own children, the interests of disadvantaged parents not to reproduce their disadvantages in their own children, the interest of society in maintaining solidarity and enhancing the quality of life by the fair and impartial selection and development of talent, and the rights of children to an open future. He argues that these interests can be balanced by rethinking the way in which education is supported, and by providing incentives for advancing public goods such as inclusion and democratic accountability.

Conclusion

The history of education is full of failed panaceas. On the one hand, the idea of choice seems to dampen this utopian spirit and introduce a necessary dose of realism into the educational debate. It allows that children are very different from one another and that parents want many different kinds of things from their children's schools. The idea is simple: allow parents to choose the school their children will attend and make that choice easier. If parents are unsatisfied with the child's school, they should not be required to buy a house in a new neighborhood to find a more satisfying educational experience. It is very difficult to argue with this reasoning. It makes intuitive sense. Most parents would like the right to move their children out of failing schools and into better ones. Yet choice, as it has been advanced, promises much more than a satisfactory educational experience for all children. It promises greater equality, more innovation, more effective parent control, less bureaucracy, higher efficiency, et cetera. In other words, it is offered not just as a solution to the extreme dissatisfaction of some parents, but as a panacea to cure all of the problems of American schools. Granted, as its advocates will argue, choice is relatively young and the idea is still growing. But we have yet to see the research that suggests wholesale choice is likely to live up to all of these claims. In the meantime, it is important to remember that American schools, public and private, exist in a context of growing inequality in many areas—health care, housing, mental health, income, and that all of these influence the state of education.

Notes

1. Jabeen Bhatti, "Felon works as chief of DC charter school: Criminal record dates back to 1987," *The Washington Times,* May 22, 2003, A1; Edd Doerr, "Vouchers fragment school populations," *Education Week* 19, no. 44, 45 (March 8, 2000); Thomas W. Goodhue, "Religious school vouchers: A one-way ticket to northern Ireland's troubles," *Church & State* 51, no. 21 (March 1998); Rethinking Schools, "No comment," *Rethinking Schools* 16, no. 21 (Summer 2002); P. Walsh-Sarnecki, "School's pupil count, curriculum questioned" *Detroit Free Press,* March 9, 2000, http://www.freep.com/news/education/school2009_20000309.htm (accessed March 14, 2000).

2. Milton Friedman, "The Role of Government in Education," in *Economics and the Public Interest,* ed. R. A. Solo 127–34 (New Brunswick, NJ: Rutgers University Press, 1955).

3. Christopher Lubienski, "Redefining 'Public' Education: Charter Schools, Common Schools, and the Rhetoric of Reform," *Teachers College Record* 103, no. 4 (2001): 634–66.

4. Milton Friedman, *Capitalism and freedom* (Chicago: University of Chicago Press, 1962).

5. Theodore J. Forstmann, "A Competitive Vision for American Education," *Imprimis* 28, no. 9 (1999); Milton Friedman, "The Case for Choice," in *Voices On Choice: The Education Reform Debate,* ed. Kenneth L. Billingsley, 91–101 (San Francisco: Pacific Research Institute for Public Policy, 1994); Milton Friedman, *Public Schools: Make Them Private,* Briefing Paper No. 23 (Washington, DC: Cato Institute, 1995); Adam Meyerson, "Education's Evil Empire," *Policy Review* (January/February 1999); Tom Tancredo, *Education Vouchers: America Can't Afford to Wait* (Golden, CO: Independence Institute, 1991); "Turning Schools Right Side Up," *Wall Street Journal,* November 16, 1999, A30.

6. John E. Chubb and Terry M. Moe, *Politics, Markets, and America's Schools* (Washington, DC: Brookings Institution, 1990).

7. Harry Brighouse, "Two Philosophical Errors Concerning School Choice," *Oxford Review of Education* 23, no. 4 (1997): 503–10; David H. Hargreaves, "School Choice and the Development of Autonomy: A Reply to Brighouse," *Oxford Review of Education* 23, no. 4 (1997): 511–15.

8. See Rob Reich's chapter in this volume; see also Lubienski, "Redefining 'Public' Education"; Christopher Lubienski, "A Critical View of Home Education," *Evaluation and Research in Education* 17, no. 2/3 (2003): 167–78.

9. Benjamin R. Barber, *Strong democracy: Participatory politics for a new age,* rev. ed. (Berkeley: University of California Press, 2004).

10. Chubb and Moe, *Politics, Markets, and America's Schools*; Paul E. Peterson, "Monopoly and Competition in American Education," in *Choice and Control in American Education: The Theory of Choice and Control in Education*, vol. 1, ed. William H. Clune and John F. Witte, 47–78 (London: Falmer Press, 1990).

11. Andrew. J. Coulson, *Market Education: The Unknown History* (New Brunswick, NJ: Transaction Publishers, 1999); Joe Nathan, *Charter Schools: Creating Hope and Opportunity for American Education* (San Francisco: Jossey-Bass, 1996).

12. Clive R. Belfield, *The Evidence on Education Vouchers: An Application to the Cleveland Scholarship and Tutoring Program*, Occasional Paper No. 112 (New York: National Center for the Study of Privatization in Education, 2006); Jay P. Greene, Paul E. Peterson, and Jiangtao Du, "Effectiveness of School Choice: The Milwaukee Experiment," *Education and Urban Society* 31, no. 2 (1999): 190–213; Alan B. Krueger and Pei Zhu, "Another Look at the New York City School Voucher Experiment," *American Behavioral Scientist* 47, no. 5 (2004): 658–98; Kim K. Metcalf, "Commentary—Advocacy in the Guise of Science: How Preliminary Research on the Cleveland Voucher Program Was 'Reanalyzed' to Fit a Preconception," *Education Week* 18 (September 23, 1998): 34, 39; Paul E. Peterson and William G. Howell, "Efficiency, Bias, and Classification Schemes: A Response to Alan B. Krueger and Pei Zhu," *American Behavioral Scientist* 47, no. 5 (2004): 699–717; C. Rouse, *Schools and Student Achievement: More Evidence from the Milwaukee Parental Choice Program* (Princeton University and the National Bureau of Economic Research, 1998); Cecilia E. Rouse, "Private School Vouchers and Student Achievement: An Evaluation of the Milwaukee Parental Choice Program," *Quarterly Journal of Economics* 113, no. 2 (1998): 553–603; John F. Witte, *The Market Approach to Education: An Analysis of America's First Voucher Program* (Princeton, NJ: Princeton University Press, 2000).

13. Henry Braun, Frank Jenkins, and Wendy Grigg, *A Closer Look at Charter Schools Using Hierarchical Linear Modeling* (No. NCES 2006–460) (Washington, DC: National Center for Education Statistics, 2006); Caroline M. Hoxby and Jonah E. Rockoff, *The Impact of Charter Schools on Student Achievement: A Study of Students Who Attend Schools Chartered by the Chicago Charter School Foundation* (Cambridge, MA: Department of Economics, Harvard University, 2004); Christopher Lubienski and Sarah Theule Lubienski, *Charter, Private, Public Schools and Academic Achievement: New Evidence from NAEP Mathematics Data*, Occasional Paper No. 111 (New York: National Center for the Study of Privatization in Education, 2006); Gary Miron and Jerry Horn, *Evaluation of Connecticut Charter Schools and the Charter School Initiative* (Kalamazoo, MI: Evaluation Center, Western Michigan University, 2002); Gary Miron and Christopher Nelson, *What's Public about Charter Schools? Lessons Learned about Choice and Accountability* (Thousand Oaks, CA: Corwin Press, 2002); Gary Miron, Christopher Nelson, and John Risley, *Strengthening Pennsylvania's Charter School Reform: Findings from the Statewide Evaluation and Discussion of*

Relevant Policy Issues, Year 5 Report (Kalamazoo, MI: Evaluation Center, Western Michigan University, 2002); F. Howard Nelson, Bella Rosenberg, and Nancy Van Meter, *Charter School Achievement on the 2003 National Assessment of Educational Progress* (Washington, DC: American Federation of Teachers, 2004).

14. Jay P. Greene, *A Survey of Results from Voucher Experiments: Where We Are and What We Know* (Civic Report No. 11) (New York: Center for Civic Innovation, Manhattan Institute, 2000).

15. Chubb and Moe, *Politics, Markets, and America's Schools*.

16. Thomas B. Fordham Institute, *Charter School Funding: Inequity's Next Frontier* (Washington, DC: Thomas B. Fordham Institute, 2005).

17. Thomas Frank, *One Market under God: Extreme Capitalism, Market Populism, and the End of Economic Democracy*, 1st ed. (New York: Doubleday, 2000).

18. See for example, Braun, Jenkins, and Grigg, *A Closer Look at Charter Schools Using Hierarchical Linear Modeling*; Sarah Theule Lubienski and Christopher Lubienski, "School Sector and Academic Achievement: A Multi-Level Analysis of NAEP Mathematics Data," *American Educational Research Journal* 43, no. 4 (2006): 651–98.

19. Donald Moore and Susan Davenport, "School Choice: The New Improved Sorting Machine," in *Choice in Education: Potential and Problems*, ed. William Lowe Boyd and Herbert J. Walberg, 187–223 (Berkeley: McCutchan, 1990).

20. Robert Kuttner, *Everything for Sale: The Virtues and Limits of Markets* (New York: University of Chicago Press, 1999).

21. Christopher Lubienski, "School Diversification in Second-best Education Markets: International Evidence and Conflicting Theories of Change," *Educational Policy* 20, no. 2 (2006): 323–44.

22. Christopher Lubienski, "School Choice as a Civil Right: District Responses to Competition and Equal Educational Opportunity," *Equity & Excellence in Education* 38, no. 4 (2005): 331–41.

23. Joe Nathan, *Charter Schools: Creating Hope and Opportunity for American Education* (San Francisco, CA: Jossey-Bass, 1996).

24. John E. Brandl, "Governance and Educational Quality," in *Learning from School Choice*, ed. Paul E. Peterson and Bryan C. Hassel (Washington, DC: Brookings Institution Press, 1998).

25. Anthony S. Bryk, Valerie E. Lee, and Peter B. Holland, *Catholic Schools and the Common Good* (Cambridge, MA: Harvard University Press, 1993); Chubb and Moe, *Politics, Markets, and America's Schools*.

26. David F. Labaree, "Public Goods, Private Goods: The American Struggle over Educational Goals," *American Educational Research Journal* 34, no. 1 (1997): 39–81; David F. Labaree, "No Exit: Public Education as an Inescapably Public Good," in *Reconstructing the Common Good in Education: Coping with Intractable American Dilemmas*, ed. Larry Cuban and Dorothy Shipps (Stanford, CA: Stanford University Press, 2000).

27. Aristotle, *The Politics of Aristotle*, trans. Ernest Barker (Oxford: Clarendon Press, 1946), 332–33.

28. See Lawrence Arthur Cremin, *Popular Education and Its Discontents* (New York: Harper and Row, 1990).

29. Labaree, "No exit."

30. Alex Kotlowitz, *There Are No Children Here: The Story of Two Boys Growing Up in the Other America* (New York: Anchor, 1991).

31. John F. Witte, *The Market Approach to Education: An Analysis of America's First Voucher Program* (Princeton, NJ: Princeton University Press, 2000).

Chapter 1

Common Schooling
and Educational Choice
as a Response to Pluralism

Rob Reich

The common school ideal is the source of one of the oldest educational debates in liberal democratic societies.[1] The movement in favor of greater educational choice, is the source of one of the most recent. Each has been the cause of major and enduring controversy, not only within philosophical thought but also within political, legal and social arenas. This chapter explores the tensions between the aspiration for common schools and the aspiration for educational choice.

My purpose is to forward two arguments. First, common schooling and educational choice cannot be properly understood without reference to the normative significance of pluralism within a society. Second, once we understand the relationship between educational choice and pluralism, we can reconcile the two aspirations and discern what I shall call the liberty argument in favor of choice.

Because school choice is the guiding theme of this volume, it may help to situate my liberty argument in light of this particular theme. There are many possible reasons to support educational choice; elsewhere in this volume arguments in favor of school choice are produced on the basis of equality[2] and economists routinely invoke efficiency as a reason to support choice-based markets in education.[3] Today, the equality and efficiency arguments have a virtual monopoly on the attention of policymakers and pundits. This is unfortunate, for it is my contention that the legitimacy of school choice is founded in liberty.

Permitting parents to select a school for their children is crucial to respecting the liberty interests of parents. To be more specific, liberal societies must protect some version of school choice because the normative significance of pluralism requires the state to respect the liberty interests of parents to rear their children in some rough accordance with their deepest ethical or religious convictions. This is not to argue that the state must always and everywhere respect the educational preferences of parents; state regulations on all schools and limitations on the educational preferences of parents in order to secure what is valuable in the common school ideal are indeed warranted. My point is simpler: a liberal state acts unjustly if it prohibits parents from any choice in the assignment of their children to a school. In short, the moral foundation of educational choice in a liberal society characterized by pluralism can be located in the liberty interests of parents.

It is important to explain at the outset my understanding of what educational choice entails. As a descriptive matter, the United States already has a version of school choice. Parents choose a school for their children when they choose what school district in which to live. Public school choice is a fact of life, insofar as it is exercised in the residential choices of families. When the differences in public school quality among cities and towns are large, as is often the case in the United States, school choice as residential choice is impossible to overlook. Its exercise is most clearly enjoyed by the relatively wealthy, who have the means to reside in localities that have high spending preferences for public schools. This fact is what fuels many equality-based arguments in favor of school choice.

However, here I pursue a more expansive understanding of educational choice. I assume educational choice to indicate the permissibility of parents to enroll their child in a public, private, or religious school, or to homeschool their child. Do parents have available choices in school assignment that go beyond publicly-funded and managed schools, regardless of whether their child would be assigned to such a school on the basis of residence or whether parents can choose from among some set of public schools? Can parents educate their child in a private, religious, or home school? If so, then educational choice exists. I do not make any assumptions or arguments here about whether educational choice, so defined, requires public funding of the schools parents choose. My interest is in establishing the reason why educational choice must be defended, not in presenting arguments about how private, religious, or home schools should be funded. The financing of a school choice scheme is a secondary matter, to be settled only after the legitimacy of school choice itself has been settled.

The relationship between common schooling and educational choice might appear to be simple. Does educational choice lead to the creation and perpetuation of separate schools? If so, then choice conflicts with common schooling. If not, then choice and common schooling can coexist. But this appearance is misleading, for how we view the relationship and assess the weight of each aspiration depends on something external to each. In particular, it depends on the normative significance we attach to the fact of pluralism, by which I mean the existence of ethical and religious diversity in a society. Whether or not we see common schooling and educational choice as in fundamental tension, merely compatible or mutually reinforcing, turns on how we interpret the normative implications of pluralism.

This chapter proceeds in four parts. In part one, I explain why we need to understand pluralism in order to understand common schooling and school choice. In the second and third parts, I explore the normative significance of pluralism for common schooling and educational choice, respectively. In the fourth part, I show how a proper appreciation of the normative significance of pluralism delivers a reconciliation of common schooling and educational choice and, therefore, a defense of educational choice. I then illustrate the liberty argument in favor of choice through a seminal United States Supreme Court decision, *Pierce v. Society of Sisters* (1925).[4] Within the American context, *Pierce* represents the legal warrant and provides the moral justification, parallel to my argument, for educational choice.

I begin, however, with a cautionary note. Little about the justice of either common schooling or educational choice can be settled decisively at the level of philosophical theory or principle. This is so for two reasons. First, the practice of schooling rests inevitably within particular social settings and historical traditions where the institutional structure of schooling reflects the community of which it is a part. Authority over education in the United States, for instance, is far more localized than in most other countries. Second, philosophy does not furnish a complete educational blueprint for all educational practice. At best, philosophy can provide a theoretical framework that shapes the making of policy and the particulars of practice. For these reasons, my goal here is not to spell out what happens when we combine common schooling with educational choice but rather to map out the key philosophical considerations involved in determining whether the ideals are reconcilable, and to provide an argument to show how they are.

The Fact of Pluralism

Pluralism is a sociological fact in liberal societies. The natural outcome of the use of human reason within free political and social institutions is a multiplicity of values and ways of life. People will be divided by their adherence to a diversity of religious and ethical doctrines that differ in their understanding of what constitutes a good life. As a result, liberal societies house citizenries divided by religious and philosophical traditions which are sometimes in conflict or even incompatible. It is the distinguishing feature of liberal societies that they attempt to secure the legitimacy and stability of political institutions amidst such pluralism. Indeed, many interpret the rise of liberalism as a response to pluralism, specifically religious diversity.

How then is the fact of pluralism related to common schooling and educational choice? Quite simply, both represent a response to cope with the political complications that arise in a pluralistic society. Let's start with common schooling. The movement to create common schools arose in the mid-nineteenth century in the United States as an effort to instill in diverse citizens a set of common values and allegiances in order to forge an *unum* from the *pluribus*. Common schools would be the vehicle in which children of all groups would be educated for democratic citizenship, in which the social cement of national identity would be laid. At times, the movement to create common schooling was unjustly oppressive of diversity because its leaders understood citizenship and nationalism in narrowly ethnic terms. But history also provides examples of common school defenders with views of citizenship and nationalism that are civic rather than ethnic. Consider, for instance, John Dewey's aspiration for the American common school:

> The intermingling in the school of youth of different races, differing religions, and unlike customs creates for all a new and broader environment. . . . The assimilative force of the American public school is eloquent testimony to the efficacy of the common and balanced appeal.[5]

The fact of pluralism, in short, makes the common school necessary in that the schoolhouse is perhaps the best vehicle available to the state to unite a diverse citizenry under common ideals and to help forge a common national identity.

If the ideal of common schooling represents an effort to respond to and shape the diversity that attends a pluralist society, the movement for educational choice must be equally understood as a response to pluralism. But rather than an effort to shape diversity, school choice represents the appropriate accommodation to such diversity. If the liberal state must refrain from compelling uniform convergence on a single set of values or one way of life, it ought to respect diverse approaches to raising children rooted in particular ways of life. Educational choice is thought to be warranted because the fact of pluralism requires that parents and communities be permitted to create schools that accord with their own values and ends. Forcing all students to attend common schools not only fails to respect the choices of parents who wish for particularistic school environments, it also runs the risk of sowing the seeds of discord in the populace. Consider, for example, the view offered by U.S. Supreme Court Justice Robert Jackson: "Probably no deeper division of our people could proceed from any provocation than from finding it necessary to choose what doctrine and whose program public educational officials shall compel youth to unite in embracing."[6] School choice, in short, is an effort, in keeping with liberal principles, that seeks to accommodate parents and groups with diverse convictions.

On this view, there seems to be an ineradicable tension between common schooling and educational choice. Efforts to inculcate common values in common schools run headstrong into efforts to respect and accommodate the diverse convictions of citizens. But must it be so? In the next sections, I examine the normative significance of the fact of pluralism for common schooling and educational choice as a prelude to showing how they can be reconciled.

Common Schools and the Normative Significance of Pluralism

Historically, the movement to establish common schooling was driven by the task of creating citizens. Early proponents of common schooling hoped through schooling to produce a unified citizenry capable of democratic self-governance. Advocates such as Thomas Jefferson, for instance, thought common schools were a prerequisite for safeguarding individual and collective liberties. "It is an axiom in my mind," Jefferson wrote to George Washington in 1786, "that our liberty can never be safe but in the hands of the people themselves, and that too of the people with a certain degree of instruction. This it is the business of the state to effect, and on a general plan."[7] Later proponents, such as Horace Mann, thought common schools were necessary not only for the general diffusion of knowledge but for the transmission of common virtues amongst an increasingly diverse populace. Schools would serve to educate children from all religious and class backgrounds, including the many newcomers to American soil, and to inculcate in them civic virtues and allegiances. The common school crusaders of the mid-nineteenth century were heavily motivated by a religious ethic, however, and they understood civic virtue to be infused with Protestant Christianity. This orientation was naturally felt to be oppressive by the increasing number of Catholics in the United States, and led to monumental struggles which culminated in the creation of a separate Catholic school system.[8] Charles Glenn has shown that the common school movements in France and the Netherlands were similarly oppressive.[9] As common schooling became established as a necessary vehicle for creating intelligent and loyal citizens from a diverse populace, it was an ideal that intertwined civic virtue with religious and ethnic allegiances. This is the historical record. It is worth recounting because it registers the intellectual roots connecting the common school ideal with citizenship and the actual institutional practices that tended to impose a dominant cultural matrix on religious and ethnic minorities.

I turn now to contemporary philosophers, who do not advocate that common schooling be cast in narrowly religious or ethnic terms. Yet, debates among liberal theorists reveal how common schooling is still understood as a response to pluralism. Consider two approaches that interpret the normative significance of pluralism in different ways, each flawed.

Take first John Rawls's defense of political liberalism, in which the aim of the state is to secure political agreement about fundamental principles of justice while remaining neutral to the reasonable but sometimes clashing and incompatible worldviews professed and lived by citizens. Here the existence of pluralism constrains what the liberal state can do in order to establish social unity; it may not seek to unite people under any one religious, philosophical, or moral doctrine. Therefore, according to Rawls, "Society's concern with [children's] education lies in their role as future citizens . . . ," not in shaping their private identities, values, or allegiances.[10] For Rawls, this implies that schools are common insofar as they all attempt to foster in children the political virtues of democratic citizenship. But they should not go beyond this. Common schools must instill a common political morality but leave private belief alone. In this vision of liberal society, because the state cannot endorse any particular comprehensive religious or moral doctrine, schools are authorized to cultivate a wide set of political virtues but must forbear from shaping the nonpublic identities of children and refrain from imposing any view of the good life on them.

This sharp demarcation between shaping public identities while leaving private identities alone is both impossible and undesirable. It is impossible because education can never be morally neutral to private life. Decisions about even such mundane matters as coeducation, or the identification of a language of instruction and school holidays, transmit the importance of certain pervasive values (e.g., the equality of the sexes and the religious traditions worthy of public recognition). Moreover, the inculcation of political virtues such as political autonomy and reasonableness cannot be accomplished without making it possible for these to be activated in a child's private life; teaching only political virtues in common schools cannot avoid spillover effects.[11] These virtues require associated skills and habits such as rational reflection and evaluation, open-minded toleration of competing viewpoints, and a willingness to engage in collective deliberation, which possess alone, and more strongly in combination, a transformative potential for the various private affiliations and allegiances of individuals. Because pluralism must be shaped in light of important civic purposes, such as the achievement of justice and the development of public reason in order to ensure the endurance of equality and freedom that make respect for diversity possible, it follows that the liberal state should not seek to be neutral in aim or outcome. Hence, the liberal state cannot and should not leave private belief untouched to the extent that Rawls suggests.

Another prominent strand of liberal theory takes the protection of diversity as the primary aim of the liberal state. William Galston, for instance, defends the "Diversity State," which "afford[s] maximum feasible space for the enactment of individual and group differences, constrained only by the requirements of liberal social unity."[12] For those to whom diversity is paramount, the fact of pluralism becomes the central point of departure for the liberal state, and these requirements of social unity are comparatively minor and unburdensome. On many such views, social unity can be achieved when public institutions convey the importance of law-abidingness and tolerance. Thus, Galston accepts the importance of a common civic education, but its aim is only to foster "social rationality," or the ability to participate in the main social and economic institutions of society. The promotion of autonomy or political virtues such as reasonableness are seen unduly to constrain diversity because they valorize choice making, critical thinking, and secular rationality. So long as children learn to tolerate their diverse fellow citizens and learn social but not secular rationality, schools have no warrant to teach children anything that threatens to interfere with or undermine diversity. In this vision of liberal society, common schooling is necessary, but its program of civic education is purposefully thin in order to allow maximum space for the flourishing of diversity.

But a vision of liberal society and common schooling put at the service of deep diversity fails for two reasons. First, when maximum feasible accommodation of diversity is the goal, the content of common civic education must be reduced to the lowest common denominator of what citizens can agree upon. This strategy may seem attractive inasmuch as it eliminates anything considered controversial, but as Eamonn Callan argues, it effectively undercuts any argument for common schooling at all.[13] If the content of common schooling is little more than tolerance and law-abidingness, few if any citizens will be motivated to send children to such schools because they will fail to teach anything even remotely approaching their most valued convictions. Second, it fails because a threadbare conception of common civic education neglects the independent interests of children in developing into autonomous persons. The arguments in favor of autonomy are varied,[14] but the essential point is that the exercise of autonomy is necessary in the political domain in order to establish legitimate and free consent to principles of justice. Autonomy also makes it possible for a child to exit a way of life and thereby precludes the inculcation of ethical servility to one's parents or ethnocultural group.

Political liberals, such as Rawls, interpret the normative significance of pluralism as necessitating a kind of liberal neutrality which restricts the pursuit of common educational goals to the political domain. Liberals such as Galston, who identify the protection of diversity as the primary purpose of the state, assign greater weight to the normative significance of pluralism. They abjure the cultivation of political autonomy, secular reason, and related political virtues in schools. Each view insists upon an important role for a common education, but the breadth of this education is circumscribed by the respective importance attached to diversity. Each view is also mistaken: first because political liberalism bleeds inevitably into the realm of the private and must engage anyway in a transformative educational project supportive of liberal democratic citizenship; and second because maximal space for diversity means an anodyne educational environment that will attract no one and because the protection of diversity should not take precedence over the interests of children in their prospective autonomy.

How then should we interpret the normative significance of pluralism for the common school ideal? First, theorists must acknowledge that invocations of common schooling have to contend with the past use of common schools to subjugate and coercively assimilate minority populations. The frequent result of such uses was not only social discord but, ironically, the stimulation of a separate system of schooling, as with the Catholic school system in the United States. Common schooling must be sufficiently responsive to the scope of diversity so that it does not impose upon children a sectarian or ethnic conception of education. The task of the common school is not to overcome pluralism, but to shape it in light of public purposes.

Second, our consideration of both political liberals and promoters of diversity helps to illuminate an absolutely fundamental aspect of the common school. Within a liberal pluralist society, the common school ideal is distinctive not for its structural features but for its substantive educational ethos and aspirations. By this I mean that common schools are not necessarily schools whose funding is exclusively public or whose admission criteria are open to all. They are schools which might be privately funded or might welcome only some particular students but which pursue a conception of common education without regard to students' or their parents' ways of life. That a privately funded school might be considered common can be seen in the example of the contemporary state of Catholic schools in the United States. Many urban Catholic schools not only appear to achieve considerable success in civic outcomes but also admit students without considering their religious background.[15] Conversely, many publicly funded schools can hardly be said to deliver anything associated with the common school ideal. Consider the educational system in Israel, in which at least four separate systems of schooling are publicly supported, included the schools of the Ultra-Orthodox Jews, which are as good an instance of separate schooling as one is likely to find. That a school which limited admission to particular students might be considered common can be seen in the various and legitimate attempts to carve out forms of restrictive schools designed only for some students. Some schools pursue common educational goals but restrict entry in order to overcome certain forms of disadvantage. Consider, for instance, schools for disabled or ill children where teachers have special training and resources, or all-girls academies whose rationale is to promote science and math achievement more effectively. Arguments might be made to show that disabled children and girls are better off when schooled with all other students. But the point is that common schooling is consistent with separating students, so long as the separation is done for reasons that accord with liberal justice.

What is fundamental to the common school ideal, then, is not its structure but its substance. A common school is marked by an educational environment that is open to ethical and cultural diversity and by a commitment to common educational goals. These common educational goals are twofold. First, schools are responsible for a civic education that teaches children what they need to know in order to be free and equal citizens in a pluralist liberal society. It is not my purpose here to settle the scope and depth of civic education. My point is only to insist, as Terry McLaughlin has put it, that "The common school has an obligation to 'transmit' the basis or non-negotiable norms which constitute the framework of a liberal democratic society,"[16] however one understands these norms. Second, as a matter of justice, schools owe children an autonomy-promoting education. Independent of a state's interest in civic education, common schools that expose children to and engage children with cultural and ethical diversity are important in cultivating autonomy.

Educational Choice and the Normative Significance of Pluralism

The fact of pluralism provides both the inspiration for and limits to common schooling. The need for a unifying civic education must be carefully balanced against an unjust oppression of the diverse convictions of citizens. To understand the normative significance of pluralism for educational choice, consider once again two different views, each flawed.

One school of thought holds parental choice to be inimical to the development of citizenship and the interest of children in autonomy. Bruce Ackerman, for instance, rejects vouchers out of hand because "most parents will refuse to spend 'their' vouchers on anything but 'education' that strives to reinforce whatever values they have . . . imposed on their children during infancy," and that vouchers would legitimate "a series of petty tyrannies in which like-minded parents club together to force-feed their children without restraint."[17] Meira Levinson's argument about the demands of liberal education are similar, concluding that schools must be detached from parental and local control, and that all forms of religious schools in the United States and Britain should be closed because they are organized around divisive conceptions of the good.[18] She also says that state regulation should be used to make private schools indistinguishable from public schools. Levinson endorses limited educational choice (among schools of different sizes and varying pedagogical approaches), but because schools cannot embody a particularistic ethos, it is choice that has virtually nothing to do with responding to the fact of pluralism. For Ackerman and Levinson, the deference accorded to the diverse convictions of parents concerning the best education for their children is small indeed.

But this is a cramped view of educational choice, for it is both unfairly dismissive and unduly suspicious of parents' interests in the education of their children. On the one hand, it fails to register the legitimate interests that parents have. Surely parents have some claim to influence the educational environment of their children, to be involved with their schooling, and to expect that schools will provide reinforcement for at least some portion of the child's home environment. It cannot be the function of schooling to oppose parental convictions at every turn; such an experience will only produce wanton moral confusion and rootlessness in children. On the other hand, the Ackerman and Levinson view assumes that, given the opportunity, all or most parents will seek to shield their children from anything except their own moral or religious universe. To be sure, some parents will do so, but how many is an empirical question and the existence of some should not rule out the possibility that others may choose schools on the basis of values fully consonant with liberal democratic citizenship. (Indeed, school choice experiments in the United States indicate that most parents seek an education for their children that will offer a stronger chance for academic achievement.) Regardless of the empirical matter, however, the point is that the existence of state interests in common schooling provide no reason to ignore parental preferences. Authority over schooling is properly shared between parents and the state,[19] and that shared authority is not inconsistent with an educational choice plan responsive to parental preferences.

For a polar opposite view, take the position of legal scholar Michael McConnell. McConnell is an ardent proponent of school choice, or as he calls it, educational disestablishment. His argument rests on the claim that educational choice is required in order to maintain a free and liberal society in the face of wide cultural and religious diversity. He fears what John Stuart Mill worried about with respect to state-provided and regulated schooling: the imposition of a standardized uniformity on children that runs counter to liberal values supportive of diversity. Moreover, citing the battles between Catholics and the Protestantism of the American common school founders and contemporary strife between devout religious believers who see in public schools nothing but rampant secular humanism, McConnell says that common schooling sows the seeds of social unrest. Thus McConnell believes that a liberal pluralist society should organize education along pluralist lines, permitting parents to choose from a marketplace of educational options, including state, private, religious schools, and homeschooling. For McConnell the deference to be paid to the diverse convictions of parents is vast, constrained only by "basic requirements of educational quality, and perhaps of minimal civic responsibility."[20]

However, rather than asserting that parents possess natural or legal rights of some sort to direct the upbringing of their children in accordance with their own understanding of the good, he thinks that citizenship and democratic values are not only consistent with but are best served by educational choice. In an interesting twist on the usual line of argument, pluralism not only requires educational choice, but so too does the transmission of democratic citizenship. It is as if a greater number of diverse schools signals for McConnell a corresponding increase in civic health. If this is true, McConnell's argument undercuts one significant foundation of the common school ideal.

In developing his argument, McConnell makes three important claims. First, he endorses a minimalist set of political virtues that citizens need in a liberal democratic society: literacy and numeracy, a rudimentary understanding of history, and a tolerant live-and-let-live attitude. Second, he says that democratic citizenship requires a moral and spiritual underpinning, a coherent rather than disjointed worldview. And third, he appeals to empirical research indicating that public schools are flooded by a moral tidal wave of consumerism and materialism and that nonpublic schools foster comparatively higher rates of civic participation, voting, and community service.

Even assuming these were true, however, the common school ideal with its attendant conception of common education would retain some force insofar as McConnell's argument does not address the child's independent interest in an autonomy-promoting education. Were educational choice to result in autonomy-undermining school environments, we would still have to weigh this result against the civic benefits of choice. But leaving this aside, McConnell's argument for educational disestablishment as conducive to civic virtue has its own internal problems. For starters, it makes of democratic citizenship a thin gruel consisting of little more than basic academic outcomes and a healthy tolerance for the beliefs and values of others. This is not the place to offer a defense of a more robust conception of citizenship, but few theorists understand citizenship as capped by the lowly hillock of tolerance; most defend at least a sense of fairness and civility. What's more, McConnell strangely enlists Rawls's conception of overlapping consensus on his behalf, claiming that since political arrangements are to be endorsed for a variety of reasons from the range of citizens' diverse doctrines, educational choice will help foster the comprehensive moral and religious worldviews of citizens undergirding the overlapping consensus. But McConnell neglects to mention that an overlapping consensus can form only through the use of so-called public reason, which requires citizens to abstract from their particularistic views and come to understand, sympathetically listen to, and learn to respond to—not merely tolerate—the diverse views of other citizens. Public reason demands far more than tolerance, but a settled disposition to treat fellow citizens fairly and with civility. It demands, as John Tomasi argues, a potentially taxing psychological reintegrative project to show how public reason can be supported by one's nonpublic affiliations and values.[21] Rawls's overlapping consensus does not support, but rather undermines educational choice of the sort promoted by McConnell.

More importantly, in some cases the consequences of educational disestablishment do threaten to compromise a child's interest in an autonomy-promoting education. McConnell prefers morally coherent school communities to public schools, because he thinks a deep grounding in particularistic views sets the foundation for democratic citizenship. But some parents and religious groups, such as the Amish, do not value autonomy because they think its exercise may lead their children away from their religious or ethical beliefs and communities. If permitted to select schools that mirror and reinforce their own beliefs in every way, some parents will not provide an education for autonomy. Deference to parental choice in education must end when parents wish to thwart the development of autonomy that enables their children to exercise the basic freedom of living a life other than that into which they were born.

Once again, we see how visions of educational choice are powered by a normative understanding of pluralism. The weight assigned to the authority of parents to choose an educational environment depends on how one interprets what must follow from the fact of pluralism. The Ackerman and Levinson view offers too little accommodation to parents and educational choice, McConnell's too much.

Pluralism should not be discounted or exalted. Put differently, the fact of pluralism should neither wholly trump, nor be trumped by efforts to secure the basis of social unity and foster citizenship and autonomy. The function of schools is not to subdue or tame an unwelcome diversity of ways of life nor to be the institutional fertilizer that permits a thousand blossoms to bloom and sustains their reproduction over time. In some sense, they must do a little of each: schools must be common insofar as they secure unity, foster citizenship, and cultivate autonomy, which will inevitably cut against some ways of life and thereby narrow the range of pluralism that would exist if educational choice was a supreme value; and schools must be responsive to parental interests in education, which opens up space for some kinds of educational choice that would not exist if common schooling was a supreme value. With a proper understanding of pluralism—seeing it as one among several important values in a liberal state—we can honor both the common school ideal and calls for educational choice. The final section shows how.

Reconciling Common Schooling with Educational Choice

The fact of pluralism is, as Rawls says, not an unfortunate condition but a natural outcome of the exercise of freedom in a liberal state.[22] But fostering pluralism is not the purpose of the liberal state, as if the only function of public institutions were to permit diversity to thrive, and the mark of a better or healthier liberal state were its ability to promote greater pluralism. Liberal states are committed in the first instance to ethical individualism—the fundamental unit of analysis is the individual and not the group or the state. Liberals view the freedom and equality of individuals as the highest political values, and the success of political arrangements is to be judged not on the basis of how they sustain or allow pluralism to thrive, but on how they promote individual freedom and equality. Of course, the best understanding of freedom and equality can be contested, but the basic point is clear: individuals have equal entitlements to define for themselves what goods and ends are most worthy according to their own lights and independent judgment, and to possess equal civic standing. Seen in this light, pluralism is the consequence of the liberal state's concern to protect individual freedom and equality, because individuals will make different choices about how to lead their lives—choices which are worthy of the state's and citizens' respect.

Given this understanding of pluralism, how should we understand common schooling and educational choice? As I suggested earlier, the fact of pluralism is a source of both personal and social meaning and enrichment but also sets up a foundational problem: what will provide the basis of the social unity of a diverse, free, and equal citizenry with shared commitments to justice without unjustly oppressing reasonable ways of life? As I argue, common schooling can be seen as an attempt to forge unity while educational choice can be seen as an accommodation to diversity. But this is not an either-or proposition. Common schooling can coexist with educational choice, in the process doing justice to individual freedom and equality and to pluralism.

Following Callan and McLaughlin, we should distinguish between common schooling and common education.[23] Common schools are schools that are open to all and that as a result may attract a mixed student body. But what matters about the common school ideal is not that a school accepts all comers and is diverse in population, but that the institutional ethos and common educational goals are part of the common school ideal. The function of common schooling must be to promote common educational aspirations, and if they fail, then they are not independently worthy of liberal approbation. To suppose that they are is to suppose, in Callan's apt analogy, "that hospitals are good or bad in a way that is independent of their effects on the health of patients."[24]

So if an institutional ethos that is open to pluralism and a conception of common education is what matters about the common school ideal, then there exists wide room for parental discretion in choosing among schools which are distinguished in a variety of ways but that all embody this educational vision. At least in principle, public, private, religious, and even home schools can be successful in achieving the right ethos and common educational vision. Whether or not they do so in practice is an empirical question, and it is the proper task of the liberal state to set regulations on all forms of schooling such that common educational goals are met.

Here, then, we see how common schooling and educational choice can be reconciled. Educational choice in a variety of contemporary forms—private and religious schools, charter schools, vouchers—are all potentially consistent with the demands of common education. As I said at the outset, it is impossible from the level of theory to determine a specific institutional blueprint for the provision of schooling. What this analysis suggests is that so long as schools embody an ethos that does not shut out diversity and that develops citizenship and autonomy, parents should be free to choose schools on the basis of how they want their children to be educated. This would include a great diversity of schools, public, private, religious, and homeschools. To be sure, it rules out some undiscriminating forms of choice, such as McConnell's proposal, whose view of democratic citizenship is threadbare and ignores the child's interest in autonomy. And it rules out schools which would refuse to expose children to and engage them with value diversity. Democratic citizenship and autonomy can be fostered only when children become aware of the existence of other ways of life, and moreover, when they engage intellectually with such value diversity. The liberal state should be wary of parents whose choices are made solely on the basis of shielding them from any and all competing views. To allow this would indeed establish a kind of parental despotism over children. As the liberal state seeks to protect the freedom and equality of all citizens, including children, it must make it possible for children to make decisions about the kind of lives they wish to lead. This does not imply the ridiculous claim that children deserve to be able to lead any life possible, or that the state should seek intentionally to increase the chance that children will be skeptical of their parents deepest convictions. It simply means that children deserve the basic freedom to lead lives other than those into which they are born, or to contest and revise the values of their parents' or cultural communities.

On some views, the achievement of these common educational goals might require side-by-side learning of diverse students. In an understanding of Aristotelian civic friendship, Randall Curren, for example, finds that students must learn to exercise certain virtues in the practice of relating to diverse others.[25] Similarly, Eamonn Callan believes that the exercise of the political virtue of reasonableness and the exercise of public reason can only be learned in deliberative settings in which students of diverse backgrounds encounter and engage each other.[26] There is a strong case to be made here, and that a diverse student body is an undeniable asset to both the democratic citizenship and autonomy-promoting goals of common education. Thus, to the extent that educational choice makes it likelier that schools will be divided along religious and moral lines, the prospects of realizing the common school ideal look dimmer. But again, the implication is not to forbid choice but to construct a framework for educational choice that does not lead to a system of schools marked by external pluralism and internal homogeneity.

Indeed, supporters of some form of educational choice include some of the strongest defenders of a common educational vision.[27] Each is deeply concerned with the common school ideal, yet sees room for educational choice that is controlled or constrained by the public purposes of education. One approach is to see separate education—schools which are not open to religious or ethical diversity and do not foster citizenship or autonomy—as permissible during the early ages when children depend most on their parents and need most a coherent moral universe to establish an initial identity. Another approach sees the common school ideal as the very rationale for endorsing choice. Richard Kahlenberg's recent proposal to create a choice system of schools integrated by socioeconomic lines, for example, assumes that such schools will not only produce better academic outcomes but also result in broader racial and ethnic diversity than currently exists in most American public schools.[28] A great many institutional arrangements for pursuing common education and accommodating educational choice will be permissible, and liberal accounts should leave the resolution of these arrangements to democratic politics.

What cannot be subject to democratic politics, however, is the legitimacy of educational choice itself. The United States Supreme Court reached the same conclusion in *Pierce v. Society of Sisters* (1925).

The case concerned an Oregon ballot initiative, successfully passed by voters in 1922, that mandated attendance at public schools for every Oregon child aged eight to sixteen. The initiative effected a transformation of compulsory attendance laws into compulsory public school attendance laws, outlawing both sectarian and nonsectarian private schooling. The Supreme Court overturned the initiative, ruling in favor of the Society of Sisters of the Holy Names of Jesus and Mary, a Catholic school, and the Hill Military Academy, a nonsectarian private school. While the case is well known in American jurisprudence and remembered for the unanimous Court's ruling that invoked the "liberty of parents and guardians to direct the upbringing of children under their control,"[29] the historical context of the Oregon initiative is largely and unjustly forgotten.

The ballot initiative represented the apex of efforts to secure common schooling against the perceived threats of immigrants, Catholics, and Bolshevism in the wake of three events: massive waves of immigration in the 1900s and 1910s, World War I, and the Russian Revolution of 1917. With the success of the Oregon initiative, a dozen other states were prepared to act in similar fashion. Along with the Scottish Rite Masons, the champion of the initiative was none other than the Ku Klux Klan. According to historians David Tyack, Thomas James, and Aaron Benavot, the Klan would recite, "I believe that our Free Public School is the cornerstone of good government and that those who are seeking to destroy it are enemies of our Republic and are unworthy of citizenship."[30]

The Klan, in effect, was wary of the pluralism—especially the religious pluralism that immigration had brought to Oregon, and sought to combat this by ensuring all children would attend common schools that would Americanize the youth. Social solidarity and common citizenship could be accomplished, the Klan evidently thought, only when private schooling was abolished. But the Klan, of course, was not making an argument in favor of what philosophers might call civic nationalism, the laudable attempt to secure civic unity without ethnocentric bias. The Klan was motivated by a conviction that White, Anglo-Saxon Protestants (WASPs) were a superior race; aliens, Catholics and Jews, and especially Blacks all were genetically inferior. But with fewer than one percent Blacks in Oregon, and with *Plessy v. Ferguson* (1896) the reigning law of the land, Blacks could hardly have been the target of the initiative. Almost certainly the target were Catholics. Stephen Carter reads the historical context of the initiative as driven primarily by antireligious and especially anti-Catholic sentiment.[31]

Somewhat surprisingly, the Supreme Court rejected the democratic majority's preferences in Oregon. While a portion of its ruling was technical, grounded in a finding that the Oregon compulsory public school attendance law destroyed the plaintiff's business and property, the key declaration of Pierce is a defense of educational choice. Noting that "No question is raised concerning the power of the state reasonably to regulate all schools,"[32] the Court nevertheless issued a ringing declaration of limited government, echoing Mill's concerns about the pernicious effects of complete state authority over schooling:

> The fundamental theory of liberty upon which all governments
> in this Union repose excludes any general power of the state to

standardize its children by forcing them to accept instruction from public teachers only. The child is not the mere creature of the state; those who nurture him and direct his destiny have the right, coupled with the high duty, to recognize and prepare him for additional obligations.[33]

Pierce thus establishes in law that the liberty interests of parents in raising their children preclude the state from acting to abolish private schools. This constitutes, in effect, the liberty argument in favor of educational choice.

It bears repeating that the liberty argument for educational choice does not establish the existence of unchallenged parental authority over schooling. To the contrary, the liberty argument establishes that the state may not act as the sole authority over schooling; it invests parental preferences about the education of their children with some weight, enough to permit private and sectarian schools as educational options for parents, but exactly how much weight to control the curriculum and pedagogy in such schools is left unsettled.

As *Pierce* recognized, the state could still regulate private schools and hold them accountable for public purposes. The battles over the accountability and financing of private schools have a long history in the wake of *Pierce*; indeed they continue today and constitute the main turf on which conflicts about school choice and vouchers are fought. These battles represent ongoing efforts to reconcile, in institutional form, the tension between aspirations of common schooling and aspirations of educational choice. No philosopher can settle, at the level of principle, the institutional design of any school system. But I hope to have shown that the two aspirations, when understood against the normative significance of pluralism in a liberal society, are reconcilable in principle. Educational choice is not merely justifiable but actually morally required in a liberal society. Liberty-based arguments are the fundamental grounds of educational choice.

Notes for Chapter 1

1. This paper is a significantly expanded version of "Common Schooling and Educational Choice," which appeared in *A Companion to Philosophy of Education*, ed. Randall Curren, 430–42 (Oxford: Blackwell Publishing, 2003). I thank Christopher Lubienski, Walter Feinberg, and the other participants in a conference on school choice held in April 2006 where I received comments on this paper.

2. See for example, Harry Brighouse, "School Choice and Educational Equality," this volume.

3. E.g., Lubienski in this volume.

4. *Pierce v. Society of Sisters*, 268 U.S. 354–35 (1925).

5. John Dewey, *Democracy and Education* (New York: Free Press, 1916), 21–22.

6. *West Virginia Board of Education v. Barnette*, 319 U.S. 624, 641 (1943).

7. Quoted in James B. Conant, ed., *Thomas Jefferson and the Development of American Public Education* (Berkeley: University of California Press, 1962), 98.

8. David Tyack and Elisabeth Hansot, *Managers of Virtue: Public School Leadership in America* (New York: Basic Books, 1982); Diane Ravitch, *The Great School Wars: New York City, 1805–1973* (New York: Basic Books, 1974).

9. C. Glenn, *The Myth of the Common School* (Amherst, MA: University of Massachusetts Press, 1988).

10. John Rawls, *Political Liberalism* (New York: Columbia University Press, 1993), 200.

11. Amy Gutmann, "Civic Education and Social Diversity," *Ethics* 105, no. 3 (1995): 557–79; Eamonn Callan, *Creating Citizens: Political Education and Liberal Democracy* (Oxford: Clarendon Press, 1997); Stephen Macedo, *Diversity and Distrust: Civic Education in a Multicultural Democracy* (Cambridge, MA: Harvard University Press, 2000); Rob Reich, *Bridging Liberalism and Multiculturalism in American Education* (Chicago: University of Chicago Press, 2002).

12. William Galston, "Two Concepts of Liberalism," *Ethics* 105 (April 1995): 516–34, 524.

13. Callan, *Creating Citizens*, 170ff.

14. See Callan, *Creating Citizens*; Meira Levinson, *The Demands of Liberal Education* (Oxford: Oxford University Press, 1999); Harry Brighouse, *School Choice and Social Justice* (Oxford: Oxford University Press, 2000); Reich, *Bridging Liberalism and Multiculturalism*.

15. Anthony Bryk, Valerie Lee, and Peter Holland, *Catholic Schools and the Common Good* (Cambridge, MA: Harvard University Press, 1993).

16. Terry McLaughlin, "Liberalism, Education, and the Common School," *Journal of Philosophy of Education* 29, no. 2 (1995): 239–55, 247.

17. Bruce Ackerman, *Social Justice in the Liberal State* (New Haven, CT: Yale University Press, 1980), 160.

18. Levinson, *Demands of Liberal Education*, 144, 158.

19. Amy Gutmann, *Democratic Education* (Princeton, NJ: Princeton University Press, 1987).

20. Michael W. McConnell, "Education Disestablishment: Why Democratic Values Are Ill-served by Democratic Control of Schooling," in *Political and Moral Education: NOMOS XLIII*, ed. Stephen Macedo and Yael Tamir (New York: New York University Press, 2001).

21. John Tomasi, *Liberalism Beyond Justice: Citizens, Society, and the Boundaries of Political Theory* (Princeton, NJ: Princeton University Press, 2001).

22. Rawls, *Political Liberalism*, 37.

23. McLaughlin, "Liberalism, Education, and the Common School"; Callan, *Creating Citizens*.

24. Callan, *Creating Citizens*, 166.

25. Randall Curren, *Aristotle on the Necessity of Public Education* (Lanham, MD: Rowman & Littlefield, 2000).

26. Callan, *Creating Citizens*.

27. McLaughlin, "Liberalism, Education, and the Common School"; Callan, *Creating Citizens*; Macedo, *Diversity and Distrust*.

28. Richard Kahlenberg, *All Together Now: Creating Middle-Class Schools Through Public School Choice* (Washington, DC: Brookings Institution Press, 2001).

29. *Pierce*, 268 U.S. 510, 535.

30. David Tyack, Thomas James, Aaron Benavot, *Law and the Shaping of Public Education* (Madison, WI: University of Wisconsin Press, 1987),181.

31. Stephen L. Carter, "Parents, Religion, and Schools: Reflections on *Pierce*, 70 Years Later," *Seton Hall Law Review* 27, no. 1194–1224 (1997); see also Richard W. Garnett, "Taking *Pierce* Seriously: The Family, Religious Education, and Harm to Children," *Notre Dame Law Review* 76, no. 109 (2000), 109–46.

32. *Pierce*, 268 U.S. 510, 534.

33. *Pierce*, 268 U.S. 510, 535.

Chapter 2

Educational Equality
and Varieties of School Choice

Harry Brighouse

Justice is the first virtue of social institutions and the institutions which regulate schooling. Education policy, like social policy more generally, should be guided principally by considerations of justice and only secondarily by pragmatic considerations. Compromises must be made with existing social forces opposed to justice in order to optimize the justice of the existing institutions. But of course, in an otherwise unjust society, there are sharp limits on what can be done to pursue justice in any given policy arena. Justice is, furthermore, complex. It is not simply captured by identifying a single value (e.g., educational equality) because other values are also important. For example, benefiting the least advantaged, or instituting preconditions for flourishing familial relationships may, in some circumstances, conflict with that value. This makes it all the more difficult to accomplish what I want in this paper—explore a particular educational reform idea in terms of its potential contribution or detriment to social justice.

So, I am going to simplify—very explicitly—by looking at the idea of school choice and considering what contribution it might make to equality in education. I am well aware of the variety of interpretations of equality in education, and I am going to simplify even further by using the vague phrase "equally good provision for each individual child" to mean equality in education. Different readers will interpret equally good provision differently depending on their conception of what constitutes a good education, and I invite them to do this, so as to abstract away from such questions. I believe that much of what I have to say about school choice stands or falls independently of which (plausible) understanding of equally good provision you adopt.

41

Most critics and opponents of school choice adopt fairly radical understandings of justice—or equality—in education. For example, they might think that equality consists in ensuring social class background and racial background have no impact at all on achievement, and inequalities of achievement that have a significantly unequal impact on the life-prospects of individual children are unjust. They might also think that other values I've mentioned, for example, instituting the preconditions for flourishing familial relationships, are either unimportant or, if important, rarely in any deep conflict with educational equality. Personally, I endorse the first part of such radicalism; and although I disagree with the second half (I think that family values have great importance and are, in our deeply unjust social conditions, frequently in conflict with educational equality) I do not disagree with it deeply—I believe that social equilibria, which combine strong support for family life and radical educational equality, are in some sense available, and that the struggle for social justice is a struggle to move toward that range of equilibria.[1]

My aim in this paper is to show that school choice is far more pervasive than many of its radical critics believe, and to show that some variants of school choice are more likely to move us toward educational equality than others. I also want to show that opposing those variants does not amount to opposing school choice because the current, de facto, system of allocation of children to schools, on the so-called neighborhood school model, involves as much school choice as any of the promising variants.[2] I don't have any kind of quantitative measure of school choice, but nor, as far as I know, does anyone else. I shall, however, make the case on an intuitive understanding of choice which I think is easy to grasp and widely shared.

How Choice Compromises Equality

No one thinks that choice compromises justice with respect to a whole range of goods, like basic consumer goods and housing. As long as incomes are distributed justly, justice requires that people get more or less what they want, within their budget constraint. The challenge to choice comes only when we consider goods like education and healthcare: goods which many people think should not be distributed purely according to people's willingness and ability to pay, even when income and wealth are justly distributed. These goods, many think, should be distributed according to different norms than regular consumer goods, and in both cases, it is common to think that they should be distributed more or less equally (where the actual understanding of equally is subject to some debate).[3] Now, it is not necessarily the case that choice compromises equality in the distribution of these goods. While allowing choice, the government could work to ensure that choice did not have the effect of some getting superior quality over others. But such action would eviscerate the main benefit of choice.

The efficiency benefits of choice depend on mechanisms that must, simultaneously, produce inequality. If choice is going to be used to improve provision of these services, then it must be because that better providers are chosen by more people. Those who choose the worse providers get worse provision. The better and worse providers have to compete. Over time this should produce improvement (if markets work as their enthusiasts claim). But at any given time there will be better and worse providers—those who have the worse providers are worse off (in one relevant respect) than those who have the better providers.

Does the observation that choice compromises equality in education or healthcare provision support the conclusion that we should reject choice as a policy tool? This is the main topic of the next section, and the answer is that it does not, at least with respect to education. First, though, I want to note that even education and healthcare are different from one another.

Both education and healthcare in childhood not only help to form the the child and provide them with the equipment to enter life-influencing competitions—most strikingly the labor market, and, less remarked on, competitions for friendship (including marriage) and access to fulfilling activities. Furthermore, we are unwilling to think of children, especially young children, as responsible for the quality of their schooling or healthcare, or of the raw materials (themselves) that those services operate on. But healthcare, especially in old age, is often valuable simply because it enables a person who has access to it to lead a more satisfactory life in the near future, rather than because it enables people to do better in longer-term competitions. For this reason it is not morally problematic when wealthy elderly people vacate queues for hip replacements in the National Health Service (NHS) by going private in the same way that it is problematic (though not necessarily wrong) for wealthy parents to send their children to expensive private schools. In fact it is not clear to me that there would be a problem of justice if wealth were justly distributed (a big if) and the state refrained from paying for, or charged a user fee for, a wide range of health-enhancing procedures for the elderly.

How Is Choice Supposed to Improve Schools?

Choice gets its impulse from two observations. The first is that parents should have a good deal of control over how their children are reared and educated as a matter of right. The less choice they have, other things being equal, the less control. I am not concerned with this observation: it is a true observation. But in so far as it is true, it has little bearing on the actual policy choices we face. The second observation is that markets in general, and choice in particular, have the nice feature that as long as consumers are reasonably well informed and face reasonably low transaction costs, and producers do not have excessive market power, productivity should improve over time, yielding, in the case of education, either better education for all (or most) or cheaper education, which is just as good as it would have been absent choice. This latter observation is true and important; it really matters that high quality education be produced at a reasonable cost by government schools in particular. It is important that it be high quality because that is the only hope that the least advantaged children have of getting a high quality education, and it is important that it be produced at reasonable cost because voters, at least in the foreseeable future, seem to impose a upper limit on tax revenues, and other important priorities vie with education for those revenues (not least illness prevention, healthcare, and income supplementation for the least advantaged).

However, enthusiasts for school choice tend to overestimate the quality of information parents have, and to underestimate or even ignore the transaction costs consumers face, as well as the power that producers have in educational markets. They tend to assume, in other words, that markets in schooling can be more perfect than they really can be.

Think first about the quality of information. The UK government goes to great lengths to produce good quality information for parents about the quality of the schools they are choosing. For over twenty years the government has constructed an elaborate set of league tables, comparing schools by looking at scores in various tests at key ages. In the United States, No Child Left Behind is moving rather slowly in the same direction. But these tables, in the United Kingdom case, include weightings of the significance of different tests which are, at best, counterintuitive, and understanding the full import takes more time and education than most parents are willing to give it. Worse, until recently the tables were constructed out of raw scores, which told parents something about the achievement levels of the students, but nothing much about the quality of the schooling. Constructing useful value-added tables is difficult. The government has instituted a scheme that will, in theory, record all relevant data (test and exam results, schools attended and a few other things) concerning every pupil from ages four to sixteen. If these data were accurately gathered, they would, in principle, allow for value-added tables. It is worth emphasizing what a massive data-gathering task this is: for example, since we know that socioeconomic background is a predicator of outcomes, quite detailed data on the (relatively frequent) movements between income deciles of children's families would be needed. There are serious problems concerning the effects of pupil mobility, and reasonable doubts that the data can be gathered accurately. The UK government has, in fact, adopted value-added measures, but has done so without solving these problems.[4] Even if these problems are overcome, however, there remain two insuperable difficulties, as Harvey Goldstein explains:

> Schools cannot be summarized by a single value-added score—they are differentially 'effective' for different kinds of pupil and in different subjects.
>
> More seriously, the numbers are smallish so that sampling error gives you very wide uncertainty intervals and this means that for anything between 60 and 80% of schools they cannot be distinguished from the overall average! Some schools do turn up as extreme but will not all do so over time, and it is also very difficult to detect schools that are changing consistently over time. In other words, for most schools there is no statistically valid way that they can be ranked. Even where you do detect an 'outlier' there may be a good reason for this over which the school has little control.[5]

On the most optimistic assumptions, value-added tables will help parents avoid (or leap at) the extremes, and not in making discriminations between the vast majority of schools that fall within the normal range.

Nor is it clear that even good value-added tables give parents relevant information. The relevant information parents need is highly peculiar—it is not how good the school is, but how high the probability is that it will be good for one's own child. Consider the parent who is confident that her child will be a high achiever in any of the available local schools. She might seek the school in which her child has the best chance of having a reasonably sized friendship network, or in which he will have the best chance of avoiding a certain kind of teasing. She might, alternatively, simply want to make sure that he avoids being at school with one or two other particular children. Some of this information might be gleaned through informal means, but most of it is simply not available at all. Now consider transaction costs. Parents face high transaction costs, and, to make matters worse, it is children, rather than parents, who bear the worst aspects of the costs. Once a child is in a school she will usually be better off in that school than moving to another, somewhat better, school, because the move, itself, harms her educational prospects and her emotional wellbeing. It takes time and emotional energy to make friends and it is more distracting from one's school work to be making new friendships than to be maintaining existing friendships. It also takes time for a teacher to get to know a child, and to tailor her instructional approach to that child's needs. One or two transitions during a school career may be fine, but a wise parent concerned with her child's prospects and happiness will avoid the numerous moves that would be needed for consumer choice to have an optimal effect on the quality of producers. Compare this with the now trivial transaction costs involved in frequent changes in one's chosen brand of breakfast cereal; markets in breakfast cereals can improve quality because consumers can switch brands numerous times a year.

For this reason and others producers (schools) have a good deal of market power. Schools must be above a certain size to be viable, so supply is inevitably restricted, and none will be exactly what the consumer wants. Any particular consumer has at most five or six schools that are realistic for them to use. The highly limited supply is a serious market imperfection. It can be diminished or enhanced, of course, by regulation; neighborhood schooling gives schools more market power than they would have some choice systems, the UK practice of allowing various forms of selection of students by schools gives them even more power.

The case for or against any particular version of choice, then, has to forgo a generalized optimism about the capacity of markets to improve productivity, and must focus specifically on the details of the scheme proposed or defended, and compare it with other schemes with respect to some desired goal. Much of what follows is an attempt at a general analytical framework to assist with that task, when the desirable goal is equality.

The Pervasiveness of School Choice

The foregoing remarks might give the impression that I am skeptical about school choice as a lever for school improvement in general and for egalitarian school improvement in particular. But school choice—parents having the power to choose which schools their children attend—is pervasive, and no participant in either the public or the academic debates argues seriously for removing it. In Western democracies, no system of allocation of children to schools eschews choice completely. Parental choice is always operative at the margins, as long as private schools are legal: anyone with the necessary funds can exit into the private sector. And within the state and public school system choice always has an impact. The issue is not whether we should have school choice, but what kind of school choice we should have.

Here, then, are three parental choice mechanisms.

1.   All OECD countries allow parents to send their children to private schools which are subject to less stringent regulation and inspection regimes than are government schools, and in some of which children can receive a much more expensive educational experience than in government schools. If they have the resources parents can choose to go private. In most OECD countries some wing of the left argues for abolishing, or at least severely curtailing, this sector; the United States is a striking exception.

2.   All OECD countries have legal housing markets, so that parents can use their resources to acquire houses in desired school districts or catchment areas for particular government schools. The extent to which the housing market enters into school choice varies. Strict rules about neighborhood schooling make the housing market the only viable arena for exercising school choice, but its effectiveness as a tool varies even then; geographically large school catchment areas and school districts make it less effective than geographically small areas and districts; having a bad transportation infrastructure makes it less effective than having a good infrastructure.

3.   Most OECD countries implement some degree of choice among government schools within a given district, especially at secondary level. Religious schools of relevant stripes, and single-sex schools, are frequently available for those who choose them; for example, in the United Kingdom most urban and suburban children can attend a Roman Catholic or a Church of England secondary school if their parents choose it and they are admitted (Roman Catholic schools normally discriminate against non-Catholics in urban areas, but more rarely in suburban areas; Church of England schools discriminate much more rarely).

The various choice schemes I discuss in the next section all allow choice to play a formal role in the allocation of children to schools; vouchers, open enrollment, charter schools, et cetera. But it is not at all clear to me that any of the schemes I describe give more scope for choice than does the neighborhood schooling model. Consider the standard neighborhood schooling system in the United States, in which children are allocated to the local school. Choice enters the picture because perceived-quality-of-school considerations affect people's house purchasing decisions. The school district (or the state which authorizes the school districts) is not itself registering or managing the choices, and schools have no direct control over who attends. But choice is there anyway. It is instructive to think of the U.S. system of public schooling as a crude and highly regulated regressive voucher system. The state (that is, the government, in one or several of its many guises)[6] gives the school more resources for your child if you live in a wealthier community. The wealthier you are, the more control you have over which school your child will attend. Schools themselves cannot reject any student; but the cumulative choices of wealthier parents crowd poorer parents out of the pertinent housing market. Therefore, the parents of the other children in the school can reject your child if they can outbid you in the housing market.

It is not impossible to alter the extent to which choice in the housing market translates into school choice. Policymakers can, if they choose, influence how easy it is for parents to select desired school characteristics by regulating the housing market, at least to some extent. So zoning boards could regulate neighborhoods to promote socioeconomic segregation by, for example, requiring large lot developments in particular neighborhoods and restricting their use to single-family homes. Alternatively they can require the integration of affordable housing into each neighborhood, thus making it harder for parents to find socio-economically segregated neighborhood schools. Policymakers could loosen the connection of schooling to neighborhood without losing it, by twinning advantaged and disadvantaged neighborhoods and using bussing or similar mechanisms to create integrated schools, rather in the way that many districts currently attempt to address racial segregation. Using zoning decisions to promote integration is, however, a very long-run strategy because it can influence only future development and not patterns within the existing housing stock. The twinning strategy has much to recommend it, but all mechanisms designed to reduce the capacity of advantaged parents to choose advantage through the housing market or through school choice runs the risk of triggering defections into the private school system. So policymakers often have limited room for maneuver.

Choice and Equality

The comments about the neighborhood schooling model help explain why choice compromises equality but do not mean that choice should be rejected. We shouldn't reject choice because there isn't a system of allocation in which choice does not play a role. The issue is not, if you like, whether choice compromises equity, but rather which feasible system of choice does best with respect to equity.

In chapter 3 of this volume, Ken Howe draws a distinction between equality-led reforms and choice-led reforms.[7] Equality-led reforms might deploy choice, but they do so only in the service of equality, either because choice will directly produce greater equality, or because permitting choice will allow policymakers the political freedom to implement other measures that will produce greater equality. Choice-led reforms see choice as a non-negotiable element of reform; valuable not because of its service to equality, but for other reasons. As should be clear, my approach in this chapter exemplifies equality-led reform; I am assuming that choice is valuable only in so far as it is a vital component of the most feasible strategy to produce greater equality. But it should also be clear by now that I regard choice as non-negotiable, not in the sense that it has intrinsic importance, but in the sense that no proposed egalitarian strategy eschews it. They all concede it as an inevitable feature of the system, whether formally (as in the case of egalitarian vouchers) or informally (as in the case of neighborhood schooling).

A great deal of opposition to the UK school choice reforms of 1981 and 1988 claims that poor parents make systematically worse choices than wealthy parents do; so the choice reforms lead to more greater socioeconomic segregation of schools and greater inequality of provision.[8] The evidence on segregation is not, in fact, clear.[9] But, it would be surprising if conclusive evidence could be found that the choice aspects of the reforms made these things worse. Prior to the implementation of the reforms, advantaged parents were already able to use choice to allocate their children to schools; they could move into the catchment area of the desired school or send their child to a desired private school, whichever suited them. Whether a system, which extends choice to all parents, is worse with respect to equality and segregation does not depend on whether wealthier parents are better choosers than poorer parents, but whether poor parents are better choosers than the state on their behalf in the prechoice era. If the state chose better in the past than poorer parents do now, then we should expect a worsening of inequality; if it chose worse, then we should expect an improvement with respect to equality and, possibly, segregation.

How well poorer parents choose for their children is an empirical question, and we should not expect the same answer in all institutional contexts;[10] similarly it is an empirical question as to how well states choose for their disadvantaged citizens. Again, there is every reason to expect states to vary on this dimension. The Netherlands, Sweden, and

Germany do better than the United Kingdom, for example, so disadvantaged parents in those countries have to meet higher standards of competence in choice-making than would disadvantaged parents in the United Kingdom, before they could be said to be better choosers than the government. Many urban schools in the United States are not good at this at all, and the state allocates children without much consideration of whether the schools will meet educational needs or interests. In fact, many states treat urban schools as policing devices rather than educational institutions. There is strong case evidence that most disadvantaged parents could choose better if they had adequate resources.

The UK government does not generally choose as badly for the disadvantaged as the U.S. government does—that is, it does not send them to schools which are as dangerous, ill-resourced, or in which learning is as unlikely to occur. But, in the United Kingdom, the question of whether state or parent chooses best is politically irrelevant—the UK education system has extensive scope for parental choice, and nothing is going to change that. Therefore, policymakers understand that they face the question of what sort of choice system to adopt and how to regulate it. This is also the question that U.S. policymakers face, only the lack of recognition that neighborhood schooling is a choice system obscures this.

At this point, I address some objections to the argument made so far, and then describe, analytically, a number of possible varieties of choice scheme. The first few are kinds of voucher schemes, but nothing particularly hangs on the term "voucher," it is just a way of making vivid the role of choice in a system.

Objections

I've argued so far that all realistic school reform proposals, including the no-reform default, deploy school choice. They differ only in how they deploy it. Egalitarians cannot ignore choice, or pretend that they have a plan in which it plays no role; they must think about how to tame it. Before proceeding to that task, I want to address two natural objections.

The first objection is that, even if all I have said so far is right, we should prefer reforms which give choice a hidden role (as neighborhood schooling does) rather than the explicit role that school choice proposals give it. Once choice is explicitly acknowledged in the design of the system, this erodes the cultural sense that schooling is part of the public sphere, and reinforces the attitude that education is fundamentally a commodity. Acknowledging choice actually creates a pressure to choose, and once parents are consciously choosing, and are aware that others are too, the stakes are raised, and the culture changes. I think there is something to this objection, but notice two things. (1) It is not an objection that focuses on the content or distribution of educational opportunity. This might well constitute a real loss, but if one were concerned strictly with educational opportunity, one would consider it an irrelevant objection. (2) In many communities (not only those which have adopted explicit choice schemes), this change has already occurred. Explicit choice schemes might worsen the situation, but there is a countervailing consideration. It is especially those who are already most advantaged—those who have choice under any system—who have adopted this way of thinking about schooling; and if explicit choice reforms prompt less advantaged parents to join them, that might improve the prospects for their children.

The second objection focuses specifically on the evidence concerning existing government voucher schemes, and, extrapolating from that evidence, argues that explicit choice schemes may be inegalitarian because they benefit not the least advantaged, but the most advantaged among the less advantaged. The evidence in question is that those who take advantage of voucher schemes, even when they are targeted to the poor, are not all of the poor, or the poorest of the poor, but the putatively most ambitious among the poor. The main beneficiaries are children whose parents have the personal resources to take up the opportunity and negotiate the voucher system.[11]

Let us suppose that explicit choice has no benefits for the lowest 10% of achievers, but does raise the achievement of the next 10 percent, thus increasing the gap between the lowest 10 percent and the rest, but decreases the gap between the next 10 percent and subsequent deciles. Has the system improved, or worsened, with respect to equality? I don't have a good answer. But whereas I have a clear intuition that equality would support holding back the top 10 percent for the sake of the bottom 10%, I do not have a clear institution that it calls on us to hold back the next-to-bottom 10 percent for the sake of the bottom 10 percent. The most advantaged among the less advantaged objection to choice has some weight, but it is not clear that, even in the worst case, egalitarians should concede it. Compare with objections to affirmative action; affirmative action primarily benefits the more advantaged African Americans, and probably does little if anything to benefit the least advantaged African Americans; most egalitarians do not take that to be a weighty objection to it.

A final objection points out that for explicit choice schemes to work efficiently and fairly, schemes have to contain a substantial supply of spare places; but this seems to be inefficient. The first part of this objection is absolutely right; in order to accommodate short-term fluctuations in demand, schools need to be able to expand and contract relatively easily, and this can only be achieved if spare capacity is built into their design (obviously, long-term decline in demand for a particular school must result in a decline in available places and, eventually, closure). But this does not, in itself, make explicit choice inefficient. Efficiency claims are always relative to some goals and some alternative. So the question is whether the extra cost of the spare capacity is greater than the extra cost of whatever alternative reform would improve the relative achievement of lower achievers equally well. The inefficiency objection has no power unless the answer to that question is yes.

Varieties of Choice

In this section I provide an analytic categorization of kinds of choice scheme, which I shall make use of when drawing lessons for policy.

Universal Unregulated Vouchers

The universal unregulated voucher is a simple subsidy to all consumers. They can use the voucher however they want, as long as it is for the prescribed purpose (schools, health insurance companies, etc.), and is not alienable (so you can't sell it and use the proceeds for something else). The voucher can be topped up by the consumer, and the providers can repel consumers through high prices or exclusionary practices. In the purest version of this (described in chapter 6 of Milton Friedman's *Capitalism and Freedom*, but not, as far as I know, practiced anywhere) the organizations running schools are independent of the government, and are not subject to special regulation, only the regulation that all firms usually face. In the less pure versions, government provides some schools, but these compete on a more or less level playing field with independent providers. This is the model suggested by the practice in higher education provisions in the United States, in which some universities are private, others state-run.

So these schemes do vary on two dimensions: (1) vouchers for private providers in a sea of public provision; and (2) the state withdraws completely from provision, leaving the field to private providers (as Friedman proposes).

All the subsequent versions vary on these dimensions too. Generally, it is reasonable to conjecture that universal, unregulated vouchers will produce high levels of inequity, and higher than standard forms of state provision. The one obvious exception is when the amount of the voucher is set at a high level and the existing system of state provision (as in the United States) is highly iniquitous. But this scenario is highly unlikely during periods of normal politics, because the forces defending inequitable state provision would have to be routed if high-level vouchers were to replace state provision.

Universal Regulated Vouchers

These involve a flat-rate subsidy to each individual, to spend, subject to regulation. Common regulations concern:

SUPPLEMENTABILITY

For example, the schools in the Milwaukee Parental Choice Program are prohibited from charging a top-up to the voucher; it is unsupplementable.[12] The Statewide Propositions which failed in Michigan (1998) and California (1994) would have allowed parents unlimited top ups. The nursery (prekindergarten) scheme in Britain also allows unlimited top-ups, though it is funded at such a sufficiently high level that some providers (including all state-run providers) can offer the service without asking for top-ups.

ELIGIBILITY OF SCHOOLS

Voucher schemes vary by how they determine the eligibility of private schools to participate. The Milwaukee scheme initially excluded schools run by religious foundations; it now permits them to participate. Florida allowed them from the start. The British nursery voucher scheme has basic licensing requirements, but allows institutions run by religious foundations. Of course, many of the state-provided institutions that participate are run in collaboration with religious foundations. Whereas most existing voucher schemes treat private schools separately from public schools, the British nursery scheme and the Dutch scheme effectively treat them the same.[13]

ADMISSIONS

Voucher schemes vary in the admissions policies they require schools to have. Strictly speaking this is an eligibility variable, but it is important enough to have its own place. The Milwaukee scheme disallows selection on any basis except that schools may reject students with special needs if they are unequipped to deal with that special need (i.e., if they already have fee-paying students with that special need they cannot reject a voucher child with it), and they are permitted to apply a sibling rule. Over-subscribed schools must select by lottery. The Swedish system requires schools to take students on a first-come first-served basis (again, with the exception of special-needs, and a sibling rule). The Dutch system allows discrimination on various bases, but the funding structure mitigates some of the disincentives schools would otherwise have to teach the least advantaged.

The degree of inequity regulated universal vouchers produce depends on the content of the regulations and the size of the voucher, but it's reasonable to conjecture that they will be highly inequitable unless they are set at a high level, and schools have very limited control over admissions.

Progressive Voucher Schemes

These vary on the same lines as the universal regulated voucher, and they are technically universal, but the value of the voucher varies according to features of the consumer. For example, the Dutch scheme is explicitly progressive: the voucher is worth more for poor children and children of immigrants and parents with low educational attainment. For this reason, some studies have found that schools with moderately high concentrations of poor children actually do quite well, as they are able to provide working conditions which enable them to attract and retain high quality teaching staff. Progressive voucher schemes are liable to be much less inequitable than other schemes, and if the vouchers are sufficiently well-calibrated to the needs of the child, that will offset worries about giving schools control over admissions because schools will have incentives to admit otherwise undesirable pupils, and schools stuck with otherwise undesirable pupils will be well compensated.

Targeted Voucher Schemes

The Milwaukee scheme is targeted because it is restricted to low-income children. Because it operates against a background of highly regressive funding of public schools, it is reasonable to think of this as a variety of progressive voucher scheme, and highly equitable. I have no doubt that the Milwaukee scheme represents an improvement, with respect to equity, compared with the preexisting system of neighborhood-based schooling.

Public and State School Choice Schemes

Public school choice schemes are unlike voucher schemes in that they exclude private schools from the set of eligible schools. This has two usual consequences. First, supply is government controlled and subject to much less variability than in a voucher scheme. Second, schools within the choice system will not automatically close just because nobody wants their children to attend them; they have to be closed by bureaucratic procedures. In other words, they are less likely than voucher schools to face hard budget constraints. However, it is not clear whether, in an extensive and well-functioning voucher scheme, private schools would face hard budget constraints because there would be political pressure for governments to bail out failing schools—at the very least in transition periods. Public choice schemes vary in at least two important ways, admission rules and districting.

ADMISSIONS RULES

In England and Wales, all parents have to express preferences about where their children will attend schools. Admissions policies vary dramatically from school to school and region to region. Catholic schools frequently use religious affiliation as a main criterion; some Church of England schools do, but others do not use it at all. Some local education authorities give proximity to school considerable weight, others much less. An adjudicator's office settles disputes among schools concerning policies in local markets. Some secondary schools select on grounds of ability, others are allowed to but do not, still others are not allowed to. Religious schools may interview parents to establish their degree of religious commitment—interviews which are likely information-rich about the potential pupils. The sibling rule is ubiquitous.

DISTRICTING

Several states in the United States have what they call open enrollment policies—ostensibly, choice policies that allow children to attend schools in districts other than the one in which they live. Technically, these schemes help to efface the barriers between school districts, and play a role in undermining inequalities of spending between districts. However, they typically allow or force districts to prefer in-district children to out-of-district children. In practice, out-of-district children can take up places which have not been filled by in-district children.

The exceptions are schemes introduced to overcome racial segregation. For example, Milwaukee, and wealthier and higher-spending neighboring school districts, operate a Chapter 20 program whereby low-income Milwaukee children are bussed to much higher spending suburban school districts at the choice of their parents. These schemes are unavoidably limited in scope. For example, the Milwaukee scheme was introduced to protect the integrity of the unequally funded, de facto, racially segregated multiple school districts in the face of judicial pressure or suffer extensive redistricting.

Some Lessons

From the above analytical comments, I am especially interested in the lessons for policy-makers and critics of education policy in the United Kingdom and the United States. I know these systems reasonably well, so I shall focus on them.

When evaluating reform proposals for any scheme of provision, whether in education, health, or other special areas, the first lesson is that it is important to attend to three particular variables:

1. To what extent do providers have the power to formally or informally select their clients?

2. To what extent does residence determine access to providers?

3. How well-calibrated is per unit funding to individual need?

The greater the extent providers have power to select, and the greater the extent to which residence determines access to providers, the more inequitable the schemes other things being equal. The better calibrated funding is to need the less inequitable the schemes (see table 2.1.)

The basic school choice system in the United Kingdom does very badly with respect to the first two variables, but better with respect to the third. As Stephen Twigg, MP, then of the Department for Education and Skills, said in evidence to the Select Committee on Public Administration investigation into *Voice and Choice in Public Services*

> Whilst there is certainly not a 300% uplift, there is a very significant difference between the per-pupil funding of Tower Hamlets,

in the deprived East End of London, which has the highest per-pupil funding in the country, and per-pupil funding in some parts of the country. It is almost double, if you compare Tower Hamlets with other parts of the country. We therefore do already, within the funding system we have, recognize that pupils from deprived backgrounds and pupils where in the early years English is an additional language, for example, should carry a greater cost because that is something the school will require in order to educate them properly.[14]

The system of neighborhood schooling in the United States does well with respect to the first, but badly with respect to the second and third. By contrast, the Milwaukee Parental Choice Program does well with respect to the first and second variables, and less well with respect to the third.

The second lesson concerns the use of evidence. It is not uncommon for advocates and critics to cite studies, demonstrating that some choice scheme or group of choice schemes has particular effects, as evidence that choice has those effects (for good or ill depending on whether they are advocates or critics). But because the details of the schemes matter in the way that I have outlined above, one can never draw general conclusions about the likely effects of school choice from studies of particular schemes. So, when looking at school choice proposals in a particular context, it is important to focus on how well the proposal does relative to what is already in place when forging or amending school legislation to attend to the variables above. When the default is highly unequally funded neighborhood schooling, opposition to some school choice proposals may not amount to opposition to choice at all, just opposition to giving less advantaged parents a counterweight to the power advantaged parents wield. If the proposal on the table is universal unregulated vouchers,

Table 2.1

Formal choice system	How equitable?
Universal unregulated voucher	Low
Universal regulated voucher	Low. Depends on contents of regulation and voucher size
Progressive voucher	High. Depends on calibration of voucher size to need
Targeted voucher	High. Depends on regulation
State school choice	Depends on regulation and funding

that may be more inegalitarian. If the proposal is for highly targeted vouchers, any good faith opposition must be pursued alongside feasible and more egalitarian alternative proposals.

This leads me to the final lesson, this time for activists and legislators who believe they are, broadly speaking, opposed to school choice. When they oppose legislation to introduce vouchers, or charter schools, or open enrollment, they are, in fact supporting school choice through the housing market, a system of choice in which the most advantaged have the most choice and the least advantaged the least choice. Sometimes, of course, they will be right; the proposed changes will be worse with respect to equality than the status quo. But even then, if they are motivated by a concern for equality, they can devise and propose amendments which limit damage, not by limiting the extent of choice, but by enhancing the likelihood that the choice system will be more, rather than less, egalitarian.

Notes for Chapter 2

1. See Harry Brighouse and Adam Swift, "Parents' Rights and the Value of the Family," *Ethics* (2006) 117(1): 80–108. Harry Brighouse and Adam Swift, "Legitimate Parental Partiality" (unpublished, on file with author).

2. There is nothing new about the observation that the traditional neighborhood schooling system is shot through with opportunities for choice; See Milton Friedman, *Capitalism and Freedom* (Chicago: University of Chicago Press, 1962), chapter 6.

3. The clearest articulation and defense of the idea that different goods should be distributed according to different distributive norms is Michael Walzer, *Spheres of Justice* (Oxford: Martin Robertson, 1983). Adam Swift and I explore the idea that, even given a single unified conception of distributive equality, different goods will be distributed in different ways in Harry Brighouse and Adam Swift, "Equality, Priority, and Positional Goods," *Ethics* (2006) 116, 3: 471–97.

4. See the tables at http://www.dfes.gov.uk/performancetables/ (accessed 2/14/2008).

5. Harvey Goldstein, personal communication, 2001. See also Harvey Goldstein, "Value-Added Tables: The Less-than-holy Grail," *Managing Schools Today* 6, no. 1 (1997): 18–19 and Harvey Goldstein, Pan Huiqi, Terry Rath, and Nigel Hill, *The Use of Value-Added Information in Judging School Performance* (London: Institute of Education, 2000).

6. Uses of the phrase "the state" can be confusing in the context of American governmental functions. I use it here in the standard sense in which it means something like "the legitimate governmental authority." It is true that school districts are governmental instruments, and that because most funding of schools is raised and spent locally, the system does not look like a regressive

voucher system, because the real inequalities of resources between advantaged and disadvantaged children within districts are not as great as those between districts, and between states. But the federal government, the State Department of Instruction, and the school district are all arms of the state in my sense. And the school district has taxing authority from the state, which gets it from the federal constitution (not the U.S. Constitution, which is a document, but the federal constitution which is the way that the U.S. government is constituted).

7. See Kenneth R. Howe, "Evidence, the Conservative Paradigm, and School Choice," this volume.

8. See, for example, Sally Tomlinson, *Education in a Post-Welfare Society* (Philadelphia: Open University Press, 2001) and Sharon Gewirtz, Stephen J. Ball, and Richard Bowe, *Markets, Choice and Equity in Education* (Philadelphia: Open University Press, 1995).

9. See Stephen Gorard, *Schools, Markets and Choice Policies* (London: RoutledgeFalmer, 2003) and Stephen Gorard, *Education and Social Justice: The Changing Composition of Schools and Its Implications* (Cardiff: University of Wales Press, 2000).

10. One unsatisfying feature of some defenses of school choice is that they treat "parents" as an undifferentiated group, asking whether they choose better than public officials, rather than disaggregating the group of parents and asking of the least advantaged whether they choose better than officials. See, for example, Joseph L. Bast and Herb J. Walberg, "Can Parents Choose the Best Schools for Their Children?" *Economics of Education Review* 23, no. 4 (2004): 431–40.

11. See, for example, the evidence concerning Milwaukee in John F. Witte, *A Market Approach to Education* (Princeton, NJ: Princeton University Press, 2000).

12. The Milwaukee scheme is, in fact, not an instance of Universal Regulated Voucher, but of a Targeted Voucher Scheme.

13. A note about the British nursery voucher scheme. It is not perceived as a voucher scheme, and many people hotly deny that it is. This is because the 1997 Labour government said it was not a voucher scheme and because, like most voucher schemes, the parents never actually see the voucher. But it is a voucher scheme.

14. See his response to Question 488, in the minutes available at http://www.parliament.the-stationery-office.co.uk/pa/cm200405/cmselect/cmpubadm/49/5012705.htm (accessed October 13, 2005).

Chapter 3

Evidence, the Conservative Paradigm, and School Choice

Kenneth R. Howe

One way to begin the philosophical enterprise . . . is to walk
out of the cave, leave the city, climb the mountain, fashion for
oneself . . . an objective and universal standpoint. Then one
describes the terrain of everyday life from far way, so that it
loses its particular contours and takes on a general shape. But
I mean to stand in the cave, in the city, on the ground. Another
way of doing philosophy is to interpret to one's fellow citizens
the world of meanings that we share. Justice and equality can
conceivably be worked out as philosophical artifacts, but a just
and egalitarian society cannot be. If such a society isn't already
here—hidden, as it were, in our concepts and categories—we
will never know it concretely or realize it in fact.[1]

Walzer's method is especially apropos for those philosophers who
would take an active role in educational policy debates. Such a role
requires participating in unfolding conversations in a way that engages
the concepts and categories in which these conversations are couched—in
the cave. There is, of course, a significant problem with Walzer's method,
perhaps more evident today than when he articulated it twenty-five years
ago: there exists more than one "world of meanings" in which concepts
such as justice and equality find their homes.

These competing worlds of meanings are intertwined with competing "paradigms" of social and educational research.[2] These paradigms
guide the choice of empirical research questions, the kinds of outcomes
perceived as important to achieve and to avoid, and the degree of perseverance displayed toward favored policies and theories. In this vein,

a "paradigm shift" occurred during the Reagan administration. The liberal paradigm, which approached education policy with the core belief that government intervention in the form of educational programs and regulations such as Head Start, Title I and Title IX, required to foster equality and justice, was displaced by the conservative paradigm, which approached education policy with the core belief that public education was trying to do too much and that government intervention was ineffective if not harmful to the intended beneficiaries. In educational research, primary concern shifted from an emphasis on equality of opportunity, as exemplified in the Coleman Report,[3] to an emphasis on competition, choice, and accountability. Indeed, Coleman himself reoriented his research in this direction in the early 1980s. By 1984, with the publication of Charles Murray's influential *Losing Ground*,[4] the conservative paradigm had gained significant momentum.[5]

Thus, school choice emerged as a real world education reform policy in a political climate saturated with the "world of meanings" associated with the conservative paradigm. It was a climate characterized by deregulation, privatization, and a reduced scope of responsibility for the state in all matters. It was a climate in which the commitment to equality in U.S. education policy inaugurated by *Brown v. Board of Education*, (1954) went into full retreat[6] and out of which market-based schemes such as John Chubb and Terry Moe's *Politics, Markets, and America's Schools*[7] provided the rationale for the expansion of school choice as it gained momentum in the 1990s.

Against this backdrop, liberal skeptics warned that an expansion of school choice would inevitably result in a less socially just educational system.[8] For, in the formulation of policy, concerns about social justice were increasingly taking a back seat to a central principle of the conservative paradigm: freeing up and encouraging market competition among schools.[9]

Not surprisingly, conservatives were unimpressed by liberal skeptics' predictions. But doubts also came from within the liberal paradigm itself. In his nuanced *School Choice and Social Justice*,[10] Harry Brighouse challenged fellow liberals on the grounds that whether or not school choice exacerbates social injustice is an open empirical question. Brighouse did not rule out this possibility, but he required that the question of the justice or injustice of school choice be evaluated against the feasible alternatives, not against an ideal standard with respect to which the status quo ante falls far short. He thus challenged those who criticize school choice as unjust to establish the claim that the introduction of school choice makes things worse vis-à-vis social justice than they otherwise would be.[11] Subsequently, in his "A Modest Defense of School Choice,"[12]

Brighouse challenges critics to show how choice could interfere with improving the education of disadvantaged students whose parents took advantage of it. Brighouse reiterates his challenges (chapter 2), emphasizing that some form of school choice has always characterized the U.S. educational system and that primary form, choice of place of residence, is especially unjust.

In an additional strand of argument set forth in *School Choice and Social Justice*, Brighouse challenges the view held by various liberals that school choice is flawed because it abandons democratic procedures as the means by which to distribute education. Brighouse labels this a red herring and contends that whether or not it is better to distribute education by democratic procedures than by parental choice is an instrumental question, in other words, a question of whether democratic procedures produce better educational results for children than parental choice procedures produce. This, too, is an empirical question and cannot be answered by appeal to the intrinsic value of democratic procedures.

In this chapter, I take up each of Brighouse's challenges and defend the skeptical liberal view. It should be emphasized here at the outset that my disagreement with Brighouse is not about general principles; he and I share a liberal-egalitarian stance, differing mainly on details. In the case of school choice, our primary disagreement results from our different views about the role of empirical evidence and how conclusive it is. We agree that empirical evidence cannot speak for itself independent of political frameworks,[13] but, as my appropriation of the notion of "paradigms" suggests, this is a deeper and more serious problem than Brighouse seems to believe. In broad strokes, I argue that the terms of school choice policymaking are dictated by the conservative paradigm and its version of "normal science." Despite growing evidence that school choice exacerbates inequality, its conservative proponents remain steadfastly opposed to the kinds of constraints on choice that egalitarians would endorse to render choice more likely to promote equality and democracy.

The Conservative Paradigm and Marketing the Market

Research in the conservative paradigm is often funded and disseminated by formidable right-wing think tanks that are motivated by an explicit commitment to expand school choice independent of the empirical evidence. For example, included in the mission statement of the foundation Milton Friedman founded, whose sole purpose is promoting expanded school choice is the following:

The Foundation serves as an indispensable resource for parents and community groups who want parental choice in education, and are ready to fight for it. Educational choice means that parents are given back a basic American ideal of freedom to choose as it applies to the education of their children. Yes, given back, for America's system was not founded in public education.[14]

Statements from other pro school choice research organizations include these:

The Cato Institute's Center for Educational Freedom:[15]

The Center's scholars seek to shift the terms of public debate in favor of the fundamental right of parents and toward a future when state-run schools give way to a dynamic, independent system of schools competing to meet the needs of American children.

The Manhattan Institute:[16]

[The Institute's] work on education reform focuses on improving two main reforms of public education: school choice and accountability. School choice reforms (including charter schools and school vouchers) are dedicated to improving the options available to parents of children in public schools, and making public schools more directly accountable to parents for education outcomes. Accountability reforms are devoted to improving educational achievement by focusing on imparting knowledge and skills and making teachers, administrators, and students accountable for success or failure.

The Heritage Foundation:[17]

The battle over who should control America's schools is a battle for the future of our nation. For decades, the quality of our schools has declined as the demands of special interests have trumped the needs of children and the dreams of parents. In recent years, however, the tide has slowly been turning: Parental choice policies are expanding state-by-state in the form of charter schools, public school open enrollment, vouchers, tax credits, and home schooling. Now there is an opportunity to turn the tide decidedly.

The Hoover Institution:[18]

> [The Institution] addresses education policy related to govern-
> ment provision and oversight versus private solutions—both
> within and outside the public school system—that stress choice,
> accountability, and transparency; that include systematic reform
> options such as vouchers, charter schools, and testing; and that
> weigh equity concerns against outcome objectives.

Given the prior commitment exemplified by these organizations,
it is not surprising that the research they produce would be favorable
toward school choice policy. Within the Hoover Institution, its fellows
include a virtual who's-who of school choice stalwarts, including John
Chubb, Chester Finn, Milton Friedman, Paul Hill, Caroline Hoxby, Terry
Moe, Paul Peterson, and Herbert Walberg. The institution's publications,
including the journal *Education Next* (cosponsored by Paul Peterson's Program on Education Policy and Governance and Chester Finn's Fordham
Foundation) are overwhelmingly favorable toward school choice.

These organizations have little interest in putting school choice to
an empirical test that could lead to abandoning it for lack of effectiveness. And this characteristic is even more evident in the case of school
choice advocacy organizations not involved in doing their own research,
such as the Center for Educational Renewal (CER) and the National
Charter Schools Clearinghouse (NCSC). In its "Charter School Guide
for Activists"[19] CER refers to growing a movement and cherry picks
research to further this purpose. In "Nine Lies About School Choice,"
CER president Jeanne Allen brashly asserts, into the teeth of considerable
counter-evidence, it is clear that school choice is "equitable" and that "it
works."[20] The National Charter Schools Clearinghouse (NCSC), which got
its start with funding from the U.S. Department of Education, foregoes
reference to any studies critical of charter schools. And this makes sense,
for NCSC's primary activity is disseminating information on how-to,
particularly how to market charter schools so as to raise money. In this
vein, the NCSC recently recommended following the advice of Dr. Steven Goldstein, president and CEO of Educational Marketing Services,
which is to "simulate a tsunami" to create the "kind of urgency we saw
in Southeast Asia."[21]

Beyond the right-wing think tanks and advocacy groups, and no
doubt bolstered by their work, school choice has gained a significant
foothold in state and federal government. Governmental educational
agencies, whose missions include facilitating the expansion of choice, not
surprisingly have little interest in critically evaluating it. For example,

the Colorado Department of Education (CDE) annual evaluations are routinely biased by the manner in which they report comparisons between student achievement produced by charter and traditional public schools without adjusting for race and income. The CDE website gives special attention to charter schools, providing information regarding founding charter schools, best educational practices, and grant funding. Like advocacy groups such as CER and NCSC, CDE's website provides no links to research or organizations critical of charter schools. It supplies links to unabashed supporters of charter schools, including CER, the Fordham Foundation, the Goldwater Institute, and the state's own Colorado League of Charter Schools.

The U.S. Department of Education (USDOE) is similar to Colorado in exemplifying an unabashedly supportive attitude toward choice and providing information useful for starting and maintaining charter schools. The USDOE also houses the Public Charter Schools Program, which provides start-up funding for charter schools. Unlike Colorado and the advocacy organizations, however, the USDOE provides access to research that has been used to question the effectiveness of charter schools. However, it is harder to find on the USDOE website than supportive how-to information. Also, the release of one important study documenting negative results for charter schools was delayed for several months.[22]

The Conservative Paradigm and Normal Science

An important part of what justifies the label "conservative paradigm" is the perseverance its proponents display toward a policy of marketization in the face of what critics from the liberal paradigm see as clear counterevidence for that policy's effectiveness. Under such conditions, debate can become thoroughly corrupted by partisan political maneuvering, where all the opposing sides care about is a policy victory for their side. If the conservative and liberal paradigms are indeed radically incommensurable, then save being mangled into a tool for marketing, empirical research on school choice is irrelevant to policymaking.[23]

But radical incommensurability does not seem to accurately depict the situation. Despite the potential for fundamental disagreement on the relevant criteria for evaluating school policy, things have not played out that way. In particular, the principle of educational equality, though no doubt weighted differently, has been taken as a given by conservatives and liberals alike. Central to the debate, particularly with respect to reducing the achievement gap, has been whether or not school choice is an effective means of closing the gap. That choice should serve to help integrate schools, or at least not further segregate them, also seems to have been widely agreed upon.[24] These two principles provide a point of contact, or commensurability, between the conservative and egalitarian paradigms.[25]

Research on school choice has settled into a phase of "normal science" as dictated by the conservative paradigm. As the number of studies has exploded, researchers have begun to focus on paradigm minutia—disputes about tiny effects and associated methodological disputes—and to lose sight of whether market-based school choice is producing the kind of meaningful improvements advocates promised. For example, in one celebrated controversy about vouchers between Harvard sociologist Paul Peterson[26] and Princeton economist Alan Krueger,[27] one dispute was whether one African American parent was sufficient for a student to be identified as African American (Krueger's approach) or having an African American mother was necessary to be so identified (Peterson's approach). Also in dispute was whether to include a groups of students for whom no baseline data was available (Krueger's position was to include them, in light of random assignment). The reanalysis performed by Krueger resulted in eliminating any positive achievement effects claimed for vouchers on the basis of the original analysis. A propos of the label "normal science," the effects that were the object of contention were too small and too isolated, with respect to racial groups and grade levels, to have any real significance for policy, in any case.[28]

From a perspective not mediated by the lens of the conservative paradigm, the results and nonresults of school choice are clear. It has produced no discernable benefit in the form of increased achievement, and has produced identifiable harm in the form of increased segregation. This was the basic finding of a 2001 RAND study, which examined both vouchers and charter schools.[29] It found no positive effects for choice schools regarding achievement, and relatively unrestricted choice systems increased segregation by race and income.

Since that RAND study, little has changed with respect to vouchers. If positive achievement effects exist, they are miniscule; and there is no good evidence to substantiate the claim that vouchers are more efficient or lead to greater social cohesion.[30]

By contrast to research on vouchers, several national studies of charter schools since the RAND study have provided more conclusive evidence indicating that the overall effects of charter schools are actually negative. Although charter schools serve a high proportion of African American students relative to public schools (a potentially positive effect), they do so in a way that increases racial and income stratification.[31] The accumulating evidence on achievement indicates that charter schools do not outperform public schools in terms of academic performance, to the extent differences are detectable. Charter schools do worse, particularly among low-income and racial minority students. Thus, if they are having any effect on achievement, it is to increase rather than decrease the achievement gap.[32]

The evolution of Colorado's charter school policy provides an instructive case study of how policymaking within the conservative paradigm is refractory to counterevidence.[33] The number of Colorado charter schools grew from one in 1993, the year the legislature passed the Charter Schools Act, to 107 in 2004–2005. Over this time, Colorado's education policy became increasing generous to charter schools. Significant changes in policy included removing the original cap of sixty; increasing the per-pupil funding local school districts are required to pass through from 80% to 100%; and requiring local districts to share virtually all forms of funding with charter schools, including capital construction. The implementation of the state-level Charter School Institute in 2004 provides its member schools with complete autonomy from local school districts. The enabling legislation was passed in response to certain local districts which had placed a moratorium on new charter schools because they had proven financially harmful to traditional public schools and exacerbated stratification by race and income.

This evolution of education policy in Colorado squares poorly with the accumulated evidence on Colorado's charter schools. In the case of student achievement, a 2004 study by SRI International[34] found no significant differences between charter and other public schools in the high-income group of schools where the percentage of low-income students was below the median for Colorado schools. Traditional public schools performed significantly better in the low-income group of schools where the percentage of low-income students was above the median for Colorado schools.[35] A parallel analysis was performed with respect to minority enrollments, and the results were also parallel, that is, there were no significant differences between charter and traditional public schools in the low-minority enrollment group, but traditional public schools were significantly better in the high-minority enrollment group.[36]

In a further analysis, SRI controlled for the proportions of minority and low-income students simultaneously, and also for school size. The general conclusion of this analysis was that "being a charter school was associated with not meeting the standard, controlling for low-income, minority students, and student enrollment."[37]

In general, Colorado's charter schools do not produce higher student achievement compared to traditional public schools for any groups, and in the case of low-income and minority students, charter schools produce lower achievement. Colorado's charter schools are thus more likely increasing the achievement gap than decreasing it.

In the case of segregation, Colorado's charter schools enroll fewer low-income (20.3 percent versus 32.1 percent); minority (32.2 percent versus 37.5 percent); and special education students (6.8 percent versus 11.1 percent) than its traditional publics schools. And these global statistics obscure the true magnitude of imbalance at the school level. For example, on average, Boulder Valley School District's four charter schools enroll slightly more minority students than the district average, 23 percent compared to 21 percent. However, this is due to one high school for adjudicated youth that enrolls fewer than one hundred students that, at 50 percent, heavily exceeds the district average; the remaining three, a middle school, K–8, and K–12) are each below the district average, at 11 percent, 12 percent, and 19 percent, respectively.

A more general illustration may be provided using the eleven Colorado districts that have at least three charter schools. These districts account for sixty-seven of Colorado's 107 charter schools (63 percent).[38] Among the charter schools of these districts, a disproportionately large number serve 75 percent or fewer minority and low-income students than their district average and a disproportionately small number serve 125 percent or more (see table 3.1).

The evolution of Colorado's charter school policy is thus significantly out of synch with the direction in which the evidence points if closing the achievement gap and avoiding increased inequality are serious considerations in policy setting.[39]

Unless the matter of the effectiveness of school choice policy is exempted from confronting the evidence, the lack of achievement gains and increased segregation, are, to stick with Kuhnian language, serious anomalies for the Conservative Paradigm.

The durability of the Coleman Report finding that nonschool factors, especially student SES, are the most powerful predictors of the achievement gap is also an anomaly.[40] For the notion that education

Table 3.1. Low-income and minority enrollments in charter schools compared to districts location

	Charter Enrollment Percentages	
	75% or fewer than district average	125% or more than district average
Low-income	65%	15%
Minority	47%	8%

reform policies such as school choice, which focus exclusively on schools, could ever do much to eliminate the achievement gap simply doesn't square with the evidence.[41]

Ideally, the response to general empirical findings that indicate choice policies are having no positive effect on achievement and are exacerbating inequality, would be to explore ways of revising policies to alter these outcomes. But this has not been the response in Colorado or elsewhere. Charter schools have been the primary growth area for school choice. Forty states currently authorize charter schools; 3600 charter schools now exist and the number is growing rapidly. The marketization rationale has come to dominate the movement.[42] Legislation enabling the formation of charter schools has been characterized by weak or no requirements on charter school enrollments regarding racial and low-income students. States that do include such requirements typically fail to enforce them.[43] Depending on how much autonomy they are afforded, particularly with respect to budgeting and fundraising, charter schools can closely approximate universal vouchers.[44]

For their part, the most visible and influential leaders in the choice movement have adopted a strategy of shouting down negative results, ignoring them, or shifting ground.[45] These tactics are illustrated in the responses by choice advocates to two studies of charter schools conducted by the American Federation of Teachers (AFT), the nation's second largest teacher's union. The first study was released in 2002.[46] Among its conclusions, it found that charter schools exacerbated segregation and failed to produce better achievement. The response from school choice advocates was immediate. They jeered the study for its alleged bias.[47] Lawrence Patrick, president of Black Alliance for Educational Options, a school choice advocacy group with significant ties to right-wing think tanks, quipped that "An AFT study on charter schools has about as much credibility as a Phillip Morris study on smoking." This remark was quickly picked up and repeated by the school choice noise machine, as other frontline school choice advocacy groups such as the Center for Educational Reform[48] and the Fordham Foundation[49] deployed it in their own denunciations of the AFT study. Chester Finn, who heads the Fordham Foundation, and who was Assistant Secretary of Education in the Reagan administration, devoted more than half of his *Gadfly* commentary on the AFT study to impugning teacher's unions. He also takes a swipe at the NEA. The RAND review[50] of the research evidence on school choice was Finn's single explicit reference to the research, with whose recommendations he took considerable liberties.[51] Otherwise, he and the choice advocacy group as a whole remained relatively silent on the RAND study despite the fact that its findings on charter schools largely agreed with those of the AFT study.

The AFT released a second study critical of charter schools in August 2004[52] that prompted a brouhaha of considerably larger proportions than the first, partly because it was reported in the *New York Times* and partly because the findings were so potentially damaging. Based on an analysis of test data from the National Assessment of Educational Progress (NAEP) program, the study concluded that on average, charter schools produced lower academic achievement than public schools, particularly in the case of low-income and minority students. In response, a mix of about thirty school choice activists and researchers listed their names in an a *New York Times* ad, paid for by CER, condemning the AFT study as well as the *Times* for reporting it. Though not participating in the ad, the Bush administration, which vigorously supports school choice, expressed its displeasure via a letter to the *Times* by Robert Lerner, commissioner of the National Center for Education Statistics (NCES).[53] Notwithstanding, in December of 2004, the NCES released its own study of charter schools, also based on NAEP.[54] The findings differed little from those of the AFT study and, like the RAND study, received relatively little heat from choice advocates.

Some of the concerns expressed about the technical limitations of the AFT study and the NCES study, for example, concerning the use of snapshot rather than longitudinal data, are legitimate. But such limitations weren't of sufficient magnitude to vitiate the findings,[55] and school choice advocates have rarely had a problem using similar data and analyses to attack the public schools. Indeed, one of the vanguard school choice researchers, Caroline Hoxby,[56] deployed snapshot data in a study, widely applauded by choice advocates, as allegedly refuting the AFT study. And Hoxby did this after including her name on the *Times* ad list criticizing the approach; she also rushed the study to press without vetting it, something else for which the AFT study was criticized in the *Times* ad. The shifty ad hoc-ing reached its peak with Chester Finn's explanation of the poor showing of charter schools by claiming they serve a more disadvantaged population of disadvantaged students than regular public schools.[57] Even if true, which it isn't,[58] this is a major departure from the view of accountability implicit in the rhetoric of "no more excuses" and the "soft bigotry of low expectations" that has been so often used by choice advocates to beat up on low performing public schools serving disadvantaged students.

As in the case of charter schools, mounting evidence casts serious doubt on the capacity of private school vouchers to improve academic achievement.[59] They skim the least disadvantaged of qualifying students.[60]

They are quite limited in scope and do nothing to help the disadvantaged students left behind—exemplifying what Jonathan Kozol calls a life boat mentality in which we save the few we can. And where religious schools are included in voucher programs, depending on the availability of alternatives, students can be coerced into opting-in to religious schools as the only way to exit inferior public schools.

So far, only targeted voucher plans that limit participation to low-income students have been implemented. Such plans diminish the centrality of choice as a value and as a mechanism because choice is not construed as a "panacea," by universal voucher advocates like John Chubb and Terry Moe,[61] but is grafted on to the public education system as a means to equalize educational opportunity for those most likely being denied it. From a larger perspective, however, targeted vouchers are in significant danger of being fashioned into a Trojan horse, deployed by the well-organized, well-financed, and highly partisan school choice movement. Polly Williams, the person most responsible for the creation of the Milwaukee voucher program, accused school choice advocates, including then Wisconsin governor Tommy Thompson, who subsequently went to work promoting vouchers in the George W. Bush Administration, of trying to "hijack" the program by expanding it to the more well-to-do.[62] The idea of universal vouchers, first proposed by Milton Friedman in 1950s, has not gone away. Indeed, Friedman created his own foundation devoted to propagating the idea in 1996, and he participates in a wide circle of right-wing think tanks that are behind the idea.[63] Friedman, the pied piper of voucher enthusiasts, says this about targeted vouchers: "I support an entering wedge in the form of a program for low-income people, but I believe it would be a very serious mistake to stop at that point."[64]

Responding to Brighouse's Challenges

Having laid the groundwork, I now return to Brighouse's challenges. In response to the first—that liberal skeptics show how school choice has actually made things worse vis-à-vis social justice than they otherwise would have been—the preponderance of the evidence indicates that school choice has failed to produce gains in achievement and exacerbated segregation. With respect to the latter, rather than reducing segregation that results from allocating schools based on place of residence, school choice has often just added another layer on top of it. Courtney Bell's article (chapter 6) in this volume helps explain why this should be so. Thus, school choice policies have produced a net harm relative to the status quo ante. Moreover, even if school choice had not produced a net harm, it could be seen as having made things worse than they otherwise would have been. For it held out the false promise of a significant improvement in public school performance on the cheap, and distracted attention from the deep social causes of inequality in schools and the kinds of measures required to make progress toward solving them.[65]

In response to Brighouse's second challenge—that liberal skeptics show how providing choice to the parents of disadvantaged children doesn't result in improving their schooling—even if those who actually participate in choice did improve their situations, a hypothesis the evidence doesn't bear out, this would not undermine the critics' case. A legitimate challenge to the skeptics must be in terms of the effects of targeted choice on all disadvantaged students, not just those taking advantage of choice. And this leads back to the general problems that beset targeted vouchers.

Now the response to Brighouse's third challenge to the liberal skeptics: to show that democratic procedures provide a better way of (allocating children to schools) distributing K–12 education than the method of parental choice. This way of putting the challenge concedes to Brighouse that democratic procedures must show their instrumental value relative to parental choice. Of course, a criterion is required on the basis of which to judge the instrumental value of a method of distribution, and I use educational equality, the same criterion Brighouse employs to evaluate the methods for distributing K–12 education. The status quo procedures for distributing K–12 education that are the alternative to school choice, policymaking by state and local school district government bodies, fit the description "democratic." Thus, the question of whether educational equality is better served by school choice than democratic procedures raises no new comparative empirical question, and accordingly may be answered by appeal to the very same empirical evidence used to address Brighouse's first two challenges.

Evidence indicates that, where educational equality is a fundamental concern, democratic procedures are better than school choice as a method of distributing K–12 education. And the case for democratic procedures is stronger when viewed in light of the fact that its chief competitor is the market-based conception of school choice associated with the conservative paradigm.

Brighouse's challenge is further weakened by the fact that democratic procedures cannot be juxtaposed with school choice in the clean way he requires because current choice policies are themselves the outcome of democratic procedures. For example, consider the role of the legislature exemplified in the successive versions of Colorado's school choice policies and laws. If progress is to be made toward greater educational equality, then it will have to be through the democratic process. Thus, egalitarian principles that constrain democratic negotiations and what policies such negotiations can yield are key. Negotiations about school choice policy will continue to go poorly vis-à-vis educational equality unless and until such constraints are put in place.[66]

Conclusion

So what, if anything, are egalitarians to do to get some traction in an educational policy arena dominated by the conservative paradigm's world of meanings? Changing the conversation about educational reform so as to diminish the centrality of choice as a value and as a mechanism is the only feasible strategy I see. Choice in some form is, indeed, here to stay. But instead of being choice-driven, enrollment policies should be choice-utilizing but equality-driven. This is the basic egalitarian rationale for targeted vouchers, which, as we have seen, turn out to be quite flawed in the overall scheme and are in danger of being hijacked. A more encouraging instantiation is Wake County, North Carolina, which includes Raleigh.[67] The attendance policy is clearly equality-driven, designed to close the achievement gap and foster integration, rather than choice-driven, though choice, particularly in the form of magnet schools, is incorporated into the policy. Unfortunately, the Wake County policy is probably feasible in only a handful of places because it depends on an interdistrict arrangement and is rooted in a thoroughgoing commitment to desegregation that began in the 1970s. Other restricted choice arrangements such as controlled choice and voluntary transfers have produced some initially promising results but are under increasing attack from the conservative paradigm for compromising parents' freedom of choice.[68]

The sources of inequality in U.S. public education are many and are deeply seated. Until and unless these are addressed, there is no reason to expect that the current choice policy alternatives of laying an expanded system of choice over such a structure, as in charter schools and open enrollment, or along side it, as in targeted vouchers, could mitigate inequality. On the contrary, it is reasonable to expect that the result would be increased inequality. That is exactly what has happened.

Notes for Chapter 3

1. Michael Walzer, *Spheres of Justice: A Defense of Pluralism and Equality* (New York: Basic Books, 1983), xiv.

2. "Paradigm" is, of course, appropriated from Thomas Kuhn, *Structure of Scientific Revolutions*, 3rd ed. (Chicago: University of Chicago Press, 1996). My meaning is intended to be broader to more fully incorporate the political forces impinging on and incorporated into empirical research, as in the conservative and liberal paradigms described subsequently.

3. James Coleman, *Equality of Educational Opportunity* (Washington, DC: United States Government Printing Office, 1966).

4. Charles Murray, *Losing Ground* (New York: Basic Books, 1984).

5. Murray himself used the concept of a "paradigm" to characterize competing perspectives on social policy. Ibid., 41.

6. See Rosemary C. Salamone, *Equal Education Under Law: Legal Rights and Federal Policy in the Post-Brown Era* (New York: St. Martin's Press, 1986).

7. John E. Chubb and Terry M. Moe, *Politics, Markets and America's Schools* (Washington, DC: The Brookings Institution, 1990).

8. See, for example, Kenneth R. Howe, *Understanding Equal Educational Opportunity: Social Justice, Democracy and Schooling* (New York: Teachers College Press, 1997).

9. Whether school choice for social justice can be successfully defended in the abstract or in other political circumstances is not within the scope of my argument. I think it clearly can be.

10. Harry Brighouse, *School Choice and Social Justice* (New York: Oxford University Press, 2000).

11. Ibid., 209

12. Harry Brighouse, "A Modest Defense of School Choice," *Journal of Philosophy of Education* 36, no. 4 (2002): 653–59.

13. Brighouse, *School Choice*, 35–36.

14. http://www.friedmanfoundation.org/about/index.html (accessed December 2, 2005).

15. http://www.cato.org/research/education/index.html (accessed December 2, 2005).

16. http://www.manhattan-institute.org/html/cci.htm#02 (accessed December 2, 2005).

17. http://www.heritage.org/research/features/mandate/2005/topic. cfm?topic=15 (accessed December 2, 2005).

18. http://www-hoover.stanford.edu/research/education/ (accessed December 10, 2005).

19. From the "Charter School Guide for Activists," http://www.edreform. com/index.cfm?fuseAction=section&pSectionID=14&cSectionID=34 (accessed February 20, 2006).

20. http://www.edreform.com/index.cfm?fuseAction=document&docume ntID=2167 &section ID=37&NEWSYEAR=2006 (accessed February 20, 2006).

21. "Charter School Fundraising," email received from NCSC, January 26, 2006.

22. American Federation of Teachers, "Charter Schools Underperforming, Repeatedly Delayed," http://www.aft.org/news/2004/AFT_charterschools.htm (accessed November 5, 2005).

23. See Kenneth Howe, "Free Market Free for All," *Education Week*, April 10, 2002.

24. Integration is most directly tied to civic education—as means of fostering democratic pluralism—but it is also related to the principle of equality, as a factor relevant to the provision of "effective" educational resources. Brighouse uses "effective" educational resources to refer to educational resources that can be taken advantage of by given kinds of students (e.g., a hearing aid for a deaf student, see *School Choice*, 138–39). The Coleman Report was the first to suggest that integrated classrooms, with the proportions of white and African American students falling within a certain range, function as an "effective" educational resource for African American students. For a recent and comprehensive examination of this issue, see Russell W. Rumberger and Gregory J. Palardy, "Does Segregation Still Matter? The Impact of Student Composition on Academic Achievement in High School," *Teachers College Record* 107, no. 9 (2005): 1999–2045.

25. Of course, there is no guarantee the ground will not shift; the rehabilitation of the principle "separate but equal" is one place this might be happening.

26. William Howell and Paul Peterson, *The Education Gap: Vouchers and Urban Schools* (Washington, DC: The Brookings Institute, 2002).

27. Alan B. Krueger and Pei Zhu, "Another Look at the New York City Voucher Experiment" (paper presented at the Conference on Randomized Experimentation in the Social Sciences, Yale University, August 20, 2002).

28. See Clive Belfield and Henry M. Levin, "Vouchers and Public Policy: When Ideology Trumps Evidence," *American Journal of Education* 111 (August, 2005): 548–67.

29. Brian P. Gill, P. Michael Timpane, Karen E. Ross, and Dominic J. Brewer, *Rhetoric versus Reality: What We Know and What We Need to Know about Vouchers and Charter Schools* (Santa Monica, CA: RAND, 2001).

30. Belfield and Levin, "Vouchers and Public Policy."

31. Erika Frankenberg and Chungmei Lee, *Charter Schools and Race: A Lost Opportunity for Integrated Education* (Cambridge, MA: The Civil Rights Project at Harvard University, 2003).

32. For a comprehensive discussion, see Martin Carnoy, Rebecca Jacobsen, Lawrence Mishel, and Richard Rothstein, *The Charter School Dust-Up: Examining the Evidence on Enrollment and Achievement* (New York: Teachers College Press and Economic Policy Institute, 2005). See also Christopher Lubienski and Sarah Theule Lubienski, "Charter, Private and Public Schools and Academic Achievement: New Evidence from NAEP Mathematics Data," (National Center for the Study of Privatization in Education, 2006).

33. The discussion of Colorado is composed largely of excerpts from Kenneth R. Howe, "Colorado's Charter Schools and the Choice/Equity Balance," *Prism* 6, no. 1 (2006): 9–12.

34. SRI International, *Evaluation of the Public Charter Schools Program: Final Report* (Washington, DC: U.S. Department of Education, 2004), http://www.ed.gov/rschstat/eval/choice/pcsp-final/index.html (accessed November 5, 2005).

35. p < .01, Ibid., 112.

36. p < .01, Ibid., 113.

37. p < .01, Ibid., 114.

38. The districts are Boulder Valley, Brighton 27J, Denver, Jeffco, Douglas County, Harrison 2, Greeley 6, Pueblo City 60, Adams 12, Colorado Springs 11, and Poudre R1.

39. It is quite clearly not such a consideration in Colorado or in many other states. See Table 1 in Frankenberg and Lee, *Charter Schools and Race,* 20–22.

40. See Rumberger and Palardy, "Does Segregation Still Matter?" and Rothstein, *Class and Schools.*

41. Rothstein, *Class and Schools.*

42. Frederick Hess, *Revolution at the Margins: The Impact of Competition on Urban School Systems* (Washington, DC: The Brookings Institute, 2002).

43. Frankenberg and Lee, *Charter Schools and Race.*

44. See, for example, Kenneth Howe, Margaret Eisenhart and Damian Betebenner, "School Choice Crucible: A Case Study of Boulder Valley," *Phi Delta Kappan* 83, no. 2 (2001): 137–46.

45. Carnoy et al., *The Charter School Dust-Up.*

46. American Federation of Teachers, "Do Charter Schools Measure Up? The Charter School Experiment After 10 Years" (2002), http://www.aft.org/pubs-reports/downloads/teachers/charterreport02.pdf (accessed November 5, 2005).

47. Julie Blair, "AFT Study Denounces Charters," *Education Week,* July 17, 2002.

48. Center for Educational Reform, "Charter Leaders Dismiss AFT Report: Teachers Union Deliberately Skews Data Against Charters" (Washington, DC, July 16, 2002).

49. Chester Finn, "The Shame of AFT," *Education Gadfly* 2, no. 27 (July 2002).

50. Gill et al., *Rhetoric versus Reality.*

51. Howe, "Free Market Free for All."

52. American Federation of Teachers, *Charter School Achievement on the 2003 National Assessment of Educational Progress* (Washington, DC: American Federation of Teachers, 2004).

53. Carnoy et al., *The Charter School Dust-Up,* 13.

54. National Center for Education Statistics, National Assessment of Educational Progress, *The Nation's Report Card. America's Charter Schools: Results from the NAEP 2003 Pilot Study* (Washington, DC: NCES, 2005–456).

55. Furthermore, a subsequent, more expansive and more methodologically sophisticated analysis has produced similar findings. See Lubienski and Lubienski, "Charter, Private and Public Schools."

56. Caroline Hoxby, "A Straightforward Comparison of Charter Schools and Regular Public Schools in the United States," http://post.economics.harvard.edu/faculty/hoxby/papers/hoxbyallcharters.pdf (accessed November 5, 2005).

57. Diana J. Schemo, "Nation's Charter Schools Lagging Behind, U.S. Test Scores Reveal," *New York Times,* August 17, 2004.

58. Carnoy et al., *Charter School Dust-Up.*

59. Belfield and Levin, "Vouchers and Public Policy"; Lubienski and Lubienski, "Charter, Private and Public Schools."

60. This claim is based on mother's level of education. Gill et al., *Rhetoric versus Reality*, 148–49.

61. Chubb and Moe, *Politics, Markets, and America's Schools*.

62. Megan Twohey, "Who Vouches for Vouchers?" *The American Prospect* 13, no. 12 (July 1, 2002).

63. There is a constellation of organizations that include the Bradley Foundation, the Walton Foundation, the Friedman Foundation, the Heritage Foundation, the Fordham Foundation, the Cato Institute, the Manhattan Institute, the Heartland Institute, and last but not least, the Hoover Institution.

64. From an interview with George A. Clowes, "The Only Solution is Competition," The Heartland Institute, December 1, 1998, http://www.heartland.org/Article.cfm?artId=12013 (accessed October 18, 2005).

65. A good treatment of the limitations of school-based reform is provided by Richard Rothstein, *Class and Schools* (New York: Teachers College Press, 2004).

66. See Amy Gutmann, *Democratic Education* (Princeton, NJ: Princeton University Press, 1999) and Howe, *Understanding Equal Educational Opportunity*, for similar elaborations.

67. Alan Finder, "As Test Scores Jump, Raleigh Credits Integration by Income," *New York Times*, September 25, 2005.

68. Amy Stuart Wells and Robert L. Crain, "Where School Desegregation and School Choice Policies Collide: Voluntary Transfer Plans and Controlled Choice," in *School Choice and Diversity: What the Evidence Says*, ed. Janelle T. Scott (New York, Teachers College Press, 2005).

Chapter 4

Intergenerational Justice and School Choice

Kathleen Knight Abowitz

Schools are institutions frequently scrutinized for their ability to promote principles of justice, and educational policies are rightly evaluated as to how well such policies attend to the needs of families and students who are least advantaged in our society. School choice policies continue to be evaluated and criticized for the ways in which various choice schemes fulfill promises of a more just system of schooling for poor families. Several chapters in this volume contribute to these debates, arguing for targeted choice policies that provide specific mechanisms for helping poor and marginalized families to take advantage of opportunities leveraged by choice schemes.[1]

The standard of justice requires that we measure how fairly our educational institutions distribute current shared, limited resources, how students and families are accorded respect in the schooling process, and how well they prepare all classes, races, ethnicities, and genders of students for fulfilling lives beyond school. School choice policies have arisen, in part, as solutions to unjust school practices. Public magnet schools were developed as mechanisms to desegregate urban school systems. Many proponents of voucher systems argue that targeted voucher schemes allowed families most harmed by inadequate public schools and least able to choose a new school through normal alternatives available to middle class parents to seek alternatives through public funding for private schooling. As choice mechanisms continue to be introduced in the United States, questions of justice remain critical.

In speaking of justice, we normally consider the extent to which policies or procedures are fair and respectful with regards to fellow human beings of our present society. Educational justice is normally concerned with the needs of the present generation of children and their future lives as workers and citizens. These formulations of justice that have informed educational policy-making are important yet incomplete, for another set of moral commitments must be considered as we evaluate the impact of various school choice policies.

Our duties to future generations merit educational focus and attention, as no society can ignore the inheritance it leaves its prospective citizens. In particular, the ecological inheritance we leave to future generations hinges in part on the way that educational institutions consider sustainability as a fundamental aim today. Policies promoting various forms of school choice should be judged not only by their potential to deliver relatively equal opportunities and outcomes among various classes and races of U.S. students today, but should also be judged by their potential to contribute to the educational goals relating to the well-being of tomorrow's generations.

This chapter attempts to broaden the justice debates surrounding school choice in the United States by showing how questions of intergenerational justice matter to educational policy in general and choice schemes in particular. If justice requires that we attend to the needs of current and future generations, then not all school choice policies are alike in terms of being able to account for these needs. In the first part of this chapter, I develop a conception of intergenerational justice, creating from liberal frameworks a broad notion of what it means for educational institutions to account for the needs of future generations. I use the idea of intergenerational justice as one of three parts of a comprehensive framework for evaluating *educational justice*, a term which will refer to the degree to which educational institutions account for equity, respect, and sustainability in their structure, procedures and programs. In the second part, I evaluate one new choice mechanism, Ohio's EdChoice scholarship program, in light of this trivalent notion of educational justice. As I show, school choice policies promoting weak or nonexistent state educational authority will not be able to meet minimal criteria for a trivalent framework of justice, and in particular will fail to guarantee that aims of intergenerational justice will be adequately addressed in choice schools. School choice models like Ohio's EdChoice Scholarship program will suffer the tragedy of the commons problem, in that market models cannot reliably guarantee educational institutions that will prepare students for environmental stewardship in the future. Other models of choice, however, are quite promising in their abilities to address a trivalent framework of justice inclusive of intergenerational obligations. School choice policies which use state educational authority to promote communal forms of schooling, and which provide incentives for sustainability education as a key curricular aim, are examples of how the educational aims of ecological sustainability and policies promoting school choice are quite compatible. Choice policies oriented toward promoting communal forms of schooling can help inject some sense of community and place and with direction, can promote knowledge and values oriented toward our obligations to future generations. In the third section, I expand on these claims.

A Trivalent Notion of Justice:
Distribution, Respect, and Transmission

What do we owe future generations? Schooling has historically been an attempt to reproduce societies, helping to pass along the social mores, knowledge, and values of each society. Education has, in its essence, a forward thinking approach. It is a project of preparing each new generation to live in the world. Yet typically in the West, we evaluate education in terms of how well it prepares current generations of students to construct their lives in individually and socially fulfilling ways. As educators, we look ahead, but only as far as the current generation.

Justice requires that we do indeed look ahead; it requires that we consider the educational prospects of an elementary school student in Camden, New Jersey, and judge how well the schools she'll attend will serve her interests as a person, citizen, worker, and family member. There are several types of justice to consider when making this evaluation. We most commonly consider distributive justice, in that we ask what kinds of scarce resources, such as good teachers, quality textbooks, or well-appointed school buildings are allocated to this student in comparison to other students in the state or nation. Distributive justice, in the liberal-egalitarian tradition, uses equality as a primary principle to evaluate how well this student fares in regards to the resources allocated to her formal education.[2] Focusing on socioeconomic factors and material goods, distributive justice is a framework that helps school choice researchers judge how various choice policies will affect the ways educational goods are allocated to various groups in our society, particularly as school choice advocates claim that their policies will do better than traditional schools at addressing the educational injustices suffered by the poor.

Yet justice is not a matter of material goods alone. Justice is also measured by how this hypothetical student in Camden, New Jersey is recognized and respected in her school. Justice as recognition looks beyond the distribution of educational dollars and capital to examine how her schools will recognize her identity, according both human dignity due to all students as well as recognizing aspects of her identity that are unique and special. Justice as recognition uses respect as a key principle to evaluate how well this student fares in regards to receiving a formal education that promotes her value as a cultural and human being. Through curriculum, discipline procedures, communications with families, and assessment processes, schools are required to acknowledge and respect the various unique cultural and other identities students bring to school. This may involve ways in which educators communicate with and regard students and their families, special curriculum units that focus on inquiry related to students' interests or cultures, or special programs for underserved students.[3] Most voucher policies provide for standards of respect chiefly through market mechanisms of free enterprise, offering families the right to seek schooling that recognizes their unique educational needs as related to cultural or other kinds of identities. Charter laws provide for respect through the potential of a combination of free market enterprise combined with the potential of civil society to help create alternative kinds of schools serving the needs of educationally underserved families using public funds. The argument goes that if smaller, more unique schools can be opened up through charter school laws, for example, these unique schools will be more likely to recognize and serve students' unique needs and interests than their larger, more impersonal public school counterparts.[4] Justice as recognition requires that school choice policies of various kinds provide for schooling that acknowledges various aspects of a student's identity, and requires that all options provide minimal levels of respect through schooling structures, procedures and curriculum.

Distribution and recognition are both justice frameworks that predict how the current generation of children will be schooled according to principles of equality and respect, but they do not provide criteria for evaluating how schools serve us beyond the current generation. When linked together, these distributive and recognition ideals account for how equity and respect, material resources and cultural recognition, are mutually constitutive.[5] Yet, in these usual formulations, neither distribution nor recognition are quite forward thinking enough. Neither of these formulations can account for the problems of ecological sustainability that face us today and in the future. Distributive justice is normally conceived as the equitable allocation of present resources to present, living generations. Recognition is conceived as allocating respect and dignity to current students and families. Intergenerational justice adds a third standard to consider in evaluating a student's formal schooling in relationship to ideals of justice. How well are schools attending to the basic needs of future generations? Schooling policies and curricula designed using criterion of intergenerational justice will provide educational frameworks that avoid causing harm to future generations. In particular, intergenerational justice helps us frame an evaluation of how well schools are preparing society as a whole and students as individuals to live sustainably, particularly with regards to scarce but necessary natural resources.

Intergenerational justice does not require predicting the future, nor does it require deciding in advance how future generations of people should lead their lives. The obligations of sustainability only extend to meeting basic human needs, the kinds we can reliably predict. "Institutions are humanly sustainable if and only if their operation does not leave future generations worse equipped to meet their needs than members of the future generation are to meet their own needs."[6] Such a definition of sustainability obligates us to consider what basic human needs future generations will have, and how present institutions, policies, and norms may take into account those future needs. Just as we are obligated to poor and marginalized families and students for whom school choice policies may be having harmful effects on educational outcomes, so are we obligated to future generations, and must examine policies with effects to sustainability.

Intergenerational justice, an idea basic to some indigenous cultures, represents a moral appeal to the rights of future citizens and our obligations to them as future inhabitants of our society. As a moral and political ideal, intergenerational justice takes seriously the responsibility to offer future generations a wide range of choices and freedoms, realizing that to do so requires protecting their vital interests through our own actions today in "managing the relationship between ecological, social, and economic considerations."[7] As Barry argues, this means

> taking seriously the idea that conditions must be such as to sustain a range of possible conceptions of the good life. In the nature of the case, we cannot imagine in any detail what may be thought of as a good life in the future. But we can be quite confident that it will not include the violation of what I have called vital interest: adequate nutrition, clean drinking-water, clothing and housing, health care and education, for example. We can, in addition, at the very least leave open to people in the future the possibility of living in a world in which nature is not utterly subordinated to the pursuit of consumer satisfaction.[8]

As a framework designed to extend the distributive and recognition ideals of justice, intergenerational justice manages the relationship between ecological, social, and economic concerns using principles of both the distributive and recognition frameworks. The principle of equality is used to evaluate whether an educational policy or practice is promoting the rights of future citizens to access vital interests such as adequate nutrition and clean drinking water, and by educating students today with regards to sustainability aims. Future generations have rights to these vital interests, and current generations are infringing upon these rights when we fail to live in ecologically sustainable ways today. The principle of respect is used in the intergenerational justice framework to consider whether an educational policy or practice recognizes the basic needs of future generations. The principle of respect calls educators to recognize future generations as unborn but potential inhabitants of the earth, who will have to share in the limited and common natural resources of the planet. Educating for justice today requires educating for respectful recognition that tomorrow's inhabitants of our society inherit both the natural wealth and ecological problems that we leave behind today.

Ultimately, intergenerational justice supplements distributive and recognition frameworks of justice with what Achterberg calls the transmission principle, which requires that "we should not hand the world that we have used and exploited on to our successors in a substantially worse shape than we 'received' it."[9] Transmission is linked to principles of equality and respect, conjoining these to a more holistic set of principles with which to evaluate educational polices, practices and ends. Intergenerational justice combines with distribution and recognition to form a triumvirate framework of educational justice, useful for evaluating how well schooling helps all students, both rich and poor, mainstream and marginalized, and present and future generations, attain an equitable, respectful, and sustainable society. How successfully have choice programs responded to principles of transmission? There is virtually no discussion in the educational choice debates regarding the criterion associated with intergenerational justice, and if sustainability aims have been served by choice mechanisms, it has been an unintended consequence rather than a central goal. A handful of private and magnet schools that have a life science or environmental emphasis have likely received more students or tuition dollars from various choice schemes, but these are peripheral consequences rather than targeted outcomes.

Evaluating schools with the transmission principle would involve judging how adequately their institutional structures, processes, and curricula prepare students to understand and participate in a society faced with balancing ecological, social, and economic concerns. While a multitude of schooling models and curricula could potentially prepare students with the knowledge, values, and skills to exist in such a society, here I outline a minimal sense of institutional criterion. Schools serve intergenerational justice when they attend to basic environmental standards in their structural maintenance, and when they deliver educational programs that include a sound grounding in the life sciences, an experiential component set in local ecosystems, and an adequate education for critical thinking and public deliberation in the context of our modern democracy. In addition, a moral education component is necessary. As discussed later, schools mindful of the transmission principle will incorporate a virtue-based approach in order to successfully incorporate criteria of intergenerational justice into effective educational programs.

Concerns of justice must be central to policy discussions in order for schooling to provide justice for current and future generations. In this section, I have sketched a trivalent notion of educational justice, examining how principles of distribution, respect, and transmission conjoin to form a complex criterion for judging how schools are serving students and their families. To better explore this trivalent notion, I examine a new policy providing educational vouchers throughout my own state.

Choice and Future Generations

There are many school choice mechanisms, from the very uncontroversial idea that parents may send their children to private schools to different kinds of voucher and charter programs (see Brighouse, chapter 2). Brighouse as well as Howe (chapter 3) find that only certain types of choice mechanisms will likely benefit the least advantaged families in U.S. society. How will choice schemes fare under a trivalent measure of justice? To explore this general question, I focus on one particular voucher program in my own state, which has an extensive record of experimentation with choice programs.

Ohio's Educational Choice Scholarship Pilot Program passed the Ohio House in March of 2006, and is now called The EdChoice Scholarship Program by the Ohio Department of Education. Ohio's EdChoice Scholarship Program follows the now periled Florida voucher system as the second effort to implement a state-wide system in which tax dollars in the form of educational vouchers can be used by qualified students to enroll in private and religious schools. In Ohio, EdChoice aims to serve students in schools with the state rankings of Academic Emergency or Academic Watch lasting longer than three years; 213 schools in 34 Ohio districts fit this description in early 2008 (up from 99 in summer 2007).[10] Ohio EdChoice began in the fall of 2006 to "offer up to 14,000 students with the opportunity to attend a participating private school of their choice."[11] Actual enrollments will be limited to those students admitted to their desired private school. The list of approximately 300 private schools accepting enrollments for the EdChoice scholarship program includes approximately 85% Christian affiliated private schools and several secular (including Montessori), Jewish, and Islamist schools.[12] These schools cannot charge families at or below 200% of the federal poverty level for supplemental tuition payments above the scholarship of $4,250 for Kindergarten through eighth grades, and $5,000 for ninth through 12th grades.

With respect to distributive justice based on principles of equity, the EdChoice program attempts to provide families in inadequate schools with educational options. It targets families in low-performing school districts and makes provisions disallowing schools from charging poor families extra tuition, requiring schools with tuition differentials to offer voluntary service activities in lieu of payments. But EdChoice, like the Cleveland Scholarship and Tutoring Program on which it is partly based, is not only limited to low-income families but is also available to those children who attend schools designated as poorly performing.[13] Insofar as EdChoice will fund tuitions to private school that provide more equitable distribution than currently exists of high-quality schooling opportunities to families in low-performing districts, the criterion of distributive justice could well be met by the EdChoice program, at least for those students who get to take advantage of the limited number of vouchers. But because of the broadly targeted nature of EdChoice, some or perhaps many of these scholarships may be used by the least disadvantaged of those attending the failing schools.[14] Because questions of distributive justice are partly empirical—to be determined by longitudinal study of the EdChoice program—these questions cannot be addressed here. Suffice to say, however, that EdChoice Ohio has expanded Cleveland's voucher program with some minor revisions, and the achievement data on Cleveland's program with respect to equity goals are at best mixed. That Ohio has made the Cleveland program a pilot for a state-wide venture is more proof that proposals to expand voucher programs, despite the egalitarian rhetoric of their advocates, do not rest on conclusive data supporting the success of these programs in more equitably distributing educational success for all children in need.[15]

The second framework of justice revolves around principles of recognition and respect, particularly difficult to make concrete in the educational realm, and made more complex by the fact that EdChoice funnels public education dollars to private and religious institutions. In Ohio, there are a number of fundamentalist Christian schools eligible to receive EdChoice scholarships, and a small handful of Jewish and Islamist fundamentalist schools as well. To the credit of EdChoice with regards to the principle of respect, fundamentalist believers will likely find more understanding and accepting educational environments for their believing children in these schools. Yet, other issues of respect are problematic from a private school point of view. These schools, for example, will likely define respect to girls and women quite differently than most public schools; they may characterize other religious or ethnic groups in unfair, slanted, or disrespectful ways. Similarly, private schools of all kinds are free to incorporate all manner of half-truths and stereotypes about people from different ethnic, racial, national, and social groups into their curricula, because of the lack of public oversight. A review of the oversight mechanisms built into the EdChoice law reveals minimal criterion and procedure for states to use in evaluating how scholarship schools are attending to minimal principles of respect and, as we shall see, transmission.

Eligible schools must comply with the Operating Standards for Ohio schools, fairly implement admission procedures, report the tuition structure of their institutions, and must administer annual state achievement tests in grades three through eighth as well as the Ohio Graduation Test, beginning in tenth grade. The Ohio Department of Education performs random visits to schools to ensure conformity to the Operating Standards, which make provisions for high academic expectations, balanced curricular representations in social sciences topics such as geography, history, and government, and for nondiscriminatory staff hiring.[16] The Operating Standards do not provide accounts of what high expectations or balanced curricular representations look like, and they do not provide criteria for fair and inclusive educational programs or practices. An official from the Ohio State Education would have safe grounds on which to close eligibility to a school with evidence only of the most obvious and flagrant defiance of basic nondiscriminatory and inclusive clauses in the Operating Standards. Again, empirical studies will have to be used to answer the sticky questions around a diverse array of private and religious schools meeting conditions of educational justice related to the principle of respect, and no studies of schools of choice, of which I am aware, address the question of respect. Most focus on questions of distribution. Yet, the educational authority to evaluate and properly address violations of the principle of respect seems extremely limited, particularly as it relates to curricular matters. Indeed, insofar as voucher programs are designed to allow maximum freedom of educational aims under the banners of freedom and pluralism, programs like EdChoice are intended to provide the state with very limited curricular control, assuming that parents will not choose learning environments that disrespect their children.

The third framework of educational justice, that of intergenerational justice, would require that the schools eligible to receive Ohio EdChoice scholarships promote policies and curricula that minimally address the principle of transmission. Schools meeting this minimal criterion would have to address ecological sustainability in their curriculum as well as in their administrative and operating procedures. Curriculum would promote content, skills, and values that are aligned with the transmission principle. Content knowledge would minimally include several basic domains: the study of sciences with a focus on life sciences, experiential inquiry into local ecosystems; and knowledge of participatory democratic governance. Skills associated with the transmission principle would include critical thinking and the participation in deliberation for shared decision making. Values promoted in the curriculum would include virtues associated with a basic responsibility to act in such a way that future generations' vital interests in clean water, air, and adequate nutrition are not harmed. Schools would, of course, do well to go far beyond these basic curricula goals to fully educate for sustainability. But, in terms of policy, the content and pedagogy of all educational programs would need to meet these minimal requirements in order to be considered as meeting the principle of transmission as required by intergenerational justice.

The sole control that the state of Ohio retains over curriculum in scholarship eligible schools consists of the requirement to administer annual achievement tests and the Ohio Graduate Test. Because schools must give these tests and report their data to the state, the department of education unofficially requires some standardized content in reading, math, science, social studies, and citizenship. These tests, based on the Academic Content Standards of the state, consist of reading and math assessments in all grades, writing assessments in grades four and seven, science assessments in grades five and eight, and social studies assessments in grades five and eight. At present, there are precious few Academic Content Standards in science or social studies that relate to knowledge, skills, or values promoting the transmission principle. Science content about the interrelatedness of ecosystems, about the finite nature of the earth's resources, renewable and nonrenewable sources of energy, and observable changes in the climate are examples of content benchmarks scattered across the grades.[17] Geography content standards include benchmarks regarding the relationship between human and physical environments, and Citizenship content standards include the role of government, the role of elections, and ways to participate in democratic governance.[18] These academic content standards, though all pointing in the proper directions toward some minimal content regarding ecological sustainability, are scattered and insufficient to direct a coherent focus on ecological sustainability as one significant aim of an educational program.[19] If private schools are motivated to use these Academic Content Standards as a basis for their pedagogy, they will find little to guide them in shaping curricula according to the minimal knowledge, values, and skills required for intergenerational justice to be served.

The EdChoice Scholarship program provides a regulated voucher scheme and retains for the state some basic powers of oversight as tools for ensuring educational justice. It attends to the redistribution of schooling resources for disadvantaged families to some extent, but vouchers can be used by rich and poor alike, as long as they are attending low-performing public schools. As such, the program can provide greater equity for some families who are able to access better private schools within a reasonable distance from their home, but will leave many other families in the same inadequate schools. With respect to frameworks of recognition and respect, EdChoice provides very minimal nondiscriminatory safeguards in the delivery of sound educational programs to all students, and for fair admission and hiring practices. However, the program provides scant criteria and no formal mechanisms for evaluating curricula, and because principles of respect and transmission require curricular aims in line with these objectives, Ohio is left with no tools to ensure that these schools are designing curriculum that meets minimal requirements for respect and transmission to future generations. Advocates of market schemes are likely to reply that as environmental programs become more pressing to the general public, schools will naturally respond to market demand and take up sustainability aims on their own, without impositions of state authority.

In his seminal essay, "The Tragedy of the Commons," Garrett Hardin reminds us that the idea of a commons requires what he bluntly calls "coersion."[20] In his example, a jointly owned piece of land can graze one hundred animals indefinitely but anything above that number exceeds the land's carrying capacity. If each shepherd is motivated to maximize his or her profits, then there will be incentives for grazing more than their proper share of animals. If ten shepherds have ten sheep each, and if one of them purchases one or two more, the profits of the other nine shepherds are cut, because all the sheep will be a little bit leaner. The shepherd with 12 sheep, however, reaps larger benefits and incurs no obvious individual costs in the process. The commons —the idea of shared, limited resources like land, oceans, and air—is harmed when humans motivated by self-interested rationality make their tragic choices. Only coercion, Hardin argued, would correct this. "The social arrangements that produce responsibility are arrangements that create coercion, of some sort." Hardin is thinking here of mutual coercion—a social contract—agreed on by social participants as a code of responsibility that all would feasibly support for their long-term interests. Taxation is the mechanism that creates coercion, as are laws that punish criminals. State-mandated schooling is another form of coercion, the necessity of which is widely agreed upon in our society. But coercion for what purpose? Schooling itself obviously provides no guarantee that students will be prepared to secure the commons for future generations. Labaree argues convincingly that most Americans today view schooling as a tool for social mobility, and education as a private good primarily used for getting a family ahead in the economic race of life.[21] Because sustainability aims to provide no immediate benefit to an individual family, and because individuals can succeed in any number of schools that ignore considerations of sustainability in their curriculum, the tragedy of the commons concept is descriptive of how a free-market educational system cannot guarantee aims of intergenerational justice.

Market-based voucher schemes, even broadly regulated ones like EdChoice, primarily operate on an idea of justice based in private property. In this libertarian framework, political institutions should protect property rights and individual freedom. Because children are widely seen by libertarian citizens and politicians as the property of their parents, schooling systems should promote a variety of options with minimal state interference in those choices. Yet the tragedy of the commons shows how all children, as adults far beyond the authority of their parents, will eventually operate in the public sphere affecting the welfare of all. The tragedy of the commons is that our freedom within it contains the seeds of our demise, and thus for future freedoms to be supported, some constraint or coercion on present freedoms is required. In order for a school to serve aims of intergenerational justice, some coericon by the state is required, because we cannot count on the good conscience of individuals in this high-stakes gamble with the future of our ecosystem.

To serve the aims of intergenerational justice may run the risk of directly conflicting with some interpretations of the respect principle. Consider a fundamentalist Christian school that refuses to teach the science of evolution on the grounds that creationism is more in line with their cultural identity as Christians. To teach evolution as dictated by national science standards would constitute a lack of recognition of their ways of life and beliefs. Families eligible for EdChoice can choose this school for their children and pay tuition through state-issued vouchers. Or consider an imaginary private school, the Milton Friedman High

School, that vigorously promotes free market capitalism through a curricular focus on capitalism, entrepreneurial skills, and the virtues of free markets. This school may reject the imposition of the aim of sustainability, seeing it as directly conflicting with their free-market ideology. These two situations present direct conflicts, and the state finds itself funding an education that is harmful to the principle of transmission because students are taught a fundamentally flawed understanding of the earth and its history, with no understanding at all of the knowledge, skills, and values necessary for sustainable living. These are cases in which we see the extent to which the principle of transmission constrains respect. Feinberg writes, "any educational system that failed to provide children, regardless of their cultural background, with the conceptual tools that are required to make a reasonable life in the modern world of science and technology is guilty of cultural neglect."[22] I interpret this to be a way of limiting the authority of cultural and familial groups from choosing educational programs that fail to prepare all students with the tools they need to live a successful life, broadly defined. I paraphrase Feinberg when I say that there should be limits on the authority of cultural and familial groups to choose schooling—to the extent that school choice should never be allowed to be a mechanism for families to avoid or neglect the aims of sustainability. EdChoice offers only the most basic limitations on the authority of the family to by-pass or avoid sustainability as an educational aim. It provides the state with no real oversight or influence over curricula, the primary vehicle through which the transmission principle is served in education. As a voucher program, EdChoice is a program based on a maximal notion of the authority of the family and a correspondingly minimal authority of the state. Thus, it is difficult to see how all but the most targeted voucher programs would fail to serve the principle of transmission. Can choice mechanisms be designed to combine the strengths of choice with qualities that can maximize an institution's ability to educate for a trivalent conception of educational justice, serving equity, respect, and transmission?

Amending Choice

I wish to defend the general idea that mechanisms for school choice should be amended and targeted rather than eradicated. Broadly regulated voucher schemes such as EdChoice fail to provide educational justice in important ways. Such schemes can produce some limited remedies for distributive justice, but their power to support minimal criterion for respect and transmission is weak. Yet some variations of choice mechanisms can be designed to create more communal social groups in which educational justice is better served, particularly as it relates to the principles of respect and transmission. Selected choice policies can promote schooling in which virtues of justice and knowledge of place can be nurtured in the educational process. Part of the coercion that Hardin seeks is the force of normative or ethical ideals that will guide us as we interact within the commons. As part of larger educational program that includes content and skills oriented toward sustainability, virtue-oriented education can serve the ideals of justice, particularly intergenerational justice, quite well. Place-based education serves ideals of justice and can be diversely utilized by many different kinds of schools, but provides a substantive local orientation to schooling through which principles of respect and transmission can be concretely studied and lived.

One of the primary appeals of school choice mechanisms like voucher programs or charter school laws is that they make the chance to attend smaller schools more widely available. Smaller schools have various general traits that appeal to families, not the least of which is their ability to develop a unique identity in terms of how they serve students, and their ability to help foster community between educators, students, and parents. Communal structures can provide educators with greater leverage to foster the virtues of sustainability, a necessary part of an education sufficient for aims of transmission.

Intergenerational justice is served when students begin to adopt an ethic of sustainability, so as to provide internal constraints on how we act in public in regards to the commons. As an abstract ideal, justice for future generations will not motivate students to reconfigure their actions based on the short-term immediate pleasures of current consumption practices. Respecting the rights of future generations does not give most individuals enough reason to act responsibly in regards to the ecosystems of which they are a part.[23] A sense of duty to the ecosystems we are part of constitutes a widely acceptable definition of the ethic of sustainability we seek. Although this duty might be very broadly defined, to adapt to a wide array of belief systems that are evidenced in schools within a pluralist democracy, virtues associated with this duty provide concrete norms and habits to shape personal action. Virtues associated with respect for others as well as respect for the environment would enable educators to more assertively educate for justice, and it would particularly make sustainability aims more concrete and able to be infused within an educational program. Smaller schools are likely better able to promote virtues associated with justice throughout their programs. Religious schools of various kinds might feasibly promote sustainability aims insofar as these are seen as compatible with religious doctrine and spiritual beliefs. Virtue-based education is particularly important to promote with respect to intergenerational justice, and the kinds of schools that are promoted by choice mechanisms may provide as good or better educational environments than public schools for sustainability education.

A related educational goal associated with intergenerational justice that may be well served by choice policy mechanisms is incorporating a sense of place through content and pedagogy. The notion of place is powerful and pervasive in the writings of sustainability education circles and a concept that is well suited to help educators seek aims of intergenerational justice through curricula and pedagogy. Sobel defines place-based education as

> the process of using the local community and environment as a starting point to teach concepts in language arts, mathematics, social studies, science, and other subjects across the curriculum. Emphasizing hands-on, real-world learning experiences, this approach to education increases academic achievement, helps students develop stronger ties to their community, enhances students' appreciation for the natural world, and creates a heightened commitment to serving as active, contributing citizens.[24]

Smith articulates place-based education as encompassing cultural studies of local communities, nature studies of those communities, real-world problem-solving, and internship and entrepreneurial opportunities. Thus, incorporating a range of traditional disciplines, place-based education acknowledges the value of interdisciplinary and experiential approaches as the best way to engage students in learning about their interdependence with local ecological and other systems.[25]

Place-based education comes from a communitarian approach to education, invoking a democratic communal ethic in its emphasis on participatory learning in local communities. A pedagogy and curriculum oriented to one's locale can promote aims of justice, as well. A sense of respect for diverse others in school and in community can be nurtured through educational programs oriented towards local cultural groups. A sense of duty to future generations can be promoted through explorations of local ecosystems and education oriented to understanding how humans can act responsibly within those ecosystems. Notions of place within this pedagogy can be broad, and its foundation in the local arenas of U.S. schooling means that our local traditions of schooling can find common philosophical grounding within this pedagogical framework. A sense of place for a charter school in Dallas can be found within the urban ecosystems, diverse human neighborhoods, political workings, and economic contingencies of that school's geographical space. Place for a Catholic elementary school in Ohio can encompass both scientific and spiritual orientations towards the study and stewardship of natural environments. As a child develops and matures through an increasingly broadened curriculum, expanding any school's sense of place beyond local confines gradually links the local and the global. A sense of place, from local to the global, can be used uniquely and flexibly to promote sustainability within a variety of pedagogical and philosophical orientations to education. A sense of place can be diversely addressed in a variety of educational environments, public and private, small and large, and targeted voucher and charter policies might be designed so as to promote this pedagogy and see it take shape through a variety of educational institutions and their diverse ideological approaches to schooling.

Schools can better serve aims of educational justice, particularly those associated with respect and transmission, if educational programs include virtues of justice and a sense of place within their scope. Returning to Hardin's perhaps unfortunate phrasing, such provisions for educational justice require some power of the state to coerce. The state, as the institutional and organizational arm of public problem-solving, is not the only vehicle for school reform, but also the entity that assumes the greatest public responsibility for ensuring educational justice. In this regard, the state's responsibility requires substantive but flexible authority over schooling, a greater authority than most voucher schemes can, by design, provide. While the aims of educational justice, particularly intergenerational justice, have benefited from considerable and creative contributions from civil society spheres spanning a range of sustainability education efforts, the state has a unique role to play. The importance of vital grassroots and civil society approaches to educational justice does not alleviate the state's duty to respond to the welfare of current or future generations.

In this exploration of a tripartite framework of justice, we examined how the principle of transmission, in conjunction with principles of equity and distribution, would impact school choice policies. Through a study of Ohio's EdChoice, we identified how this broadly targeted voucher scheme will not adequately serve the principles of distribution, respect, and transmission in particular. In programs like EdChoice, the state is empowered to attend to some of the injustices of distribution, as it can redistribute educational dollars to motivated families who wish to pursue educational opportunities that are otherwise unavailable to them in their failing public schools. It can also help families seek educational environments that recognize and respect their child's unique interests and identity. Yet, EdChoice provides negligible state authority to fully provide for the principles of respect and transmission. To provide for these principles of educational justice, the state needs to use some coercive power over curriculum, wisely and judiciously. Without these curricular aims, there is no way for the state to ensure educational justice in choice mechanisms such as the EdChoice program—or in most loosely regulated charter school laws. As I have proposed here, regulating choice to serve these aims can use the power of smaller schools to educate in ways that serve the aims of sustainability—if the state is given some flexible authority to ensure that educational justice is served in all schools receiving state tax dollars.

Notes for Chapter 4

1. See Kenneth R. Howe, "Evidence, the Conservative Paradigm, and School Choice," this volume; and Harry Brighouse, "School Choice and Educational Equality," this volume.

2. John Rawls' social contract theory is the leading formulation of distributive justice today. See John Rawls, *A Theory of Justice* (Cambridge, MA: Harvard University Press, 1971). Philosophers of education who have adapted a Rawlsian framework to evaluate school choice schemes include Harry Brighouse, *School Choice and Social Justice* (New York: Oxford University Press, 2000).

3. I speak here of something like what Feinberg (1998) calls "minimal recognition," which he describes here:

> minimal recognition in the classroom requires that a teacher understand children's cultural background and the way it influences their responses to certain situations. Here minimal recognition might entail fitting one's teaching into the style of the cultural group with which one is working, dressing as they expect a teacher to dress, and allowing their meanings to be reflected in discipline and classroom management. If the group does not value competition, for instance, the teacher might not decide to use it as a way to encourage achievement. Recognition is provided in order to aid the child's performance or comfort in the classroom, and it may or may not have any importance for the culture itself. (p. 169)

See Walter Feinberg, *Common Schools/Uncommon Identities: National Unity and Cultural Difference* (New Haven, CT: Yale University Press, 1998).

4. See Kathleen Knight Abowitz, "Charter Schooling and Social Justice," *Educational Theory* 51, 2 (Spring 2001): 151–70.

5. David Schlosberg (2003) argues for joining distribution and recognition with processes that ensure participation of all citizens. He follows the work

of Nancy Fraser (1997) in advocating for linking various frameworks of justice to create a more comprehensive political theory of justice. Issues of justice are, for Scholosberg, trivalent, demanding equitable distribution, recognition, and participation. See David Scholosberg, "The Justice of Environmental Justice: Reconciling Equity, Recognition, and Participation in a Political Movement," in Andrew Light and Avner de-Shalit (Eds.), *Moral and Political Reasoning in Environmental Practice* (Cambridge, MA: The MIT Press, 2003): 86. See also Nancy Fraser, *Justice Interruptus: Critical Reflections on the "Postsocialist" Condition* (New York: Routledge, 1997).

6. Clark Wolf, "Intergenerational Justice," in R. G. Frey and C. H. Wellman (Eds.), *A Companion to Applied Ethics*. (New York: Blackwell Publishing, 2003): 292.

7. Mike Mills, "The Duties of Being and Association," in J. Barry and M. Wissenburg (Eds.), *Sustaining Liberal Democracy: Ecological Challenges and Opportunities* (London: Palgrave, 2001), 164.

8. Brian Barry, "Sustainability and Intergenerational Justice," in A. Light and H. Rolston III (Eds.), *Environmental Ethics: An Anthology*. (New York: Blackwell, 2003): 493.

9. Routley and Routely 1982, 123, quoted in Wouter Achterberg, "Can Liberal Democracy Survive the Environmental Crisis? Sustainability, Liberal Neutrality, and Overlapping Consensus," in *The Politics of Nature: Explorations in Green Political Theory*, Andrew Dobson and Paul Lucardie, Eds. (New York: Routledge, 1993), 96-7.

10. Ohio has compiled a list of public schools that fit the criteria at the EdChoice Web site: http://www.ode.state.oh.us/GD/Templates/Pages/ODE/ODEDetail.aspx?page=3&TopicRelationID=92&ContentID=9341&Content=46494 (accessed on March 21, 2008).

11. "Fact Sheet," EdChoice—Ohio's Educational Choice Scholarship Pilot Program, Ohio State Department of Education web site: http://www.ode.state.oh.us/GD/Templates/Pages/ODE/ODEDetail.aspx?page=3&TopicRelationID=92&ContentID=9341&Content=46494 (accessed March 21, 2008).

12. "Participating Private Schools," Ibid.

13. Cleveland's program gave priority to students from lower socioeconomic groups but all students within the targeted district were eligible, including those students previously attending private schools.

14. Questions of eligibility are already being raised, as families in eligible districts who currently send their children to private school have been caught enrolling their students in public school temporarily in order to receive EdChoice scholarships. See Jennifer Smith Richards, "Vouchers Abused, State Says," *The Columbus Dispatch*, 7 June 2006. Available: http://www.dispatch.com/news story.php?story=dispatch/2006/06/07/20060607-A1-01.html (accessed on June 11, 2006).

15. The Cleveland voucher program has been the subject of a longitudinal study conducted by the Indiana Center for Evaluation. See Jonathan Plucker et. al., "Evaluation of the Cleveland Scholarship and Tutoring Program: Summary Report 1998–2004," (Bloomington, IN: Center for Evaluation and Education Policy,

February 22, 2006, http://ceep.indiana.edu/projects/PDF/200602_Clev_Summary.
pdf (accessed on June 11, 2006). Another recent study on the Cleveland voucher
program parallels the Indiana report: Clive R. Belfield, "The Evidence on Education
Vouchers: An Application to the Cleveland Scholarship and Tutoring Program,"
National Center for the Study of Privatization in Education, Teachers College,
Columbia University, January 2006, http://www.ncspe.org/publications_files/
OP112.pdf (accessed on June 11, 2006). Howe, in "Evidence, makes the point
nicely that expanded voucher plans such as Ohio's are expanding not because
they deliver on promises of equity but for ideological reasons.

16. "Operating Standards for Ohio Schools," Ohio Department of Education, http://www.ode.state.oh.us/GD/Templates/Pages/ODE/ODEDetail.
aspx?page=3&TopicRelationID=313&ContentID=5769&Content=37299 (accessed
March 21, 2008).

17. The Ohio Science Academic Content Standards are available at http://
www.ode.state.oh.us/GD/Templates/Pages/ODE/ODEPrimary.aspx?Page=2&T
opicRelationID=305 (accessed March 21, 2008).

18. The Ohio Social Studies Academic Content Standards are available
at http://www.ode.state.oh.us/GD/Templates/Pages/ODE/ODEPrimary.aspx?
Page=2&TopicRelationID=305 (accessed March 21, 2008).

19. I am aware of no state that has sustainability aims coherently addressed in its content standards, with the partial exception being Wisconsin's
Model Academic Standards for Environmental Education, a set of guidelines that
the Wisconsin Department of Education offers and encourages districts to use.
Use of the model academic standards (available in a variety of content areas)
is voluntary only. See http://dpi.wi.gov/standards/pdf/envired.pdf (accessed
March 21, 2008).

20. Hardin's focus in the essay is overpopulation of the earth, and his
solution is in part to abandon the notion of a welfare state; thus, I borrow from
his ideas quite selectively here. Garrett Hardin's essay, "The Tragedy of the
Commons," was originally published in Science on December 13, 1968. Available:
http://www.garretthardinsociety.org/articles/art_tragedy_of_the_commons.html
(accessed March 21, 2008).

21. David Labaree, "Resisting Education Standards," in *Readings in So-
ciocultural Studies in Education*, 5th ed., Eds. Kathleen Knight Abowitz and Kate
Rousmaniere, 233 (Dubuque, IA: McGraw Hill Custom Publishing).

22. Feinberg, Common Schools/Uncommon Identities, 85.

23. "It is evident that our behavior is not, in fact, motivated by the ob-
servance of the rights of others most of the time—indeed there is very little of
'what we do' that can be explained in this way." See Mike Mills, "The Duties
of Being and Association," in John Barry and Marcel Wissenburg (Eds.), *Sustaining Liberal Democracy: Ecological Challenges and Opportunities*, 171 (New York:
Palgrave, 2001).

24. David Sobel, *Place Based Education: Connecting Classrooms and Communities* (Great Barrington, MA: Orion Society, 2004), 7.

25. Gregory A. Smith, "Place Based Education: Learning to be where we
are," *Phi Delta Kappan* 83 (8) (April 2002), 584–94.

Chapter 5

The Politics of Parental Choice

Theory and Evidence on Quality Information

Christopher Lubienski

School choice is an appealing abstraction for many different reasons, not the least of which is that choice is a foundational value in both a democratic republic and a market economy. The general idea is attractive to advocates of family values as the appropriate way to organize educational decision-making around parental prerogatives. Prominent liberals have endorsed school choice as a means of making access to good schools more equitable, especially for disadvantaged children. A few libertarians have argued that it is useful as a means of rolling back state control in an important area of life that should otherwise be under the purview of individual control. Perhaps most importantly, the idea suggests an economic logic, matching diverse consumers to various producers for effective and efficient provision of educational services.[1]

It is important to note that all of these rationales hold that the primary, decision-making role is to be taken on by the parent. This assumption makes sense for a number of important reasons. Parents are thought to be best positioned to know the strengths and interests of the child, and are situated to use that information in acting on the child's behalf. This is a crucial assumption, though, particularly with economic theories of school choice premised on the individual use of information that will then drive system-wide improvements. Thus, the parental prerogative in education has both a philosophical or moral component, and an empirical claim as well. Although scholarly debates have developed around whether or not parents are inherently able to exercise choice in the best interests of their children, surprisingly little attention has been paid to the quality and availability of the information necessary for parents to make those decisions.

99

There are strong arguments to position parents at the center of the educational decision-making process, and yet there are philosophical issues and empirical evidence that together problematize overly simplistic assumptions about the primary role of parents as an exclusive authority on children's education. This analysis suggests the need for a much more complex understanding of the advantages and pitfalls to the different roles parents play in guiding their children's education. In this chapter, I offer an overview of the politicized debate on parental choice in education, identifying the primary perspectives brought to that discussion. Then my analysis highlights the two most common arguments about parental choice, suggesting serious shortcomings with both of these ideas. Consequently, I suggest a different basis for judging the merits of claims for parental choice, based on democratic and economic criteria; that is, rather than arguing whether or not parents are able to choose widely, this analysis suggest that we need to consider the extent to which quality information is widely available. The analysis then outlines a framework for understanding the different types of information typically available to parents in choice schemes, and describes a brief empirical exercise designed to assess that information. The concluding discussion demonstrates that more useful types of information are least likely to be available to parents, thereby hindering parental choice as an effective vehicle for equity and effectiveness in education.

The Politics of Parental Choice

Parental choice of schools is an increasingly important topic in public policy-making, moving far beyond the obscure essay published by Milton Friedman advocating vouchers in the 1950s.[2] Nations such as Chile heeded this advice in developing voucher programs for students to choose schools across public and private sectors, while England, Wales, New Zealand and other countries developed comprehensive choice programs primarily within the public sector. In recent years in the United States, several states have instituted voucher plans and tuition tax credits, most states have embraced the charter school movement, and countless jurisdictions have implemented various forms of open-enrollment choice schemes. Furthermore, choice is an integral part of the Bush administration's policies, serving as the basis for the federally-funded voucher program in Washington, DC, the penalty for failing schools in No Child Left Behind, and a controversial element—in the form of federal vouchers—in the president's annual budget proposal.[3]

Obviously, with annual spending on education in the hundreds of billions of dollars, the question of control over education is likely to be fiercely contested, and school choice represents a major change in the control and distribution of those resources. Consequently, groups with an interest in the current system of educational governance—the education establishment of teachers unions, administrators, school boards—have typically opposed many school choice proposals, particularly vouchers that move control further away from traditional forms of governance. This position is often supported by civil rights groups, liberal advocacy organizations, and think tanks. Quite often this position is defended on the grounds of equity, access, and accountability.

On the other hand, a wide range of interests have coalesced around the general idea of parental choice of schools for a number of competing, if not conflicting, reasons. Some newer civil rights groups have emerged, sometimes from community organizing, arguing that school choice is the new civil right, giving poor students more equitable access to the same options traditionally enjoyed by the affluent. Family advocates have made the case that decisions about schooling should fall within the parents' purview, and returning that function to parents will strengthen the institution of the family. While more often associated with conservatives, parental choice is also attractive to neoliberal apostles of efficiency and effectiveness—a perspective that also draws substantially from the ranks of centrist Democrats.

These perspectives are of particular interest to this current analysis. In fact, conservative and neoliberal arguments about appropriateness, efficiency, and effectiveness are some of the most compelling arguments for making families the ultimate arbiters of education decision-making. Indeed, there is something very appealing—and very American—about putting parents back in charge of schooling decisions, making this topic treacherous territory for critics of school choice.[4] Quite often, otherwise fruitful debates about school choice expire on this issue, as proponents charge critics with a failure to trust parents to make education decisions about their own children. More ominously, concerns about the impact of targeted, means-tested programs open critics up to the charge that they do not trust poor or minority families to control their children's education when it is commonly accepted for affluent communities.

It is important to note that the economic objectives of efficiency and effectiveness are all premised on the crucial component of information. Without quality information on school options, parents cannot be expected to make the most reasoned decisions of behalf of their children, both in terms of academic quality and programmatic fit. In the absence of a critical mass of consumers, appropriately armed with information about the relative effectiveness of their different options, any choice-driven system, in education or otherwise, lacks the force required to fuel innovation and the pursuit of quality. And even if enough informed consumers are present and engaged to drive innovation in a field, unless knowledge of quality is widely distributed, only some consumers will be positioned to select the most effective options—leading to overall inequities.

Many choice advocates are aware of these potential problems, but believe that market dynamics themselves can and will solve these information problems. Perhaps most prominently, Joseph Bast and Herbert Walberg have given these issues considerable thought, and argue that market mechanisms largely remedy these concerns. They point to both hypothetical processes representing how markets should work in education, and empirical evidence of consumer behavior in the school sector.[5] Specifically, they point to three findings in the research literature to support this view:

- Survey data showing that parents give ratings to schools that are similar to the ratings given by experts—indicating that parents have the information necessary to make reasoned choices.

- Survey data showing that parents are primarily interested in academic quality—indicating that they are not making foolish choices for their children based on peripheral issues.

- Achievement data demonstrating that the exercise of choice leads to gains in academic achievement—indicating that consumer choice can drive improvements in quality.

Furthermore, regardless of academic quality and achievement concerns, many choice advocates contend that parental choice should be encouraged simply because it is the right thing to do. For some, particularly libertarians, choice is an end in itself; liberating consumers to pursue their preferences is a paramount concern, and gains or losses in achievement are beside the point.[6] This is a particularly strong position when used to argue that disadvantaged communities should be afforded choice. In those cases, it can be argued that students trapped in failing schools generally deserve choice, and that, in particular, communities traditionally marginalized in the common school model have the most to gain from finding schools that better match their preferences. For others, the elevation of parental control in education is a moral imperative, because it reasserts the rights of parents as the ultimate arbiters of a child's education. This view is most effectively articulated in the prolific homeschooling movement, but it also holds true for many other advocates of school choice, who see the opportunity to roll back the inappropriate incursion of the state into the private domain of family life.

Analyzing Arguments for Parental Choice

The two main arguments for parental choice are, therefore, philosophical and empirical. The philosophical argument is premised on a view of the appropriate role of the family in relation to the state. The empirical argument refers to research on the use of information in education markets, but is heavily influenced by theoretical perspectives regarding how market mechanisms should work in education. Here, I examine each of these arguments further, in order to get beyond simplistic assumptions and consider the implications of each.

Parent Roles and Rights in Education

The simple insight, that parents are best able to exercise responsibility over their children's education, is quite appealing and seemingly self-evident. Indeed, there are many cases where this is obviously true. However, the question is not whether this is typically the case, but whether or not this is to be a guiding principle for shaping public policy. In that regard, there are three essential issues that need to be addressed that are too often neglected in assumptions about the appropriate role of parents in their children's education.

The first is an institutional one. Parents act as proxy consumers for their children in schools, as they do in other areas of life: medical care, nutrition, religion, and so forth.[7] Yet, with regard to different social institutions, proxy consumers play different roles, depending largely on their knowledge and the nature of a specific sector. For instance, parents purchase food and clothing in the business sector for their children based on their assessment of preferences, costs, and availability, and so forth. Similarly, institutions such as politics and religion are left almost exclusively to the parents to instruct the child as they see fit. However, in more specialized sectors, parents often defer to experts with arcane knowledge on technical issues such as medical care. The question, then, is whether education is best characterized as a market, politics, or science. But this is a question neglected in the discourse on parental choice, which advances largely from the assumption that education is akin to the inculcation of political or religious values, often played out in a market arena where parents can shop for the right educational services for their children. While education does indeed embody these types of qualities, it is also the case that education requires some outside expertise (that is, moving beyond the role of advocate) in diagnosing and treating each learner—a consideration denied in the rhetoric about parental control.

The second issue is a democratic concern. Families have an interest in reproducing their values in the next generation. Thus, parents look not only to childrearing and church, but also to institutions such as education to reinforce, or at least not contradict, the values that they emphasize in the home.[8] This is widely agreed to be a primary interest of the good parent. However, a democratic society, particularly one with any pretensions of meritocratic fairness, also has an interest in providing equitable opportunities for autonomous citizens. Because family backgrounds provide an inequitable basis for determining future opportunities, with some children receiving a much greater advantage from their families, democratic societies typically look to education to provide both equity and autonomy for individuals. In a sense, this means that schools need to break the cycle of poverty and affluence that so characterize modern market societies. That is, one of the primary purposes of schools in a democratic society is to make a child's family factors meaningless for success in school and life. Similarly, parents typically demand that children respect their authority, but a truly democratic society should encourage children to question authority.

The third issue involves the place of the child in a democratic society. Choice advocates often point to a parent's prior right to determine their children's education, guaranteed in agreements such as the Universal Declaration of Human Rights, which trumps claims of other interests.[9] Although it is assumed that, as a parental right, parents will act in the child's best interests, but this assumption is largely irrelevant. Instead, this parental right is often articulated and exercised in the manner of a property right. Yet, parents do not own their children, nor are they the only recognized authority with respect to the child. The broader public also has both a right and responsibility to care for the child's interests. Although parents are typically positioned to be the primary agent in looking after the child, it is generally accepted that democratic societies also exercise an over-riding prerogative over a child's welfare, particularly in instances where a parent is unwilling or ill-equipped to make wise choices on behalf of the child. Although it can take many forms, this public interest is typically articulated through the role of the government in areas such as education.

Evidence on the Use of Information

While these three concerns problematize simplistic claims that a parent's position makes him or her an exclusive authority in education, they are not necessarily the only issues in evaluating parental choices in education. It is also important to consider the empirical evidence on parental choice of schools. As noted above, information is the key component, so it is essential to understand the information available to parents in making school choices. Bast and Walberg highlight three forms of evidence on parents choosing schools.[10] They claim that evidence supports the classic economic idealization of a rational consumer, proving that parents are inherently better positioned to make such choices than, say, a government bureaucracy. A careful and more balanced review of the research on these three points suggests a much more complex picture, problematizing easy assumptions about parents, information, and academic quality.

SCHOOL RATINGS BY PARENTS ARE SIMILAR TO THOSE DONE BY EXPERTS

To support this point, Bast and Walberg cite three studies indicating that parents' ratings and ranking of schools were accurate on specific criteria. However, the studies they cite actually contradict that thesis. One study examines parental satisfaction with schools.[11] Yet, contrary to the thesis that parents are necessarily accurate judges of school quality, the majority of parents were incorrect in their assessment of school quality, according to the data reported by the authors: only 44 percent were highly satisfied with the highest performing schools, and 15 percent of parents were highly satisfied with the worst schools. Another study, from New Zealand, noted that parent assessments of high-quality schools were probably based on the socioeconomic characteristics of the students, rather than actual evidence of school quality.[12]

    In fact, a comprehensive research literature suggests that parents do not necessarily agree with objective assessments of school quality. In research on parents' school choices in Chile, a nation with a much more comprehensive market model for education than those in the United States and New Zealand, studies have found parents had tenuous sources of information, and were largely incorrect when asked to identify high and low quality schools in their area.[13] And in a comprehensive study of U.S. mathematics achievement on the National Assessment of Educational Progress, Lubienski and Lubienski note that demand for certain types of schools does not necessarily correlate with school performance.[14] After controlling for student demographics, charter schools were actually performing significantly beneath the level of public schools, despite much mentioned waiting lists; more importantly, students in self-described conservative Christian schools, which are the fastest growing segment of the private school sector, are almost a year behind their public school counterparts while higher performing Catholic and Lutheran schools often struggle to attract students.[15] Similarly, evidence that parents are using vouchers to send their children to higher performing schools is less than compelling.[16] The most recent research on student gains suggests that choice schools are *less* effective at promoting academic growth.

Indeed, much evidence indicates that parents have different perceptions than school choice advocates do around general issues of school quality. President Bush's 2006 State of the Union address called for a dramatic ramping up of math and science training, a theme echoed by many business leaders and school reformers. But parents are generally satisfied with the amount and quality of instruction their children receive in these areas.[17] Moreover, much to the chagrin of choice advocates, parents often see more value to the local public schools than reform advocates believe they should.[18] Surveys have repeatedly demonstrated that the people thought to be best positioned to make assessments of school quality, "those who are closest to and most familiar with the situation,"[19] tend to give relatively high marks to the schools they know the most: the local public school that their children attend.[20] Either parents are in error regarding the quality of their local schools and therefore by implication are incapable of judging school quality, or experts calling for drastic moves to market models for schooling are inaccurate in their own assessment of schools. Thus, the issue is much more complex than some of the simplistic rhetoric would indicate.

Parents are Primarily Interested in Academic Quality

The notion that parental preferences for schools revolve around issues of academic quality is a key element in the rational consumer idealization in much of the thinking on school choice. Specifically, economic logic holds that the parents are primarily interested in the academic quality of a school because this will in turn enhance economic prospects for their children.[21] This focus on academics for future labor market prospects actually limits schooling in both public and private sectors to a general comprehensive uniformity.[22] On the one hand, Bast and Walberg seek to support this notion by citing four sources showing national and local survey research in which parents identify academic quality as the most important criterion in selecting a school.[23] On the other hand, there is a substantial research literature, both survey and behavioral, from the United States and other nations suggesting that parents choose for a number of reasons besides strictly academic considerations.[24] This is not to say that parents do not choose schools based on academic quality, but that many other considerations (e.g., location, convenience, uniforms, sports, or student demographics) also come into play, making for a much more complex picture than is portrayed in the rational-consumer idealization. In fact, since school choice moved into the national spotlight, this question has been debated, and the literature hardly reflects the consensus implied by the four sources cited by Bast and Walberg.[25]

Of course, there are problems with citing survey data to support any contention on this issue. Most importantly, surveys are notoriously unreliable when people are asked to express preferences on controversial topics compared to when they actually reveal their true preferences away from public scrutiny. For instance, although few parents cite racial composition of schools as a factor in their choices,[26] it is, in fact, perhaps the most immediate bit of information they seek when considering different schools.[27] Furthermore, many of these studies survey parents who have chosen to use a voucher or private school, presenting a problem with selection bias. Finally, while parents may say that academic quality is a high priority, this does not mean that they actually have hard information on that issue. For instance, recent studies of school marketing in competitive environments suggest that evidence of academic quality is not a prominent theme in school promotional materials; instead, schools often seek to attract families through images of White or Asian American students, information about extracurricular opportunities, or symbols associated with exclusive schooling, rather than, say, test scores.[28] This trend may be cause for concern. Even if parents act on perceived academic quality, school officials may recognize and respond to incentives to shape those perceptions through surrogate information on school quality that highlights racial and socioeconomic criteria.[29] Competitive dynamics may promote sorting on these factors, and undercut incentives for school improvement.[30]

PARENTAL CHOICE LEADS TO GAINS IN ACADEMIC ACHIEVEMENT

The dynamics set in motion by parental choice are thought to lead to more effective schools overall.[31] This is a crucial claim. As Bast and Walberg note:

> Higher academic achievement by students attending schools of choice, after controlling for family socioeconomic status, could be evidence that parents are choosing wisely. However, it could also be evidence that competition produces better schools . . . even if parents are not choosing wisely, the fact that producers must compete or that choice motivates parents to be more engaged in their children's schooling may lift their children's academic achievement.[32]

To support this claim, Bast and Walberg cite twenty-five studies on a number of school choice programs, including public school choice, private schools, charter schools, and voucher programs.[33] Many of the studies do not report original research, but instead summarize existing research, so they cannot be said to offer new evidence on this issue. More importantly, a review of these studies indicates a much more complex picture than is implied in the effort to support this claim. For instance, a study by Grogger and Neal is cited as evidence of a positive and statistically significant private school effect on academic achievement.[34] In fact, Grogger and Neal's study of National Education Longitudinal Study of 1988 data found no statistically significant effect for Catholic schools on mathematics achievement for students in the suburbs, but a modest advantage for White students, and larger gains for minority students in urban areas; no private school effect was found for secular private schools.[35] This is a significant omission, in view of the Bast and Walberg thesis about the competitive impact of choice, since nonreligious private schools may be more susceptible to market-like forces than Catholic schools, which can rely on the more inert patronage of parishioners. Other studies cited show similarly mixed results. Furthermore, causation is often implied, but cannot be supported by the data or analysis. For example, they cite a study of inputs and achievement of Catholic and public school students in New York as proof that achievement "growth is greater in Catholic schools than in public schools."[36] However, the authors do not indicate that they used longitudinal data, nor does it appear that they controlled for student demographics—two fatal errors if one is to demonstrate that a school type, and not family factors, caused achievement growth. Many of the other studies cited to support this claim are actually just summaries of previous studies that have also been contested on methodological grounds.[37]

Not only do the authors engage in a selective interpretation of these studies, they appear to offer a very selective review of the literature. Other studies not cited found no academic advantage for schools of choice, and a few found a negative effect. For instance, studies by Rouse and Miron and Nelson of achievement in voucher and charter programs, respectively, do not support the thesis that school choice necessarily leads to greater achievement gains.[38] In a longitudinal study, Figlio and Stone found a small but statistically significant negative effect for religious schools for White students, but a positive impact for minority students.[39] More recently, using national samples, Lubienski and Lubienski found schools of choice to be trailing noncharter public schools in mathematics achievement after implementing appropriate controls for student demographics.[40] And Belfield found a negative private school effect in his rigorous study of the Cleveland voucher program.[41] These few studies are offered not to prove that choice has a particular impact on student achievement, but to demonstrate that the picture is much more complex than what is implied in support of the claim that choice generates gains in academic achievement.

Towards a Deeper Understanding of Parent Information on School Quality

In view of these difficulties in substantiating the thesis that parents are positioned to make the best choices for their children's schools, it makes sense to take a deeper look at the issue. Indeed, there are serious shortcomings with the question itself when it is framed as "Can parents chose the best schools for their children?" or "Can people be trusted to decide for themselves?"[42] Such representations of the issue treat parents as monolithic, ignoring substantial evidence that parents' views of schools and information can be diverse and socially situated.[43] Furthermore, as noted above, framing the issue along strictly individualistic and consumer lines negates any broader social or democratic interest in a child's education. Therefore, hypotheses such as "Parents would do a better job choosing the schools their children attend than 'experts' working for governments,"[44] while falsifiable, largely miss the point. Rather than asking if parents *can* make informed choices (when for many the answer is obvious), it makes more sense to ask whether the requisite knowledge or information about different options is of sufficient quality, widely available and equitably distributed.

A Framework for Assessing Information on School Quality

To that end, I offer three dimensions to consider in evaluating information that could be employed in selecting a school: insights into productive processes, the nature of the good or service,[45] and information that encourages horizontal and vertical differentiation. Although there is a strong case to be made that education exhibits many of the primary aspects of a public good, we can assume here, for the sake of argument, that schooling is primarily a private good, and can therefore be treated as a commodity.

First, to understand information on the quality of any consumable good, it is important to consider what aspect of the good is being illuminated for the consumer by that information.[46] For many goods, such as a car or a computer, consumers look for information on the quality of the finished product.[47] For others, such as health care, the quality of the production processes is a key concern.[48] With schooling, for instance, a diploma may be important, but it tells us little about the quality of the school experience. More accurate assessments of quality come from evaluations of the educational processes in a school (e.g., teaching, class composition and size, etc.). However, productive processes are not always apparent to consumers, leading to asymmetries of information between producer and consumer that put the customer at a relative disadvantage. The clarity of productive processes can be represented on a scale, where more obvious processes are transparent to the consumer, somewhat complex or hidden processes are translucent, while opaque processes are more obscured or even removed from the consumer's view. As noted below, schooling involves some aspects that are inherently difficult to make apparent to the consumer.

Second, just as information on productive processes can be important to consumers, different goods themselves exhibit different types of qualities, qualities that are conveyed to the consumer in different ways. Some goods exhibit qualities that are readily apparent to consumers before purchase and consumption. For instance, we can usually decide if fruit is ripe, or if a sweater fits, and use that information in making a selection. Such qualities then allow consumers to make choices based on other factors as well, such as price and availability, and competitive marketing for these search goods tends to offer information on those criteria.[49] However, important aspects of other types of goods are not readily apparent to consumers before purchase, in the case of experience goods such as canned food or a movie; while, for credence goods, important qualities may never be really known, for instance, the effects of an herbal supplement, or the actual effects of higher octane gasoline on an engine. In these cases, marketing tends to play upon the information asymmetries enjoyed by the producer, further obscuring information on quality by appealing to emotions or allegiance. Therefore, it is useful to consider the types of information available about a good: whether the information makes softer emotional appeals, or provides direct or hard evidence of product quality or effectiveness.

Third, in any competitive market, producers or providers are expected to differentiate their product or service from those of competitors.[50] While assessments of the diversity of different options can be made by examining the qualities of actual products, more important for the present purposes is the information made available to consumers regarding the differences between products. In sectors such as education it is important to note whether that information identifies differences between different options arranged on a vertical scale of different-but-equal programs, or on a horizontal scale of quality.[51] If the information focuses on the former, that could indicate niche marketing to diverse preferences. If the information focuses primarily on the latter, that could indicate a monolithic conception of quality, but it could also suggest competitive incentives to enhance market position by attracting more preferred customers.

A Brief Exercise to Consider Information on School Quality

In order to better understand the question of parent information on school quality, the following short exercise examines whether or not the requisite knowledge or information to make such choices is widely available and of sufficient quality. Information on schools has become increasingly available, as Bast and Walberg note:

> In the case of K–12 schooling, the supply of information about school quality is large and growing. Many states now issue school report cards that are sent to parents, available on Web sites, and widely reported in newspapers. No Child Left Behind (NCLB), the federal school accountability act, requires a significant increase in student testing, school ranking, and reporting of results to parents. Standard & Poor's has a Web site . . . that provides extensive information on most public schools in most of the country, as do many state-level think tanks and civic organizations.[52]

So, while comparative information on different schools is readily accessible due largely to the internet, little is known about the actual nature and quality of that information available to parents in selecting a school. In 2005, we reviewed forty Web sites to examine the nature of information on school quality.[53] Web sites were located through web searches for information made available to parents on school quality and ratings. These include many prominent national, state, and local-level databases focusing on public and private schools in the K–12 range, and are run by government agencies, community organizations, school associations, and policy groups. Many offer school report cards in line with the requirements of NCLB. While information is available in other formats as well, the Web-based approach allowed us to access not only information on individual schools, but also comparative information that would be most useful to local parents evaluating the quality of their neighborhood school, as well as to other parents considering transferring their child or moving to a new community.[54]

With regard to the different dimensions to consider in evaluating the nature and quality of information available on the Web, it appears, first, that the productive processes of schools remain relatively translucent or opaque. Remarkably few Web sites—only three of forty—offered information on things such as a school's academic program or theme, much less curriculum or pedagogy. Instead, the most common type of information has to do only with inputs such as student-teacher ratio, student characteristics, and outcomes such as test scores, graduation, and drop-out rates, with the productive processes only implied—the infamous black box of schooling.[55] This is not surprising because productive processes in schools are quite esoteric, and any given school's effects on outputs are confounded by other things such as family backgrounds of students and the peer effects of their cohort. Obviously, this is a complex issue.

Secondly, although these websites often represent themselves as offering hard information on school quality, there is actually very little direct information on school effectiveness—a key element if schooling is to be treated as a search good. Information on schools can be understood within a range of types, from more emotional appeals to direct evidence of quality—in the case of schools: effectiveness. Of course, these Web sites are not commercial (at least for the schools), so there is no overtly emotional aspect to them. Yet, neither is there much effort to present actual evidence on school effectiveness, admittedly a difficult metric, but a key consideration if parental choice is to drive school improvement. While more Web sites (fourteen) offered information on test scores than any other type of information (graduation and drop-out rates were a close second), only four made any effort to distinguish the school's effect from other variables such as student demographics in shaping academic outcomes. This is a critical concern, since raw test scores may tell us more about who attends a school, rather than the impact of that school's program on academic achievement. To estimate a school's effect, the information would have to account for student backgrounds, compare achievement at schools with similar demographic profiles, or offer a value-added assessment of individual student growth over time. Such analyses require the ability to control simultaneously for numerous factors known to impact student achievement. Few Web sites attempt to do any of this. The problem, then, is that efforts to drive improvement by arming parents with information on school quality are not likely to have an effect if that information is lacking. Indeed, the information available does not position schooling as a search good, but instead suggests an experience or credence good—leaving consumers in a position of relative disadvantage.

Finally, the information made available to parents through this set of Web sites appears to encourage vertical sorting of students, rather than diversification of options on a horizontal scale of different-but-equally-valued options. Only 10 percent of the Web sites included information on school programs, while 50 percent of the Web sites offered information on student characteristics or the associated outcome of student achievement. Thus, parents are provided with a basis for judging schools drawing largely on information about who attends different schools, rather than the programs offered in them.

Implications

This brief exercise suggests that more useful types of information are least likely to be available to parents. The educational processes in schools are relatively esoteric and largely obscured from the direct observations of current and potential consumers. Since schooling does not appear to lend itself to easy comparisons between options based on explicit indicators of quality, as it would if it were a search good, competition between providers by itself is unlikely to generate the information necessary for consumers to make informed choices.[56] Instead, with experience or credence goods, extra-market remedies such as licensing, regulation, or accreditation are often necessary in order to compensate the consumer in light of informational asymmetries favoring producers.[57] Unfortunately, many of those extra-market mechanisms are represented here with these Web sites, and yet quality information appears to be rare.[58] Furthermore, the information that is available has little to do with program diversity, and more to do with socioeconomic distinctions between students, suggesting incentives for families and schools to sort themselves by such characteristics, thereby voiding incentives for school improvement, innovation, and equitable access to diverse options. Of course, it is likely that many parents get information on schools from social networks—the word-of-mouth means of gathering information on options.[59] However, it is important to note that these networks tend to be relatively homogenous, so that information disseminated through such channels will not be equitably distributed.[60]

As noted earlier, there are many justifications for parental choice of schools, and most school choice plans depend on the informed participation of parents. As former Secretary of Education Rod Paige observed in championing NCLB: "there is no more powerful advocate for children than a parent armed with information and options."[61] Such assertions, while simple, eloquent, and appealing, appear to be more of a statement of belief than of fact. This analysis finds the empirical and the philosophical aspects of such claims to be problematic in light of both their own internal logic and evidence on the dynamics of school choice in the real-world context. The issue of parental choice of schools is much more complex than these simplistic assertions indicate. Instead of debating whether or not parents are able to choose the best schools, it is important to consider whether the requisite knowledge or information is readily available to those who most need it. The question is centered largely on the issue of school quality, which is difficult for researchers to identify even with advanced statistical measures, and is also difficult to convey to potential consumers. Yet more useful types of information are least likely to be available to parents, thereby hindering parental choice as an effective vehicle for equity and effectiveness in education. This does not mean that parents are incapable of choosing wisely—a claim that is obviously not supported by this analysis. However, the remarkable scarcity of quality information problematizes easy assumptions about informed parental choice of schools as the basis for public policy.

Notes on Chapter 5

1. For a fuller explanation of these positions, see Christopher Lubienski, "School Competition and the Importance of Symbols in a Market Environment," in *To Educate a Nation: Federal and National Strategies of School Reform*, ed. Carl F. Kaestle (2007b).

2. Milton Friedman, "The Role of Government in Education," in *Economics and the Public Interest*, ed. Robert A. Solo, 127–34 (New Brunswick, NJ: Rutgers University Press, 1955).

3. Michelle R. Davis, "Latest Bush Voucher Plan Faces Skepticism," *Education Week* 25 (February 22, 2006): 32, 38.

4. Joseph L. Bast and Herb J. Walberg, *Let's Put Parents Back in Charge!* (Chicago: Heartland Institute, 2003).

5. Joseph L. Bast and Herb J. Walberg, "Can Parents Choose the Best Schools for Their Children?" *Economics of Education Review* 23, no. 4 (2004): 431–40; see also Herb J. Walberg and Joseph L. Bast, *Education and Capitalism: How Overcoming Our Fear of Markets and Economics Can Improve America's Schools* (Stanford, CA: Hoover Institution Press, 2003).

6. Kenneth R. Howe, *Understanding Equal Educational Opportunity: Social Justice, Democracy, and Schooling* (New York: Teachers College Press, 1997).

7. Harry Brighouse, *School Choice and Social Justice* (Oxford: Oxford University Press, 2000).

8. Bast and Walberg, "Can Parents Choose the Best Schools?"

9. Daniel Monk, "Problematising Home Education: Challenging 'Parental Rights' and 'Socialisation,' " *Legal Studies* 24, no. 4 (2004): 568–98.

10. Bast and Walberg, "Can Parents Choose the Best Schools?"

11. Caroline M. Hoxby, "If Families Matter Most," in *A Primer on America's Schools*, ed. Terry M. Moe, 89–125 (Stanford, CA: Hoover Institution Press, 2001).

12. Edward B. Fiske and Helen F. Ladd, *When Schools Compete: A Cautionary Tale* (Washington, DC: Brookings Institution Press, 2000). This practice, although rational from the consumer's perspective, can also be problematic because it indicates incentives for providers to promote themselves based on evidence of the social characteristics of their students, rather than evidence of academic quality (see below; see also Chrisopher Lubienski, "School Competition").

13. Viola Espínola, "The Educational Reform of the Military Regime in Chile: The School System's Response to Competition, Choice, and Market Relations" (doctoral dissertation, University of Wales, Cardiff, 1993); Varun Gauri, *School Choice in Chile: Two Decades of Educational Reform* (Pittsburgh, PA: University of Pittsburgh Press, 1998).

14. Christopher Lubienski and Sarah Theule Lubienski, *Charter, Private, Public Schools and Academic Achievement: New Evidence from NAEP Mathematics Data*, Occasional Paper No. 111 (New York: National Center for the Study of Privatization in Education, 2006).

15. See Stephen P. Broughman and Kathleen W. Pugh, *Characteristics of Private Schools in the United States: Results from the 2001–2002 Private School Universe Survey*, No. NCES 2005–305 (Washington, DC: National Center for Education Statistics, U.S. Department of Education, 2004).

16. Clive R. Belfield, *The Evidence on Education Vouchers: An Application to the Cleveland Scholarship and Tutoring Program*, Occasional Paper No. 112 (New York: National Center for the Study of Privatization in Education, 2006).

17. Jean Johnson, Ana Maria Arumi, Amber Ott, and Michael Hamill Remaley, *Reality Check 2006: Are American Parents and Students Ready for More Math and Science?*, Education Insights (New York: Public Agenda, 2006).

18. Thus, there is a degree of irony when former Heritage Foundation analyst and Bush (II) administration education official Nina Rees says: "To some extent, when you offer something new to low-income parents or to any parent

group, initially you're not going to have a surge signing up because they don't know what it is and the procedure to sign kids up is somewhat complicated." See Susan Saulny, "Tutor Program Offered by Law Is Going Unused," *New York Times*, February 12, 2006. Similarly, conservative commentator John Stossel cites parental choice advocate Kevin Chavous in arguing that parents do not understand about school quality: "If you're like most American parents, you might think 'These things don't happen at my kid's school.' A Gallup Poll survey showed 76 percent of Americans were completely or somewhat satisfied with their kids' public school. Education reformers like Kevin Chavous have a message for these parents: If you only knew. Even though people in the suburbs might think their schools are great, Chavous says, 'They're not. That's the thing and the test scores show that.' Chavous and many other education professionals say Americans don't know that their public schools, on the whole, just aren't that good." See John Stossel, "Stupid in America: How Lack of Choice Cheats Our Kids out of a Good Education," *20/20*, originally aired January 13, 2006.

19. Bast and Walberg, "Can Parents Choose the Best Schools?" 433.

20. Lowell C. Rose and Alec M. Gallup, "The 31st Annual Phi Delta Kappa/Gallup Poll," *Phi Delta Kappan* 81 (September 1999): 41–58; Lowell C. Rose and Alec M. Gallup, "The 35th Annual Phi Delta Kappa/Gallup Poll of the Public's Attitudes toward the Public Schools," *Phi Delta Kappan* 85 (September 2003): 41–56; Lowell C. Rose and Alec M. Gallup, "The 37th Annual Phi Delta Kappa/Gallup Poll of the Public's Attitudes toward the Public Schools," *Phi Delta Kappan* 87 (September 2005): 41–57.

21. Bast and Walberg, "Can Parents Choose the Best Schools?"

22. Byron W. Brown, "Why Governments Run Schools," *Economics of Education Review* 11, no. 4 (1992): 287–300. Bast and Walberg do note—and I agree—that it is presumptuous to assume that academic achievement is the ultimate measure for school success. (There are, after all, other goals for schools that are often neglected in reform rhetoric: socialization, democratic citizenship, integration, tolerance, etc.) However, this is certainly the metric that is elevated by reform discourse on school effectiveness, so it is important to consider. See Ibid.

23. Bast and Walberg, "Can Parents Choose the Best Schools?"

24. For example, Gauri, *School Choice in Chile*; A. Molnar, "Charter Schools: The Smiling Face of Disinvestment," *Educational Leadership* 54 (October 1996): 9–15; Harvey B. Polansky, "School Choice—Panacea or Failure?" *School Business Affairs* 64 (June 1998): 44–45; Kevin B. Smith and Kenneth J. Meier, *The Case Against School Choice: Politics, Markets, and Fools* (Armonk, NY: M. E. Sharpe, 1995); Amy Stuart Wells, "The Sociology of School Choice: Why Some Win and Others Lose in the Educational Marketplace," in *School Choice: Examining the Evidence*, ed. Edith Rasell and Richard Rothstein, 29–48 (Washington, DC: Economic Policy Institute, 1993).

25. Bast and Walberg, "Can Parents Choose the Best Schools?"

26. Mark Schneider, Melissa Marschall, Paul Teske, and Christine Roch, "School Choice and Culture Wars in the Classroom: What Different Parents Seek from Education," *Social Science Quarterly* 79, no. 3 (1998): 489–502.

27. Mark Schneider and Jack Buckley, "What Do Parents Want from

Schools: Evidence from the Internet," *Educational Evaluation and Policy Analysis* 24, no. 2 (2002): 133–44; see also Steven Glazerman, "School Quality and Social Stratification: The Determinants and Consequences of Parental School Choice" (paper presented at the annual conference of the American Educational Research Association, San Diego, California, 1998); Jeffrey R. Henig, "The Local Dynamics of Choice: Ethnic Preferences and Institutional Responses," in *Who Chooses? Who Loses? Culture, Institutions, and the Unequal Effects of School Choice*, ed. Bruce Fuller and Richard F. Elmore (New York: Teachers College Press, 1996).

28. Christopher Lubienski, "Public Schools in Marketized Environments: Shifting Incentives and Unintended Consequences of Competition-Based Educational Reforms," *American Journal of Education* 111, no. 4 (2005): 464–86; Christopher Lubienski, "School Choice as a Civil Right: District Responses to Competition and Equal Educational Opportunity," *Equity and Excellence in Education* 38, no. 4 (2005): 331–41; Christopher Lubienski, "School Competition"; Christopher Lubienski, "Incentives for School Diversification: Competition and Promotional Patterns in Local Education Markets," *Journal of School Choice* 1, no. 2 (2006): 1–31; Christopher Lubienski, "Marketing Schools: Consumer Goods and Competitive Incentives for Consumer Information," *Education and Urban Society* 40, no. 1 (2007): 118–41.

29. Bast and Walberg, "Can Parents Choose the Best Schools?" 431, emphasis added.

30. Christopher Lubienski, "Public Schools in Marketized Environments"; Christopher Lubienski, "School Competition."

31. Caroline M. Hoxby, *Do Private Schools Provide Competition for Public Schools?* Working Paper No. 4978 (Cambridge, MA: National Bureau of Economic Research, 1994).

32. Bast and Walberg, "Can Parents Choose the Best Schools?" 436, emphasis in original.

33. Ibid.

34. Jeffrey Grogger and Derek A. Neal, "Further Evidence on the Effects of Catholic Secondary Schooling," in *Brookings-Wharton Papers on Urban Affairs 2000*, ed. William G. Gale and Janet Rothenberg Pack, 151–202 (Washington, DC: Brookings Institution Press, 2000).

35. This finding caused Eric Hanushek to wonder, in his commentary, how parents could violate basic economic logic by paying for an underperforming service when a superior alternative is free of charge. See Ibid., 196.

36. Paul E. Peterson and Herb J. Walberg, "Catholic Schools Excel," *School Reform News* 6, no. 7 (2002), 12.

37. See, for instance, Alan B. Krueger and Pei Zhu, "Another Look at the New York City School Voucher Experiment," *American Behavioral Scientist* 47, no. 5 (2004): 658–98; Alan B. Krueger and Pei Zhu, "Inefficiency, Subsample Selection Bias, and Nonrobustness: A Response to Paul E. Peterson and William G. Howell," *American Behavioral Scientist* 47, no. 5 (2004): 718–28; Kim K. Metcalf, "Commentary—Advocacy in the Guise of Science: How Preliminary Research on the Cleveland Voucher Program Was 'Reanalzyed' to Fit a Preconception," *Education Week* 18 (September 23, 1998): 34, 39; John F. Witte, *Reply to Greene,*

Peterson and Du: "*The Effectivenss of School Choice in Milwaukee: A Secondary Analysis of Data from the Program's Evaluation*" (Madison, WI: Department of Political Science and The Robert La Follette Institute of Public Affairs, University of Wisconsin-Madison, 1996).

38. Cecilia Elena Rouse, *Schools and Student Achievement: More Evidence from the Milwaukee Parental Choice Program* (Princeton, NJ: Princeton University and the National Bureau of Economic Research, 1998); Gary Miron and Christopher Nelson, *What's Public About Charter Schools? Lessons Learned About Choice and Accountability* (Thousand Oaks, CA: Corwin Press, 2002).

39. David N. Figlio and Joe A. Stone, *School Choice and School Performance: Are Private Schools Really Better?* Discussion Paper No. 1141-97 (Madison, WI: Institute for Research on Poverty, 1997); see also David N. Figlio and Joe A. Stone, "Are Private Schools Really Better?" *Research in Labor Economics* 18 (1999): 115–40.

40. Lubienski and Lubienski, *Charter, Private, Public Schools*; Sarah Theule Lubienski and Christopher Lubienski, "A New Look at Public and Private Schools: Student Background and Mathematics Achievement," *Phi Delta Kappan* 86 (May 2005): 696–99.

41. Belfield, *The Evidence on Education Vouchers.*

42. See, respectively, Bast and Walberg, "Can Parents Choose the Best Schools?"; Ronald S. Brandt, "Can People Be Trusted to Decide for Themselves?" *Education Week* 19 (January 12, 2000), 34, 38.

43. For example, Stephen J. Ball, Richard Bowe, and Sharon Gewirtz, "Circuits of Schooling: A Sociological Exploration of Parental Choice of School in Social Class Contexts," *Sociological Review* 43, no. 1 (1995): 52–78; Courtney A. Bell, *All Choices Created Equal? How Good Parents Select "Failing" Schools*, Occasional Paper No. 106 (New York: National Center for the Study of Privatization in Education, 2005); Sharon Gewirtz, Stephen J. Ball, and Richard Bowe, *Markets, Choice and Equity in Education* (Buckingham, UK: Open University Press, 1995); Schneider et al., "School Choice and Culture Wars."

44. Bast and Walberg, "Can Parents Choose the Best Schools?" 432.

45. For brevity, I use the term "good," while understanding that education and other "consumables" can also be described as a service.

46. See Lubienski, "Marketing Schools."

47. In those cases, process innovations (as opposed to product innovations) may lower production costs, but are largely irrelevant to the consumer as an immediate consideration in making a choice.

48. Burton A. Weisbrod, "Institutional Form and Orgaizational Behavior," in *Private Action and the Public Good*, ed. Walter W. Powell and Elisabeth S. Clemens, 69–84 (New Haven, CT: Yale University Press, 1998).

49. Praveen Aggarwal and Rajiv Vaidyanathan, "The Perceived Effectiveness of Virtual Shopping Agents for Search vs. Experience Goods," *Advances in Consumer Research* 30 (2003): 347–48; Michael R. Darby and Edi Karni, "Free Competition and the Optimal Amount of Fraud," *Journal of Law and Economics* 16 (1973): 67–88; Philip Nelson, "Advertising as Information," *Journal of Political Economy* 81, no. 4 (1974): 729–54; Jean Tirole, *The Theory of Industrial Organization* (Cambridge, MA: MIT Press, 1988).

50. Of course, producers at the low end of a hierarchy have an incentive to minimize distinctions between their product and those of their more prestigious competitors, while those at the high end of the scale attempt to exaggerate any differences. In education, policymakers have used reforms such as charter schools to encourage diversification of options so that parents have a greater set of choices.

51. Gerhard Glomm, Doug Harris, and Te-Fen Lo, "Charter School Location," *Economics of Education Review* 24 (2005): 451–57.

52. Best and Walberg, "Can Parents Choose the Best Schools?" 433.

53. Corinna Crane and Jeff Graham assisted on this research.

54. For analyses of other forms of parental information, see Lubienski, "Incentives for School Diversification" and Lubienski, "Marketing Schools."

55. Patrick J. McEwan, "The Potential Impact of Large-Scale Voucher Programs," *Review of Educational Research* 70, no. 2 (2000): 103–49; John W. Meyer, "Innovation and Knowledge Use in American Public Education," in *Organizational Environments: Ritual and Rationality*, updated ed., ed. John W. Meyer and W. Richard Scott, 233–60 (Beverly Hills, CA: Sage Publications, 1992).

56. Gregg Garn, "Moving from Bureaucratic to Market Accountability: The Problem of Imperfect Information," *Educational Administration Quarterly* 37, no. 4 (2001): 571–99.

57. Walberg and Bast focus on market mechanisms to deal with asymmetric information. In particular, they point to information from producers, repeat purchases, and "personal and public sources of information." See Walberg and Bast, *Education and Capitalism*, 65. However, schooling does not lend itself to repeat purchases, which would be required to punish bad providers; and children, not the choosers, are the ones who have to pay a price in this idealized "discovery process" (Bast & Walberg, "Can Parents Choose the Best Schools? 433; Brighouse, *School Choice and Social Justice*; Lubienski, "Marketing Schools"). And, as this analysis shows, information from producers, as well as personal and public sources, can be more limited than these authors assume.

58. Although the internet is certainly just one means of accessing information on schools—and, of course, access to the internet is not equitably distributed—it is fast becoming a primary method for gathering information on schools (as Bast and Walberg note in "Can Parents Choose the Best Schools?"). Indeed, while gaps in access exist, we might expect the most demand for high quality information from the relatively sophisticated consumers with internet access.

59. Lubienski, "Public Schools in Marketized Environments."

60. Lubienski, "School Competition"; Mark Schneider, Paul Teske, Christine Roch, and Melissa Marschall, "Networks to Nowhere: Segregation and Stratification in Networks of Information About Schools," *American Journal of Political Science* 41, no. 4 (1997): 1201–23.

61. WrightsLaw, "No Child Left Behind Act—Final Regulations Published," December 2, 2002, 6.

Chapter 6

Social Class Differences in School Choice

The Role of Preferences

Courtney A. Bell

Rational Choice Theory (RCT) is used by many school choice researchers to elegantly and simply portray parental choice.[1] Parents gather information, have preferences, are constrained by circumstances, and make choices.[2] When aggregated up, these choices force schools to improve or close. The RCT portrayal of parental choice is both thin and powerful; but it treats a crucial construct—preferences—as exogenous to the inquiry.[3] In these portrayals, parents have preferences but it is outside the purview of the theory to investigate why parents have the preferences they do. The social, cultural, and historical contexts which shape preferences are not accounted for.

Inquiry into the social and cultural factors shaping parental participation in schooling suggests the assumption of exogeneity may be problematic. Recent scholarship documents how parental participation varies by race, social class and immigration status.[4] Parents, teachers, and administrators do not share the same definition of what it means to be involved in a child's education, which results in parents interacting with schools in very different ways.[5] In particular, all parents do not have access to the forms of capital (i.e., time, knowledge, and social connections) schools presume are most valuable for facilitating student success. The documented differences in parental participation suggest that preferences for schools may also differ systematically in ways not yet explored.

In this study, I examine the assumption of exogeneity by investigating the relationship between parents' preferences and the social context of the local schooling market. Drawing on longitudinal interview data from thirty-six urban families, I describe how interactions between schools and parents shape and bound parents' preferences. I focus on the degree to which preferences are stable over time and independent of the schooling market. I argue that schools are not neutral partners in the development of preferences and suggest that preferences should not be treated as exogenous in rational choice models of parental behavior.

I begin with a brief discussion of the existing literature on parental preferences and participation in education. After an explanation of the sample and methodology, I describe how interactions shaped parents' preferences. I analyze the resources upon which parents drew to mediate those interactions. Finally, I consider the degree to which preferences are exogenous to the schools parents selected and what this might mean for future choice research.

What Do Parents Prefer?

There has been a great deal of research into parents' stated preferences. However, much less work has sought to understand why parents have the preferences they do. When researchers ask parents what they prefer, the responses are unsurprising. Parents prefer schools that are academically superior.[6] They prefer schools that match their values.[7] They desire schools that are safe[8] and schools with fewer poor children and children of color.[9] With few exceptions, these preferences appear to be so fundamental as to be shared with parents in New Zealand, England, Scotland, and Chile.[10]

There is disagreement on the degree to which parents prefer to have their children with peers that look like them, the own-group preference. This disagreement rests in part on the distinction between stated and revealed preferences. Studies that ask parents to state factors that influenced their decisions find that parents value academic characteristics more than other factors, including the demographic make-up of the student body.[11] If we assume however, that parents' preferences are revealed in the characteristics of the schools they actually select, evidence suggests parents prefer schools with higher socioeconomic status students and lower proportions of students of color.[12] It appears then, that "parents do care about academics but they also care very much about school demographics—something they will not admit to verbally."[13] It is important to note though, these preferences are deeply intertwined with the politics and history of the choice context.[14]

While the past twenty years of parental choice studies have taught us much, they have not illuminated the logic of parents' preferences. We know little about why parents prefer what they do. This is due to the assumptions we often make about the nature of preferences. For example, preferences are assumed to be independent of external circumstances such as local choice policies. Preferences are also assumed to be fixed over time. Parents want what they want, regardless of what they learn as the choice process unfolds. These assumptions lead to a straightforward understanding of choice: parents are consumers who have a priori preferences and make choices based on their preferences and constraints.[15] The causal mechanism which links parents to their actions operates in a single direction: parents' preferences and constraints determine a particular choice. The implicit separation of parents from their sociohistorical contexts minimizes or ignores the interactions between schools and parents that occur throughout a child's career. This is particularly problematic because research suggests those interactions shape parents' perceptions of their child's education.[16]

In order to better understand the relationship between parents' preferences and the schooling context, three questions frame this study: (1) In what ways do interactions with schools shape parents' preferences? (2) How, if at all, do those interactions differ by social class? And (3) how does a parent's social class mediate her ability to make sense of those interactions?

Methods

Previous work relies almost solely on retrospective interviews and questionnaires of parents after they have already opted out of traditional public schools.[17] Although these data shed descriptive light on important issues, they do not allow researchers to explore and understand the dynamic, situated aspects of parental reasoning. Researchers are limited to asking parents to retrospectively rank factors that influenced their choice of school (e.g., reputation, teachers, and resources). The problems with self-report data and memory have long been a topic of discussion among both social science researchers and biographers. As Campbell and Stanley note, the data "provide very limited help, since the rival sources of difference are so numerous."[18]

This study addresses the issues of hindsight bias and cross-sectional data through a longitudinal comparative case study of thirty-six urban parents' thinking prior to their children attending sixth or ninth grade.[19] The transitions from fifth to sixth and eighth to ninth grades are ones in which many children move from elementary to middle, or middle to high school. At this juncture, parents might be particularly willing to consider alternative schools. I followed parents through this time period, interviewing them three times over the nine months before, during, and after they selected schools for their children. The study's design rests on a purposeful sample of parents who previously sent their children to five different types of schools: neighborhood public, magnet, charter, nonreligious private, and religious private (see table 6.1). This design maximizes diverse prior choices as a proxy for diverse parental thinking.[20] The longitudinal aspect of the design allowed me to study the dynamic, situated nature of parents' thinking vis-à-vis the local choice market.[21]

There is a long history of choice in Weldon,[22] a large Midwestern city. However, until recently, choice was available only through choice of residence or attendance at tuition-based private schools. This changed dramatically eleven years ago when the state passed its charter law. Since then, Weldon has been the site of much charter activity. As of 2001, parents living in Weldon and the adjacent ring of suburbs enjoyed choice options which include some ninety-eight charter, 393 private, forty-eight magnet, and 341 traditional public schools.

Table 6.1. Parents' previous school status, school type, & racial background, by social class proportion

	Social Class Status		Participants
	Poor & Working Class	Middle Class	
Previous school status			
Failing	.36	.25.	.61
Nonfailing	.25	.14	.39
Previous school type			
Neighborhood	.14	.06	.20
Magnet	.17	.06	.23
Charter	.25	.08	.33
Religious	.03	.11	.14
Secular private	.03	.08	.11
Racial background			
African American	.56	.33	.89
Latino and Hispanic	.03	.00	.03
White	.03	.06	.09

Data Collection

Parents were interviewed three times, in February–March, June–July, and October–November. The first two interviews took place in person, in a location selected by the parent, most often in the parents' homes. A handful took place in the child's school, the parent's place of employment, or a restaurant. The final interview was conducted by phone. The first interview averaged sixty minutes, the second, forty-nine minutes, and the final, thirty-four minutes. Interview data was collected in three waves, thus providing the opportunity to develop grounded theories[23] which informed the second and third interview instruments. The three interviews moved from semistructured to structured in order to develop trust with the participants as well as gain an understanding of the categories and ways parents thought about choice. Between waves of data collection, all the interviews were transcribed and entered into N*6, a qualitative software program. Preliminary analyses were conducted between rounds of data collection.

Three types of data displays were used between interviews: a family choice history, a summary of the interview, and a categorization of the interview. The family choice history is a figure that summarizes where all of the children in the family have gone to school and why the parents chose those schools. The summary of the interview—which was shared with parents at their second interview—was an attempt to convey to the parent my understanding of their story. The final data display was a categorization of the interview. The interviews were very chatty and many topics—some unrelated to school choice—were discussed. The categorization was treated as a sorting mechanism, rather than a coding scheme. Somewhat dissimilar and vastly unequal text was allowed into the same category. The categories, like the summaries, were a first pass. They were meant to help me reduce the data but not so much as to lose potentially interesting, yet undiscovered facets of the choice process. Together, these three data representations, each focused on a slightly different dimension of choice, acted as the basis for the development of categories and hypotheses that could be tested in subsequent waves of interviews. This method of iterative conceptual development allowed me to take advantage of the highly nuanced, descriptive nature of the interview data.[24]

Data Analysis

Data were reduced and summarized as described above. Transcripts were analyzed for preferred school features, features of the previously selected school, the set of schools under consideration, the schools applied to, visited, and rejected from, as well as demographic information about the family. Interviews were broadly coded for any interactions parents had with schools. Those interactions were then coded into resources, networks, school influences, longitudinal changes, and incidentals. The final codes were information, extracurricular, networks, expectations, and salience of preference. Comparisons were then able to be made between parents of different social class backgrounds within each coding category.

As analyses revealed the importance of social class in parents' abilities to navigate school systems, parents were assigned a social class group—poor, working-class or middle-class. Because this was a relatively small study, these three broad groups captured the range of social class experiences among the parents. This is consistent with other studies of this size and scope.[25] Parents' social class status was assigned based on the parents' income, autonomy in the workplace, and education level. Less then $39,000 was considered lower income, $39,000 to $88,000 was considered middle income, and over $88,000 was considered to be upper income. These cut points were determined by dividing the income distribution in Weldon and the inner-ring of suburbs into thirds so that one third of people fell into each category. Parents' occupations were divided into the following categories: no job, routine, semiroutine, lower supervisory and technical, small employers and own account workers, intermediate, lower managerial and professional, and higher managerial and professional. Parents' education was categorized as follows: did not complete high school, completed high school or GED, some college or certified training program, completed college, some or completed graduate education. Social class status was determined by taking account of all three factors. In most cases, assignment was straightforward. In the couple of cases that had somewhat conflicting markers, my knowledge of the parents and their context helped me assign group membership.

How Interactions Shape Preferences

Interactions with schools shaped parents' preferences in at least three ways. Interactions shaped (1) what parents expected from their children, (2) the resources available to facilitate the choice process, and (3) the salience of particular preferences. The evidence for these interactions is in different forms: as a set of schools under consideration; as characteristics of schools (e.g., location, standardized test scores, teacher quality); and as ideals which cut across more than one school characteristic or are related to the child or family (e.g., a school that would allow the child to be a kid, a school with a sense of community, a place that would allow the child to grow). These three ways of discussing schools reflect the ways parents explained their preferences. In the sections that follow, I detail cases that are representative of other parents in the study. I also note the instances in which a parent's experience is not typical of her peers. These analyses document the ways in which parental preferences are co-constructed with schools over time suggesting that preferences cannot be considered to be exogenous, existing a priori inside a parent's head, unrelated to the larger social and historical context.

Expectations

Weldon parents hoped their children would aspire to great things—have a steady fulfilling job, have a family, and be a happy person. But their expectations, or what they thought might actually happen, differed, in part because of their interactions with schools.

Over the course of their children's school careers, interactions with schools often reinforced parents' previously held expectations for their children. For example, Mr. Dish, a middle-class White father has two children who have dyslexia. Mr. Dish does not, however, view Tasha's (fifth grade) and Terrell's (seventh grade) dyslexia as anything that will stop his children from accomplishing was he expects them to. Mr. Dish explained that he "expect[s] them to do well in school, develop people skills, and be leaders." Mr. Dish's interactions with schools reinforced his belief that his children could and would be successful students. His children's schooling experiences consistently confirmed Mr. Dish's expectations.

In selecting a middle school for Terrell, Mr. Dish sought out a school with a strong special education program in dyslexia and one that would continue the high-level science instruction the children's magnet middle school provided. Mr. Dish selected Wilson Middle School for Terrell and was very pleased. The special education teachers at Wilson are trained in the Thompson method, a method particularly well-suited to Terrell's form of dyslexia. Terrell progressed so much at Wilson that his reading markedly improved and he made the honor roll for the first time. While Terrell was never a bad student, his success at Wilson reinforced Mr. Dish's expectation for school success.

Two years after selecting Wilson for Terrell, Mr. Dish decided to send Tasha to Wilson. During November of Tasha's sixth grade year, Mr. Dish reported that she was doing very well, bringing home good grades, and liking school. Tasha's attendance at Wilson seemed to be helping her achieve.

One thing I've noticed is that she's working very hard. She was a good worker at [the middle school] but she is working even harder at Wilson. I think the resource room is really important to her. They get a lot of emotional support. I haven't had reason to doubt my reasons for putting her there. It might even be working better than I anticipated.[26]

The targeted support at Wilson helped Tasha succeed. Unlike some parents, whose school interactions make them doubt their children's capabilities, Mr. Dish's interactions with schools reinforced his belief that the children could be academically and socially successful. When Mr. Dish hypothesized that the targeted support Wilson offered Terrell would help him succeed, he was right. When Mr. Dish hypothesized that Tasha would benefit from the teachers at Wilson he was right. These are just two of the experiences Mr. Dish recounted for me; there were many more. Each interaction reinforced Mr. Dish's belief that his children were capable, academically successful students.

In contrast to Mr. Dish, Mrs. Brown's expectations were reinforced through negative interactions. Mrs. Brown, a middle-class African American civil engineer, had clear expectations for Sebastian, her fifth grade son. "My son doesn't have to be CEO of anything. I just want him to be happy but I want him to be able to have a conversation with anyone and not feel that, 'Well, I haven't read *Moby Dick* so I don't know what the heck they're talking about.' I want him to be able to communicate and understand easily. And not have to shrivel away because of lack of knowledge."[27] In addition to these broad expectations for her son, Mrs. Brown read and used books such as *What Every 5th Grader Should Know*, to help her determine if Sebastian was making the progress he should.

Early in Sebastian's education experiences, Mrs. Brown chose an elementary school she loved. Umoja Academy was a small African-centered private school that focused on academic excellence. In September of second grade, Sebastian's teacher left the school and he had a string of long-term substitutes. As the school year went by, Mrs. Brown grew more and more anxious because she felt he was falling behind. She complained to the school administration and, while they promised they were working on it, Mrs. Brown had Sebastian take a reading assessment at a private company. "Sure enough, it showed that he was behind in his reading so I had a private tutor for at least eight months, maybe a year."[28] When Mrs. Brown decided to remove Sebastian from Umoja, she had trouble finding a school for him. She went through one round of entrance exams but he was too far behind grade level. The schools would not take him. As tutoring began to help Sebastian catch up, Mrs.

Brown had him take another round of entrance exams. He passed and began third grade in a new school.

Mrs. Brown's experiences with Umoja and the schools for which Sebastian took exams reinforced her expectations for Sebastian's academic achievement. When she sensed Sebastian was falling behind, the reading assessment and entrance exams revealed she was right. After tutoring and retaking the exams, Sebastian was accepted at the school Mrs. Brown desired. Mrs. Brown knew both what Sebastian was capable of and what kind of school environment would support that learning. Her somewhat negative interactions with schools confirmed those expectations.

Middle-class parents used their resources to mediate the interactions with schools that reinforced their expectations for their children. For example, Mrs. Brown went to the administration of Umoja before she decided to move Sebastian. She used financial resources to determine Sebastain's reading level. She drew on books and her cultural understanding of success to determine if her son was developing as she expected. Mr. Dish developed very close working relationships with Terrell's teachers at Wilson. Thus, as he thought about where Tasha should go to school he drew on those social ties to gather excellent information which helped him determine that Tasha's form of dyslexia would also benefit from the Thompson method. Furthermore, the history of Mr. Dish's positive, trusting relationships with the resource room teachers made it more likely that those teachers would do all they could to help Tasha succeed.

In contrast to middle-class parents, poor and working-class parents did not have as many resources with which to blunt the influence of school interactions. For example, Mrs. Carol, a poor African American mother, had repeated negative interactions with her son's schools. Her expectations for Denzel, her eighth grade son, dropped repeatedly as he continued to struggle. Denzel hates school. The year prior to the study, Mrs. Carol explained that Denzel did everything in school but his work. His teachers said he was an enjoyable child to have in class; he didn't give them any trouble but he just wouldn't do his work. Mrs. Carol tried everything she knew. She lectured him, she threatened him, she took away his privileges. At Christmas, she only bought Denzel essentials—one outfit, winter boots, and one shirt—while her other two children got at least some of the things they wanted. She exclaimed, "He's not going to get nothing until I get a good report card from him." Mrs. Carol did not find out until May that Denzel was to be retained. She was frustrated that the school was able to contact her to ask for a conference about the retention but they didn't contact her in enough time for her to do something about it. But she felt there was little she could do to change the situation once she was actually in the conference. "Then, when they started showing me the records, the reason why he didn't pass, what can I say? He wasn't trying to do nothing." Mrs. Carol explained, however, that Denzel wasn't held back because he couldn't do the work, he was held back because he chose not to do the work. In her words, Denzel is the type who does the minimum to get by. Though Denzel did much better in eighth grade the second time around, he still did not get good grades. Each time a report card would come and grades were barely passing, Denzel would tell his mother "I'm going to start doing my homework. I'm going to do better. I'm going to bring my grades up." When Mrs. Carol would attend conferences to talk with teachers, they would reiterate the same message—Denzel needs to do his work.

Mrs. Carol's expectations grew more and more limited the more she interacted with the school. In her second interview, Mrs. Carol explained, "I never used to think this but I really hope I can get him through high school. That's what I'm focused on. Graduating." In thinking about potential high schools Mrs. Carol did not expect Denzel to be successful at more challenging schools, thus limiting the schools she was willing to consider.

> [If] I'm sending him to public school for free and he's going there and he's not putting forth no effort, then I would really be fighting a losing battle to spend all my money and send him over there [pointing to the private school down the street] and he's still . . . 'Cause you've got to be motivated to learn, you know, and that starts from within. And . . . that's what . . . I'm working on getting him motivated. And that's hard.[29]

Let us review Mrs. Carol's circumstances. Denzel hates school and Mrs. Carol did not know what else to do. She had exhausted her resources. When Denzel was held back, he did not change his behavior, and Mrs. Carol's expectations sank correspondingly lower. Mrs. Carol did not have the social and cultural resources valued by schools to mediate her interactions with her son's school. Mrs. Carol did not question the school's judgment that Denzel's problem was Denzel. She did not blame the school or argue for different treatment from his teachers. She did not point out that the school was in part responsible for Denzel's achievement. She felt there was nothing to say when school officials showed her the evidence that Denzel had not been doing his work. Thus, while Mrs. Carol's expectations grew more and more narrow, she also did not have resources that could have changed that outcome.

The majority of parents (72 percent) across social classes had school interactions that reinforced expansive expectations or positively changed their expectations for their children. However, of the parents whose school interactions reinforced or shifted expectations toward more narrow expectations, 90 percent were poor or working-class parents. Poor and working-class parents disproportionately experienced school interactions that did not help them reenvision their child's future. In these cases, children were not academically successful so school was a problem to be solved. It was not a place to make parents' dreams come true.

As Mrs. Brown's and Mr. Dish's interactions demonstrate, middle-class parents had interactions that were challenging or negative. However, they had many resources to help them mediate those interactions. Using social, financial, and cultural capital, middle-class parents were able to locate and draw on the advice, opinions, and knowledge of people external to the school. From psychologists to reading specialists, to books about what your fifth grader should know, middle-class parents had access to nonschool resources which helped them mediate school interactions. Though poor and working-class parents discussed their child's schooling with their friends, fewer of them had expertise that was useful to mediating school interactions. Most of the professionals to which poor and working-class parents had access, were themselves members of the school community. This made it difficult to get another opinion or perspective. Poor and working-class parents also did not have personal histories of successful schooling. Many did not complete high school, or if they did, they had been unable to find jobs that provided a comfortable living.

As Lareau documents, differences in resources can be accompanied by cultural differences in what parents perceive to be the division of labor between home and school.[30] Mrs. Conwell explained a view common among poor and working-class parents regarding that division of labor. She said:

> I always tell the teacher if there is something I can do to make this job easier, please feel free to let me know. Because my job is not to make your job hard. Because you're training my child to be out here. You know? You have the proper training to train her; . . . to give her those academics that she needs to be successful. Not me. My job is to have her know how to act. Your job is to teach her what she needs to know.[31]

While middle-class parents also want their children to behave and not be a problem in school, they generally talked about their role in

education differently. Mrs. Feagin explained how she viewed her engagement in her sons' educations.

> I try to expose them to different kinds of opportunities and
> create learning experiences where they can survive and thrive.
> Not perish. And I really advocate for them when I think some-
> thing is going to give them a better education. I want to work
> with [the middle school]. I don't want to just "They're not
> giving me what I want so Michael is out of there." If they're
> giving me 80% of what I want, I can work within the system
> to give me the other 20% of what I want.[32]

Mrs. Feagin's sense that she knows what she wants for her children
and that she has the skills, time, and confidence to work with the school
to have those desires met, is very different from Mrs. Conwell's view.
If these two views can be thought of as pieces of a larger framework
through which parents understand school interactions, poor and working-
class parents' perspectives are less likely to mediate any interactions that
contrive to negatively influence parents' expectations.

Scholars spend a great deal of time and energy trying to understand
the role parents' expectations and aspirations play in their children's
educational attainment. My point here is not to enter into that conversation. Instead, these data show how parents' expectations can be both
reinforced and changed through their interactions with schools, thus
shaping parents' preferences for the next school. These cases suggest
that parents had different resources for mediating school interactions.
Parents were generally optimistic about their child's academic progress.
They were also realistic. And by partially defining what is realistic for
a child, schools played an influential, yet undocumented, role in the
construction of parents' preferences.

Access to Resources

Children's fifth and eighth grade schools were repositories of resources
for parents' decision making. Through their interactions with schools,
parents came into contact with resources that shaped which schools they
were aware of and preferred. School interactions provided parents the
opportunity to develop both human and social capital.[33] Parents gained
new knowledge about their children, choice policies, processes, strategies, and potential schools. Classmates' parents and school professionals
shared advice and information. Some even made phone calls and wrote

letters of recommendation necessary for admittance to selective schools. While quality information is crucial to the functioning of any market,[34] I focus here on the resources described above that have not yet been documented in the school choice literature.

The types of resources explained above are most often discussed as the resources parents draw on to help them make their decisions. This way of thinking about resources emphasizes parents' agency in the choice process. Parents must take advantage of resources available to them; they must make an effort. There is however, another way to understand these resources. Resources must be present in order for parents to exert agency. Thus, effort is necessary but not sufficient in the school choice process. The following examples illustrate the how specific resources are more or less present, depending on one's social class background.

Learning about Schools and Strategies

For some parents, the social networks at their child's school provided resources that made certain schools possible. Mrs. Erhardt, a middle-class mother of five, struggled with where she was going to send Anise, her eighth grade daughter. There was a family tradition of attending St. Christopher High School, but the neighborhood around the school was becoming unsafe and student enrollment was dwindling. Mrs. Erhardt entertained the idea of sending Anise to St. Luke, St. Christopher's suburban counterpart. But St. Luke was a forty-five minute drive from Mrs. Erhardt's home and that kind of time commitment seemed almost impossible. Mrs. Erhardt gathered information about three potential religious schools that were closer to home, academically acceptable, and had basketball teams in which Anise could participate. After talking to mothers of Anise's friends, Mrs. Erhardt and three other mothers decided they would carpool to St. Luke. Prior to these conversations, St. Luke was not a possibility, it was just too far away. After the conversations, Mrs. Erhardt spent the better part of four months convincing her husband that St. Luke was worth the additional effort. Mrs. Erhardt's network provided a resource (other parents to carpool) that made a previously unattainable school, possible.

School-based social networks often connected parents to extracurricular activities. Those activities then connected parents to new networks of parents with different or additional information. For example, some parents knew about Springboard, a technology program for urban youth, designed to increase student achievement and teach about technology so that students might consider a career in the field. The program is designed and run by one of Weldon's largest technology firms. Both Mrs. Webb and Mrs. Brown heard about Springboard from other mothers at their children's schools. When they enrolled their children in Springboard, they met parents who lived in different parts of the city. Those parents provided information about schools that Mrs. Webb and Mrs. Brown found influential. Mrs. Brown explained, "They know every school in the city. When Sebastian was in session, we all would talk. That's where I get a lot of my information." They also learned strategies that might help their children gain admittance to selective schools. For example, Mrs. Brown learned that she should write a letter of introduction to the principal at one of the magnet schools. Mrs. Webb learned strategies to get recommendations quickly from teachers and school principals. Many parents connected to other networks through extracurricular activities originally discovered through their school-based network. These extracurricular networks provided information that shaped parents' preferences for particular schools.

Learning About One's Child

In addition to the schools and strategies parents learned through school interactions, they also learned more about their children's needs. Parents developed knowledge about the school characteristics and environments that facilitate their child's success. For example, Mrs. Jordan, a working-class, African American mother, quickly learned that her sixth grade daughter, Beverly, did not do well in large classrooms or schools that enforced zero tolerance policies for behavior. Taller than all the other children and diagnosed late, in the fourth grade, with a severe learning disability, Beverly was always in trouble. Mrs. Jordan felt that Beverly's learning disability made her unable to keep up with the other kids in school. Mrs. Jordan explained the academic reasons Beverly acted out.

> A lot of it was due to the fact that the public school did not recognize the trouble she was having. The teacher would say "Okay, everybody, let's take out your math." And [Beverly thought] "I have to do something to get out of this class so I won't have to be able to do this math." So I think this pretty much all started back from like kindergarten public school when they didn't recognize that she was having more of a learning disability then she was having a behavioral problem. So it became a behavior issue.[35]

Beverly's behavior problems spilled over into her relationships with other students. When peers would tease Beverly, she would hit them. Mrs. Jordan tried many strategies, from reasoning with Beverly to sending her to the school psychologist, but none worked. After attending two schools prior to fifth grade, Mrs. Jordan finally found a private school that worked. That school shaped her preferences for a middle school which she chose two years later.

The classes were small (less than ten students), and there were many extracurricular activities. Beverly participated in these activities and began to make friends. She was included socially, invited to birthday parties and to friends' houses for play dates. Beverly began to learn how to handle her learning disability and make progress toward grade level. Through these interactions spanning fifth and sixth grade, Mrs. Jordan came to learn that the small class size, extracurricular activities, and individualized attention around academics worked together to facilitate Beverly's success. During the study, Mrs. Jordan searched for middle schools with those characteristics, expanding her search to schools that were as far away as a twenty-five minute drive one-way. She preferred and was determined to find a school with the same characteristics that helped Beverly become more successful in elementary school.

Unlike Mrs. Jordan, who changed elementary schools twice before finding an environment that worked, many parents do not have to switch schools to learn what their children need. As children have different school experiences, parents learn what helps their children succeed. Because so many of these experiences take place in school or with peers from school, the institution of schooling shapes what parents believe is necessary and desired, thereby shaping parents' preferences for school characteristics and particular schools.

Across social class groups, schools presented parents with opportunities to gain knowledge, strategies, information, and assistance from the amassed resources every school had. And parents of all social class backgrounds took advantage of these resources. Particular resources are not, however, equally valuable for advantaging one's child in the competition of schooling.[36] Middle-class parents tended to come into contact with advantaging resources. These resources made it more likely their child would succeed on traditional dimensions such as getting into selective schools, doing better than most children on standardized tests, or attending schools with high proportions of wealthier, and often, whiter students. Advantaging resources included but were not limited to professionals making phone calls to their social contacts in other schools, advice about how to align a sequence of schools for the best possible college or high school acceptance, test taking courses, strategies for getting one's child into a prestigious magnet school, other parents to carpool, and recommendations of professionals such as psychologists, special needs experts, and school consultants.

In contrast, poor and working-class parents came into contact with remediating resources. These resources tended to help parents figure out how to solve problems their children were having as well as catch them up to grade level. Remediating resources included summer school, tutoring, programs designed to expose children to the arts, programs for high school dropouts, post-high school options such as the military or trade school, and mentoring programs designed for struggling students. All parents had access to resources that influenced their child's school experience and, therefore, their preferences for future schools. However, the resources at middle-class parents' schools were more likely to advantage middle-class children in the competition of schooling than similar resources at poor and working-class parents' schools.

This is not to say that all middle-class parents had exceptional networks that informed them of the right schools or preferences. Some middle-class parents, like Mrs. Robinson, felt very alone and isolated during the choice process. She explained, "I don't really have anyone to talk to about this. My friends' children are older. Things are different now." Some of the middle-class parents were surprised and did not know of resources that could help them gather information and choose. Mrs. Robinson explained that having to find a nonneighborhood school was "something new, something foreign. I don't know how to do this. I haven't done this before. So it's uncomfortable. I'm just baffled—overwhelmed having to go through this." While Mrs. Robinson's network was not representative—most White, middle-class parents' networks provided resources and support in the choice process—there were a few middle-class networks that were not the rich resource typical of the group.

These findings should not be interpreted to suggest that poor and working-class parents only came into contact with resources that pointed them toward the wrong schools or preferences. Mrs. Gunnison got advice about a high-performing middle school from her daughter's elementary school guidance counselor. Mrs. Thomas learned about a college preparation program for her eighth grade son from the other mothers at her son's middle school. And Mrs. Morales learned about a high-performing magnet school that offered language instruction from a parent night at her daughter's elementary school. But these examples were not the norm. The vast majority of resources amassed in poor and working-class parents' schools were unlikely to support high academic achievement without many other, more substantial interventions on the child's behalf.

Salience of Particular Preferences

Rational Choice Theory presumes that preferences are stable over time. This assumption was reasonable for some parents. However, many Weldon parents' preferences changed over time, in interaction with the choice context. For example, as parents watched their children develop through fifth or eighth grade, they changed their minds about the school features most important to their child's success. As circumstances changed, parents' preferences shifted. Some children did not get picked in the lottery for a charter school that was over subscribed. Other children did not pass the tests necessary to attend certain magnet schools. Developments such as these caused many parents to reevaluate, shifting their preferences while doing so.

Parents recognize the tenuous influence of their preferences. Almost to a person, parents had contingency plans. They thought to themselves, if not this school, then perhaps this one. If not that one, then I could live with this other one. These contingency lists, which often exist only in a parent's mind, can be conceived of as a rank ordering of the parent's preferences. Schools at the top of the list maximize the largest number of preferences while schools lower down on the list contain preferences parents are unwilling to compromise. Thus, these lists provide insights. Consistent with other research that documents how parents of different social class backgrounds deal with schools,[37] Weldon parents have different resources to make it more or less likely they will end up with a school high on their preference list. Middle-class parents had greater resources to mediate the external circumstances contriving to move them further down their lists. Poor and working-class parents used the resources they had, but experienced more difficulty than did middle-class parents.

Mrs. Hawill

Mrs. Hawill, a married, middle-class African American mother of twin eighth graders, explained early on that she wanted a very challenging school for her daughter, Alecia. By her mother's description, Alecia is a bright young lady who gets very good grades. She keeps to herself, has a few close friends, and loves to read. She has her future mapped out, right down to where she wants to go to college and medical school. Alecia has researched schools and expenses. She knows what kind of grades she needs, and she is planning ahead. Mrs. Hawill believes Alecia will be a doctor someday and wants to provide her every opportunity to reach that goal. In February, Mrs. Hawill focused on getting Alecia into the best school possible. She was considering a very prestigious private school in the suburbs and two magnet schools, all three of which are widely considered elite schools.

In the spring, Alecia took exams for the private school and two of the academic magnet high schools in Weldon. While she passed the private school test, Mrs. Hawill explained that they just couldn't figure out how to pay the tuition.

> The only reason she's not going to Upland Hills is that her mother [Mrs. Hawill], well her family, didn't have the money to send her. And they said they had a scholarship but the only way they could give her that scholarship is if I were to claim her as a single parent and go on ADC. She told me that I was in the worst bracket, middle class. You don't make enough to be rich and you make too much to be poor. So you'll have to quit your job so we can give the scholarship all the way through. Ok. Now, let's think about this. What are we going to eat?[38]

There were also problems with the two magnet schools. Alecia was not accepted, despite the fact she scored in the eighty-first percentile on the exam.

> They didn't take her. And we've been in a battle. There were children in her class who scored less than Alecia and they got in and she didn't. So, I've been meeting with people down at Weldon Public Schools. I have a meeting with [the superintendent] scheduled for the 15th of this month. And I told the last person I met at the school administration building that if [the superintendent] couldn't get me an answer, I would be calling the news and they can get me an answer. Her best friend got in and she was a 79%. It's who you know. That's what it is. Why take the test if they aren't going to use it. There was a boy who scored in the 60% percentile. He got in and she didn't.[39]

These unexpected developments left Mrs. Hawill in need of other school options for Alecia. In June Mrs. Hawill had applied to another magnet school, a charter school, and went to visit a religious school. Mrs. Hawill fully expected Alecia to be attending one of the elite schools described above, but external circumstances contrived to make this impossible. Thus Mrs. Hawill's description of what she wanted shifted. She was hoping to find Alecia a small school nearby that offered an orderly, positive learning environment, where she could be with her friends and get a good education.

In the fall, Mrs. Hawill selected Edin, a magnet school, that was close to home and attended by many of Alecia's friends. Mrs. Hawill chose Edin over the religious school because it "didn't seem worth the money for what you got." She also selected Edin over a charter school because the charter school was just adding a ninth grade, and although the middle school had an excellent reputation, Mrs. Hawill was unsure about the high school. She also felt the charter school was too far away although it was no further away than the three schools Mrs. Hawill originally considered.

The criteria Mrs. Hawill focused on to decide between the second set of schools differed from her earlier criteria of academic achievement and career preparation. Mrs. Hawill continued to prefer schools that would advance Alecia, however, because her options were narrowed, another set of school characteristics factored into Mrs. Hawill's thinking. Mrs. Hawill did not completely change the set of characteristics she preferred. Instead, the rank ordering of Mrs. Hawill's desired characteristics shifted. A small school and orderly environment became more salient as she was forced to accommodate to external circumstances.

Mrs. Wise

A similar shift happened for Mrs. Wise, a working-class, African American mother of Sarah, a fifth grader. Mrs. Wise applied to and preferred Bedrock Middle School, an academic magnet middle school near her home. In February, Mrs. Wise spoke at length about wanting a selective, challenging school that would allow Sarah to continue her current academic success. Bedrock met all of these preferences. However, Mrs. Wise did not hear from the school for a long time. When she called in April, the school secretary indicated that she should have already heard. "I assume she didn't get in because we didn't get a letter. But I'll tell you, I'm about sick of them. They are really disorganized." Even in February,

Mrs. Wise had gathered information about four additional schools. She did not want to have "nowhere" to send Sarah. With prospects worsening for Bedrock, Mrs. Wise attended a city-wide information session where she learned of Lincoln Magnet Middle School. She spoke with the principal, learned about Lincoln's programs and felt that this would be a great second choice school. Although Sarah did not know anyone at Lincoln, Mrs. Wise felt she would adjust. She explained, "As long as I know the school is good and she likes it, the drive, a fifteen minutes one way, is worth it." Sarah was accepted. In early June, however, Mrs. Wise ran into an old friend, who is a teacher at Forward Academy, another magnet school, closer to Mrs. Wise's home. Forward takes an innovative, personalized approach to education and Mrs. Wise was very impressed with the school. She enrolled Sarah at Forward, where Sarah spent her first week of sixth grade. At that point, however, Mrs. Wise got a call from Bedrock indicating Sarah had been accepted and could begin the next week. Even though Sarah was happy at Forward, Mrs. Wise switched her to Bedrock. She felt it had uniforms, Sarah's friends, and she trusted its reputation more than Forward's.

The ordering of Mrs. Wise's preferences shifted when Sarah initially did not get into Bedrock and as she explored other schools. Originally, the emphasis was on school reputation, a challenging curriculum, and the chance for Sarah to remain with her friends. When Mrs. Wise considered Lincoln, she emphasized Lincoln's community feel, challenging curriculum, and a strong administrator. When Sarah was enrolled at Forward, Mrs. Wise discussed Forward's small class size, high parental involvement, individualized attention, and the recommendation of her friend. In spite of the fact that Mrs. Wise's preference for particular school characteristics shifted over the choice process, there were aspects that remained constant. Mrs. Wise preferred schools that were selective (all of her top choices were magnet schools which required applications for admissions), supportive of Sarah's development, and close to home. Like Mrs. Hawill, Mrs. Wise always wanted good academics, but as the process unfolded and she interacted repeatedly with schools, other characteristics were placed higher on her list.

Preferences shift regardless of a parent's social class background. There were however, important differences between how middle-class, and poor and working-class parents experienced and dealt with these shifting preferences. Middle-lass parents had resources that facilitated their ability to get what they wanted when school interactions contrived to shift the salience of particular preferences. For example, Mrs. Hawill did see the superintendent of Weldon Public Schools and he explained that there had been a mistake. In the end, Mrs. Hawill was able to get

Alecia into her second choice school, Jefferson, which was an academic magnet school. This was not a trivial difference as more than 80 percent of students at Jefferson are at grade level, while less then 50 percent are at grade level in Alecia's ninth grade school, Edin. Another middle-class eighth grader, Orlando Jones, did not pass the standardized test to get into Weldon's high schools. His father, a city employee with many connections to people on the school board, had two personal friends offer to pull strings for Orlando at one of the academic magnets. Mr. Jones ultimately decided this would not be good for Orlando and enrolled him in a religious school with a strong academic reputation. Mr. Jones' upper middle-class income allowed him to cushion Orlando's failure on the tests so that he could still attend a good school. For middle-class parents like Mrs. Hawill and Mr. Jones, their interactions within the schooling context were upsetting but they were not devastating. These parents had resources—money, time, personal connections, and knowledge of how to work the system—that allowed them to advocate for their children and enable them to attend schools with desirable characteristics that were higher up on their contingency lists.

Poor and working-class parents used their available resources to mediate their interactions with schools, but more often then not, they ran into roadblocks their resources could not overcome. Mrs. Wise used her networks to the best of her abilities but she did not have friends in leadership positions who offered to pull strings like Mr. Jones did. She was forced to wait for Bedrock to admit Sarah. In contrast to another middle-class mother in a similar situation, Mrs. Wise did not know that she could write a personal letter to the principal asking for a meeting, a tactic that worked for the middle-class mother. It did not occur to Mrs. Wise that the school would make special accommodations for Sarah if Mrs. Wise displayed the cultural capital valued in the school choice process.

Other poor and working-class parents had similar experiences. Mr. Williams was told by his first choice charter school that he needed to supply his granddaughter's birth certificate in order for her to attend the school. Because he and his wife had unofficial custody of his granddaughter and the relationship with his daughter-in-law was complicated, he knew he would not be able to get his granddaughter's birth certificate in time for the school's deadline. He did not feel it was right to ask for special treatment and he did not want to explain to the school the complex family dynamics that made it difficult to get the birth certificate. He withdrew her application. Another working-class mother, Mrs. Foster, did not feel she could ask her daughter's teacher for a recommendation letter on short notice so she did not apply to a school she liked very much. A middle-class mother, in a similar situation, wrote the letter for her child's teacher and asked the teacher to sign it—something the teacher was more than happy to do. This strategy did not occur to Mrs. Foster. Even if it had, it is unclear whether or not Mrs. Foster would have elected to write such a letter.

Parents of all social class backgrounds used their resources to mediate their interactions with the choice market. They shifted their preferences and attempted to find schools and situations with which they felt comfortable. Poor and working-class parents were at a particular disadvantage in mediating these interactions because they had fewer resources. Middle-class parents had the financial, social, and cultural resources to cushion the various changes they inevitably faced. While there was no difference in parents' satisfaction with the choice process, poor and working-class parents ended up with schools further down their contingency lists than did middle-class parents.

Evolving Preferences for a Developing Child

As researchers, we tend to think of children as students. We focus on school-related development—whether or not students are at grade level or have discipline problems. In contrast, parents think of their children as children. They view them as people who need to grow and develop socially, emotionally, and intellectually. Parents' broad view of their children results in them paying careful attention to many dimensions of fit between a given school and their child.

In the preceding analyses I argue that parents' interactions with the schooling environment shape their preferences. However, there were other ways preferences were shaped. For example, parents' preferences changed when their child began behaving in a new way. Mrs. Bordon, the mother of an eighth grader, Clyde, explained in our first interview that Clyde had recently begun changing dramatically. He quit Boy Scouts; his grades had dropped; and he was leaving his room a mess where before he kept it clean and tidy. Clyde also was complaining about where his parents planned for him to attend high school. Mrs. Bordon was worried. She and her husband had never doubted that Clyde would attend St. Christopher, the religious high school many of the children from Clyde's middle school attended. She explained, "Before all this started happening, he was going to St. Christopher. But now, I don't know. I'm worried about forcing him." Over the course of the nine months, Mrs. Bordon began to investigate the local public school Clyde wanted to attend. Initially, she was very nervous about the students that attended Harvey

Smith. She was also worried that moving from a small school to a large comprehensive high school would increase the possibility Clyde would get lost or wind up with the wrong group of kids. She also felt very strongly that the religious education Clyde received since kindergarten should be a continuing part of his development as a young man. In the spring, Mrs. Bordon went to meet the principal and teachers of Harvey Smith. She allowed Clyde to take driver's training over the summer with other Harvey Smith children. And she learned that one of Clyde's classmates from his middle school would be attending Harvey Smith. After a conversation with the mother of that child, Mrs. Bordon began to feel more comfortable with Harvey Smith as an option.

Mrs. Bordon's preference for Harvey Smith evolved over time. She went from preferring a small religious high school to a large public high school. She addressed her concerns for religion and high academic standards by laying down conditions for Clyde. He could stay at Harvey Smith as long as he continued to participate in church and he kept his grades up. "If he doesn't do that, he'll be right back at St. Christopher next year." Mrs. Bordon's reaction to her son's changing actions and desires was very common among parents, in particular among parents of eighth graders. As their children changed, parents' preferences shifted. Rather than loyally sticking to a specific preference, parents like Mrs. Bordon rethought their preferences in order to make choices that would support their child's development.

Conclusions

I began by explaining that RCT treats preferences as exogenous to choice models. Choice models do not predict preferences, nor is there a systematic relationship between variables in the models and preferences. Further, these preferences are presumed to exist independent of the particular schooling market in which the parent exercises choice. Furthermore, preferences are presumed to exist in a stable hierarchy in parents' heads.

The data presented here suggests these assumptions are flawed. Parents' preferences are shaped by their interactions with schools and therefore are not stable over time. Preferences shift during the choice process in response to the messages parents gather from schools about what to expect from their child as well as the resources available at their child's current school. Finally, the rank order of preferences shifts when external forces make certain schools impossible to choose. In short, preferences shift, change, and interact. They are not the independent, disconnected, unsocialized, ahistorical constructs our models presume.

Further, parents of different social class backgrounds do not have similar resources to interpret and mediate school interactions that shape preferences. It is important to emphasize here that poor and working-class parents used the resources they had available to them. They did not simply sit back and hope things would work out. But as others have documented,[40] non-middle-class social and cultural capital is not as valuable for advantaging children in a schooling system that privileges middle class ways of knowing and being. In pointing out that poor and working-class parents had fewer resources to mediate their interactions with schools, I am not saying they cared less, were less engaged, or somehow were just not as crafty in getting their way. I am suggesting that in the competition of schooling, social class status, among other things, confers differential advantage for parents' whose class position matches that of schools. This advantage has implications for choosing schools even though this need not be the case. Some schools, such as Comer schools (schools that participate in the Great School Development Program) and some African-centered schools, enact very different ways of engaging parents and their children. Unfortunately, and for the most part, schools expect, value and reward middle-class cultural capital to the exclusion of other instantiations of capital.

These findings have implications for both our empirical and conceptual understanding of choice. Perhaps most importantly, the empirical methods we use to investigate choice must become more reflective of the complex phenomenon under investigation. Current models of choice should not presume preferences are exogenous. There are methods commonly employed in economics and political science to account for endogeneity problems in many areas of policy. School choice should be no different. Relying on assumptions that are false is likely to lead to inaccurate models and misguided public policy. Furthermore, gold standard research on choice should not rely on crosssectional accounts of preferences that occur after the parent has selected a school. These analyses reflect hindsight bias and do not give us an accurate portrayal of the preferences and constraints shaping parents' actions, therefore adding little to our understanding of choice markets.

Straightforward models of human behavior advance inquiry in all areas of study. But such models have their limits. If we do not pay careful attention to the ways in which those models obscure and render irrelevant other, more nuanced and complex ways of understanding behavior, we may facilitate the stagnation of scientific understanding. This study, and others like it, provides empirical data which suggest the dominant choice paradigm must be amended. To ignore these data does a significant disservice to both the behavior we try to understand and the field we try to advance.

Notes for Chapter 7

1. For example, Joseph L. Bast and Herb J. Walberg, "Can Parents Choose the Best Schools for Their Children?" *Economics of Education Review* 23 (2004): 431–40.
2. I use the term "parents" in this article; however, my data confirm what has been documented by David, West, and Ribbens. School choice is primarily, even in two-parent, mother-father households, a task controlled by mothers. See Miriam E. David, Anne West, and Jane Ribbens, *Mother's Intuition? Choosing Secondary Schools* (London: Falmer Press, 1994).
3. Exogeneity is a technical term used by economists to indicate that a particular variable is external to the model being described with a particular equation or set of equations. In other words, when one presumes a variable is exogenous, there is no relationship between that variable and the variables being modeled.
4. Angela Calabrese Barton, Corey Drake, Jose Gustavo Perez, Kathleen St. Louis, and Magnia George, "Ecologies of Parental Engagement in Urban Education," *Educational Researcher* 33, no. 4 (2004): 3–12; Gustavo Perez Carreon, Corey Drake, and Angela Calabrese Barton, "The Importance of Presence: Immigrant Parents' School Engagement Experiences," *American Educational Research Journal* 42, no. 3 (2005): 465–98; Tiffani Chin and Meredith Phillips, "Social Reproduction and Child-Rearing Practices: Social Class, Children's Agency, and the Summer Activity Gap," *Sociology of Education* 77, no. 3 (2004): 185–210; Erin McNamara Horvat, Elliot B. Weininger, and Annette Lareau, "From Social Ties to Social Capital: Class Differences in the Relationship between Schools and Parent Networks," *American Educational Research Journal* 40, no. 2 (2003): 319–51; Amy Stuart Wells, "African-American Students' View of School Choice," in *Who Chooses? Who Loses? Culture, Institutions, and the Unequal Effects of School Choice*, ed. Bruce Fuller, Richard F. Elmore, with Gary Orfield (New York: Teachers College Press, 1996).
5. Annette Lareau, "Social Class Differences in Family-School Relationships: The Importance of Cultural Capital," *Sociology of Education* 60 (1987): 73–85; Annette Lareau, *Home Advantage: Social Class and Parental Intervention in Elementary Education* (Philadelphia: Falmer Press, 1989).
6. David Armor and Brett Peiser, *Competition in Education: A Case Study of Interdistrict Choice* (Boston: Pioneer Institute, 1997); Mark Schneider, Paul Teske, and Melissa Marschall, *Choosing Schools: Consumer Choice and the Quality of American Schools* (Princeton, NJ: Princeton University Press, 2000).
7. R. Kenneth Godwin, Frank R. Kemerer, and Valerie J. Martinez, "Comparing Public Choice and Private Voucher Programs in San Antonio," in *Learning*

from School Choice, ed. Paul E. Peterson and Bryan C. Hassel (Washington, DC: Brookings Institution Press, 1998); Valerie E. Lee, Robert G. Croninger, and Julia B. Smith, "Equity and Choice in Detroit," in *Who Chooses? Who Loses?* ed. Bruce Fuller, Richard F. Elmore, and Gary Orfield.

8. Armor and Peiser, "Competition in Education"; Lee, Croninger, and Smith, "Equity and Choice in Detroit."

9. Armor and Peiser, "Competition in Education"; Jeffrey R. Henig, "Choice in Public Schools: An Analysis of Transfer Requests among Magnet Schools," *Social Science Quarterly* 71, no. 1 (1990): 69–82; Mark Schneider and Jack Buckley, "What Do Parents Want from Schools? Evidence from the Internet," *Educational Evaluation and Policy Analysis* 24, no. 2 (2002): 133–44.

10. David, West, and Ribbens, *Mother's Intuition?*; Edward B. Fiske and Helen F. Ladd, *When Schools Compete: A Cautionary Tale* (Washington, DC: Brookings Institute Press, 2000); Varun Gauri, *School Choice in Chile: Two Decades of Educational Reform* (Pittsburgh, PA: University of Pittsburgh Press, 1998); Sharon Gewirtz, Stephen J. Ball, and Richard Bowe, *Markets, Choice, and Equity in Education* (Buckingham, England: Open University Press, 1995); Ron Glatter, Philip A. Woods, and Carl Bagley, "Diversity, Differentiation and Hierarchy: School Choice and Parental Preferences," in *Choice and Diversity in Schooling: Perspectives and Prospects,* ed. Ron Glatter, Philip A. Woods, and Carl Bagley, 7–28 (London: Routledge, 1997); Philip A. Woods, Carl Bagley, & Ron Glatter, *School Choice and Competition: Markets in the Public Interest?* (London: Routledge, 1998).

11. For example, Mark Schneider, Melissa Marschall, Paul Teske, and Christine Roch, "School Choice and Culture Wars in the Classroom: What Different Parents Seek from Education," *Social Science Quarterly* 79, no. 3 (1998): 489–501.

12. Armor and Peiser, *Competition in Education*; Brian P. Gill, P. Mike Timpane, Karen E. Ross, and Dominic J. Brewer, *Rhetoric versus Reality: What We Know and What We Need to Know about Vouchers and Charter Schools* (Santa Monica, CA: Rand, 2000); Roslyn Arlin Mickelson and Stephanie Southworth, "When Opting Out Is Not a Choice: Implications for NCLB's Transfer Option from Charlotte, North Carolina," *Equity & Excellence in Education* 38, (2005): 1–15.

13. Schneider and Buckley, "What Do Parents Want from Schools?" 141.

14. See Bekisizwe S. Ndimande, chapter 10 for an explanation of these issues in South Africa.

15. Schneider, Teske, and Marschall, *Choosing Schools.*

16. Jay MacLeod, *Ain't No Makin' It: Aspirations and Attainment in a Low-Income Neighborhood* (Boulder, CO: Westview Press, 1995).

17. Armor and Peiser, *Competition in Education*; Bretten Kleitz, Gregory R. Weiher, Kent L. Tedin, and Richard Matland, "Choice, Charter Schools, and Household Preferences," *Social Science Quarterly* 81, no. 3 (2000): 846–54; Schneider, Teske, and Marschall, *Choosing Schools*; Gregory R. Weiher and Kent L. Tedin, "Does Choice Lead to Racially Distinctive Schools? Charter Schools and Household Preferences," *Journal of Policy Analysis and Management* 21, no. 1 (2002); John F. Witte, *The Market Approach to Education: An Analysis of America's First Voucher Program* (Princeton, NJ: Princeton University Press, 2000).

18. Donald T. Campbell and Julian C. Stanley, *Experimental and Quasi-experimental Designs for Research* (Boston: Houghton Mifflin, 1965), 7.

19. The larger study includes forty-eight urban and suburban parents. The analyses reported here focus only on parents living in the city of Weldon. For a more detailed description of the sampling procedure used please see Courtney A. Bell, "Parents' Views of School Choice: An Unexamined Perspective" (doctoral diss., Michigan State University, 2004).

20. For a full description of the sampling strategy, see Courtney A. Bell, "All Choice Created Equal? How Good Parents Select 'Failing' Schools," National Center for the Study of Privatization in Education, Columbia University, http://www.ncspe.org/publications_files/OP106.pdf (accessed December 10, 2005).

21. I use the term market here for ease of communication. As Henig has pointed out, however, a more accurate term may be quasi-market. See Henig, "Choice in Public Schools."

22. All names are pseudonyms. Parents selected their own and their children's pseudonyms.

23. Barney G. Glaser and Anselm L. Strauss, *The Discovery of Grounded Theory: Strategies for Qualitative Research* (Hawthorne, NY: Aldine, 1979).

24. Matthew B. Miles and A. Michael Huberman, *Qualitative Data Analysis: An Expanded Sourcebook*, 2nd ed. (Thousand Oaks, CA: Sage, 1994).

25. Lareau, *Home Advantage*; Annette Lareau, *Unequal Childhoods: Class, Race, and Family Life* (Berkeley: University of California Press, 2003).

26. Third interview with Mr. Dish.

27. First interview with Mrs. Brown.

28. Ibid.

29. First interview with Mrs. Carol.

30. Lareau, *Home Advantage*.

31. First interview with Mrs. Conwell.

32. Second interview with Mrs. Feagin.

33. Though non-school-based social networks were important to the development of social capital and therefore parents' preferences, I exclude an analysis of capital through such networks because the focus of the paper is how interactions with schools shape preferences. I consider non-school influences on parents' preferences in other analyses of this data (e.g., Bell, "Parents' Views of School Choice"; Bell, "All Choice Created Equal?").

34. See Harry Brighouse, "School Choice and Educational Equality," this volume; or Christopher Lubienski, "The Politics of Parental Choice: Theory and Evidence on Quality Information," this volume.

35. First interview with Mrs. Jordan.

36. Lareau, "Social Class Differences"; Lareau, *Home Advantage*.

37. Calabrese Barton, et al., "Ecologies of Parental Engagement"; Carreon, Drake, and Calabrese Barton, "The Importance of Presence"; Erin McNamara Horvat, "The Interactive Effects of Race and Class in Educational Research: Theoretical Insights from the Work of Pierre Bourdieu," *Penn GSE Perspectives on Urban Education* 2, no. 1 (2003): 1–25; Horvat, Weininger, and Lareau, "From Social Ties to Social Capital."

38. Second interview with Mrs. Hawill.

39. Ibid.

40. Calabrese Barton, et al., "Ecologies of Parental Engagement"; Horvat, Weininger, and Lareau, "From Social Ties to Social Capital"; Lareau, "Social Class Differences in Family-School Relationships"; Lareau, *Home Advantage*; Lareau, *Unequal Childhoods*.

Chapter 7

Managers of Choice

Race, Gender, and the Philosophies of the New Urban School Leadership

Janelle T. Scott

Reformers are restructuring the governance, leadership, and structure of urban school systems in profound ways. Reminiscent of elite, mostly White male twentieth-century reformers—"old" school managers who professionalized public school leadership and worked to standardize *and* differentiate instruction according to scientific and business principles (Tyack, 1974)—the new iteration of school leadership comes from outside of the traditional educational establishment, and questions the qualifications and expertise of educational professionals who have largely followed the professional trajectory set by the early reformers. Namely, traditional school leaders tend to attain certification from higher education institutions and acquire experience as classroom teachers and school principals before assuming positions in school district leadership.

An under-examined contemporary trend is that of the new school leaders whose influence is helping to restructure school systems through a variety of school choice and privatization measures. Coming largely from the private and corporate sectors, these reformers are predominantly White men and have focused on school choice, privatization, alternative certification, teacher unions, test-based accountability, and small schools as means for urban school reform. Given that the student demographics of most urban school districts tend to be majority African American and Latino children from low-income families, this analysis places race, gender, and social class at the center of its inquiry. Specifically, the chapter examines the identities, philosophies, funding sources, and political networks of the new school leaders.

I examine the growth of private, for-profit and nonprofit education management organizations and charter school management organizations (EMOS & CMOs), from a race, class, and gendered critical perspective. Specifically, I demonstrate that three leadership terrains: individual charter school founders, for-profit EMO executives, and non-profit CMO executives are important areas for empirical study as areas where White men have become this century's school managers—managers of school choice—operating in a contemporary context in which governments and philanthropies are more inclined to fund private ventures than at any other period of American history. Given the demographics of the managers of choice in comparison to the almost exclusively low-income African American and Latino students their companies, funding, and advocacy target, it becomes necessary to frame this analysis within a political sociology of education reform that attends to the complicated racial dynamics in the history of education and also considers contemporary issues of racial and social class inequality.

Historical Context of Educational Leadership:
Race and Elitism

From its early origins of elite White men, to its community control-influenced diversity, the management and leadership of school districts has been a contested terrain in the politics of education. An under examined contemporary trend is the new school leaders, the managers of choice. These reformers are predominantly White men and focused on school choice, privatization, alternative certification, and small schools as means for urban school reform. This chapter examines the networks, ideologies, and systemic effects of these contemporary managers of choice.

Historians and sociologists of education have documented the rise of school and school district leadership and management as professions in the early-twentieth century. As public schools were transformed from small, community-run institutions to large urban systems, administrative progressives, a loosely configured network of business leaders, political elite, and university faculty called for and implemented reforms that would centralize urban school governance in ways that mimicked corporate governance. These reformers realized their goals with increased bureaucratization and specialization of the education profession. Schools of education developed programs in administrative science, and managers trained in these programs went on to reshape the governance and management of urban school systems.

Administrative progressives invented school and school district leadership as fields of study and as professional tracks, and largely reserved such positions for White men.[1] The original elite school managers designed the modern urban school systems and experimented with governance structures and loci of control in their search of the one best system, all the while excluding or limiting the participation of women of all races, poor men, and men of color in leadership positions. Following the Civil Rights Movement and Feminist Movement, White women and people of color began making modest inroads into school and district leadership. Indeed, given increased government oversight over equalizing opportunity, the public sphere—including school districts, the military, and federal and state government—became a somewhat protected space where people of color and women were able to build careers and attain middle-class status.[2]

As people of color and women began running schools and districts in greater numbers, and as the backlash against school desegregation, multiculturalism, and compensatory programs took hold, so emerged derisive critiques from elites outside education about the urban systems and schools they controlled, asserting that expertise existed not just outside school systems, but primarily in the private sector, a space historically dominated and reserved for White men.[3] Moreover, critics alleged that educators and leaders in public schools were the cause of lackluster school performance. There is general agreement from researchers, practitioners, and policy makers that the conditions under which poor children and children of color are educated is in need of improvement, but the causes attributed to these conditions vary greatly, as do the remedies proposed. In the last twenty years, the policy spotlight has been on market-based solutions to the challenges facing urban schools, including the adoption of charter school laws, voucher programs, management of schools by for-profit and nonprofit private companies, and the school choice provisions of the No Child Left Behind Act. These initiatives have reshaped the demographics of public school leadership in ways that have not been adequately explored in school choice research.

In this chapter, I examine the growth of private, for-profit and nonprofit education management organizations and charter school management organizations (EMOs & CMOs), from a race, class, and gendered critical perspective. Specifically, I demonstrate that three leadership terrains: charter school founders, for-profit EMO executives, and nonprofit CMO executives are important areas for empirical study as areas where White men have become this century's school managers—managers of school choice, distinguished by considerable profit to be made in a contemporary context in which governments are more inclined to fund private ventures. Given the demographics of the managers of choice in comparison to the almost exclusively low-income African American and Latino students their companies, funding, and advocacy target, it becomes necessary to frame this analysis with a political sociology of education reform that attends to the complicated racial dynamics in the history of education.

Early Architects of African American Education

Watkins details the political and ideological assumptions of the White architects of Black education in the early twentieth century, finding that they valued maintaining the social order, building profits for industry by training Blacks to be manual laborers. Although Black architects, such as DuBois and Washington, argued for their visions of Black schooling, Watkins argues that due to prevailing power disparities, they were ultimately minor players who were unable to significantly redress the inadequate schooling conditions for African American students in public schools. Writes Watkins, "Political sociology allows the interrogation of human actions and interactions within the context of power. Power is viewed in terms of wealth, property, access, inheritance, and privilege."[5]

Watkins's framing of the historical shapers of Black schooling has modern applications. Whereas, the context about which he wrote considered the role of education for newly emancipated Blacks, the twenty-first century context is one in which a global economy has rendered large segments of the United States labor force redundant, where jobs for high school graduates are increasingly low-status and low-paying, and where access to higher education is shrinking. Black men find themselves more likely to be incarcerated or under the arm of the criminal justice system than in school. It is also a context in which unprecedented advancements into public school leadership, the educational professoriate, and the school superintendency have been made by women and people of color. At the same time, public schooling is under increased scrutiny of federal and state departments of education, and student learning is measured by standardized tests, which have become the benchmark of school quality and hurdles for students to ascend. There is a pervasive sense from the citizenry that most urban public school systems are failing. School choice through charter schools, alternative small schools, vouchers, and private management is currently the most popular educational reform; policy makers propose choice as a remedy to school failure.

As new school managers influence schooling from the outside, through school choice reforms that allow for a greater role for the private sector in public education, many professors of educational leadership emphasize issues of democracy, inclusive and multicultural curricula, social justice, and access to pedagogy that fosters critical thinking to student teachers and aspiring school leaders.[6] These scholars largely prepare students to follow traditional routes to school leadership. This represents an intriguing shift in education, where experts, who have followed the path to professional legitimacy mapped out by early administrative progressives: certification, securing advanced degrees, working in public school systems, find that very legitimacy questioned and challenged by those with little or no public school experience. In particular, leaders and researchers of color who tend to work in predominantly minority school systems or focus upon multicultural perspectives and social justice, find their work especially critiqued.

Locating the New School Managers: EMOs and CMOs

Conservative critics, especially, have blamed traditional university preparation programs, along with the bureaucratization of school administration for the lackluster performance of U.S. schools.[7] Following in this tradition of critique, though coming from a diverse ideological stance, the new school managers tend to position themselves as external reformers of an educational establishment that is entrenched, hostile to innovation, averse to risk, and unwilling to change.[8] They advocate school choice based on a two-pronged argument. First, they favor school choice because of its association with market values, and claim that the consumers of schooling—parents—should determine whether or not schools stay open.[9] Second, they increasingly argue that school choice is a civil rights issue; traditional civil rights organizations such as the Urban League and the National Association for the Advancement of Colored People (NAACP) have disagreements about the validity of this position.[10]

Through the choice movement, private management of public schools has proliferated since the early 1990s. More specifically, there are now over 3,300 charter schools in forty-two states, the District of Columbia, and Puerto Rico. In tandem with charter school reform is the rise of for-profit and nonprofit school management organizations. Given the opportunity to recreate public education that charter school reform, in theory, provides, one might expect that minority communities—those most disaffected with public schooling—would be the ones to embrace the private school management trend, but that is not the case.

Almost exclusively, White men have started this new arena of educational leadership. In my review, I was able to identify only a few EMOs and CMOs started by women or people of color. Education management organizations have mostly targeted themselves to low-income, low-performing school districts, charter schools, and schools made up predominantly of students of color with their services.[11] Regardless of the targeted population, EMOs and CMOs promise greater service than public bureaucracies, although the practice has been more complicated; some are regarded as reform models, while others are not.[12] Rather than focusing on the mixed performance of these companies, however, I focus on who has started them, what they believe about public education and the students they serve, and who supports them.

Female and Leaders of Color in Public Schooling

Because of the trends in who is starting EMOs and CMOs, educational privatization can be understood not simply as a shift in the public and private spheres or a way to improve educational outcomes for children of color, but also as a way for White men to preserve an elite and privileged space in educational leadership and policy.[13] While traditional educational leadership remains a profession in which the majority are White men, people of color and women have increased their presence in the field. Between 1987 and 1994, the percentage of women principals grew by 11 percent in elementary schools, and by 5 percent in secondary schools. Men, however, continued to comprise the majority of school principals at both levels, 58.9 percent in elementary and 85.2 percent in high school, though salaries between men and women became comparable. In 1994, 10 percent of principals were Black, 4.1 percent were Hispanic, and 84.2 percent were White. Of those leaders of color, 35 percent of urban school principals were minority and tended to work in large school districts, and 69 percent of minority principals worked in high minority schools, with 50 percent or more students of color.[14] The picture painted by these statistics is one of progress, albeit slow.

Despite a history of discrimination, people of color and women have made inroads into public school leadership. They have done so by acquiring educational credentials and rising through the ranks, starting as teachers, then principals, and finally, in school leadership positions.[15] For them, the bureaucracies set up by the administrative progressives allowed for a somewhat predictable, if imperfect, professional trajectory. While Watkins argues that White reformers set up an inferior system of schooling for African Americans, others hold that the leadership of African Americans during this period should not be discounted, and that a commitment to community and social justice distinguished them.[16] In addition, researchers have identified the unique strengths that African American women superintendents bring to their work:

> Benefits include opportunities to serve as role models for culturally diverse students, providing a more humanistic and relational style of leadership, and a unique understanding and commitment to ensuring equitable educational opportunities for all students in the present climate of educational reform.[17]

Still, leadership over school systems for leaders of color often comes when hope for reform has faded. School boards often appoint leaders of color as a last resort to educational turmoil in a district, when resources and political will are scarce, leaving them in precarious positions over struggling school systems.[18] The new school leaders, then, are often unwittingly critiquing the leadership of people of color.

Charter Schools: The Gateway for the New School Managers

Many scholars of private sector involvement in public education note the phenomenon is long standing. Public schools have always relied upon the private sector for some educational services, including textbooks, construction and cafeteria services.[19] While it has been common for districts to contract out for some services, including school construction, textbooks, and food service, it has been rare for school boards to privatize teaching or whole-school management. Such proposals are met with suspicion by teachers and community members, who feel their ability to participate in shaping school curriculum and governance is usurped under such arrangements; going against the democratic purposes of public education.[20]

In the early 1990s, school districts and states again contracted with the private sector for management of schools. Advocates encouraged this trend, convinced that contracting out would result in better educational experiences. Some even argued that all schools should be contract schools.[21] Importantly, districts brought these companies in under the auspices of providing better educational experiences, particularly in high-poverty school districts serving students of color. Educational Alternatives, Inc. (EAI, later known as the TesseracT Group), received contracts to operate schools in Hartford, Connecticut and Baltimore, Maryland in the early

1990s. Thus, as in the 1970s, educational privatization in the 1990s was framed as a solution to urban school failure.

While private management of Hartford and Baltimore faltered, with the founding of the Edison Project (later Edison Schools), a new wave of private management of public schools began. The proliferation of charter school legislation around the country, beginning in 1991 in Minnesota, helped create a market for a variety of EMOs to flourish. According to Michael Sandler, chair of the Education Industry Association, a Washington, DC-based group formed to bolster the image of EMOs, "The outlines of a genuine industry came more clearly into focus with the arrival of charter schools, which accelerated the opportunity for private companies to deliver offerings to schools."[22] Indeed, in 2004, 81 percent of schools managed by EMOs were charter schools, and most of these were located in Michigan and Arizona, states where charter school legislation tends to be less regulatory.[23] According to data from NCES (2001), in Michigan, Black students make up 51 percent of the charter school enrollment—a state in which 75 percent of the charter schools are run by EMOs, and in which African American students comprise only 20 percent of the public school enrollment. In Ohio, 30 percent of Community Schools contracted with EMOs. In Florida, EMOs operate one-third of all charter schools.

Characteristics of EMO Managed Charter Schools

Nelson, Drawn, Muir & Van Meter (Nelson) surveyed for-profit management of charter schools around the United States.[24] They found that privately managed charter schools tended to be much larger than other charter schools and were approximately the size of large, urban public schools. They estimated that whereas the average size of a charter school in 1997–1998 was 137 students, in the same year, the average size for an EMO-run school was 400; the average size for a traditional public school was 475 students.[25] A study of Michigan's charter schools is one of the few statewide studies to mention EMOs, and reinforces many of Nelson and colleagues' findings. Though charter schools tended to be small, EMOs tended to operate large schools, and thus, a larger percentage of Michigan charter school students are enrolled in EMO-managed schools.[26]

Nelson also found that EMO-managed schools served, on average, fewer special education students; 3.8 percent compared to 10.2 percent in school districts. The companies serve students from economically disadvantaged backgrounds about as much as school districts—32.8 percent. The district average surrounding these schools tended to be higher, however, at 47.9 percent.

While these data imply that EMOs could be engaging in selectivity of their student populations, they tell us very little about who the founders of EMOs are. While it is important to consider the educational achievement, opportunities to learn, and characteristics of students served in such schools, it is vital that research consider who EMO and CMO founders are—especially since their careers are predicated on serving the very high-poverty communities of color that have historically been poorly served by public and private institutions.

Exploring the Institutional Terrain of the New School Managers: Networks, Ideology, and Funding

A review of position statements as found on websites, speeches, and other related documents reveals a set of shared beliefs about schooling and the role of the new managers in education reform and their advocacy of school choice. These beliefs, I find, are both implied and articulated. In addition, the managers engage in similar networking practices and receive funding from identical private sources. Summarized, their shared beliefs include:

- A belief in standardization while also espousing local control
- A belief in the power of parental choice
- A belief in efficiency and corporate management
- A belief in hybrid forms of school finance—public and private, and a tendency to be funded by identical agencies
- A belief in boards of directors, and the use of politically-connected individuals as members
- A belief that traditional educators have caused the racial achievement gap
- A belief that schools of education cannot adequately prepare teachers or leaders
- A belief that school choice is the sole or primary remaining civil rights issue

In the next several sections, I will explore these issues, paying attention to key EMOs, CMOs, and their financial supporters. First, Table 7.1 depicts a layout of the founders of EMOs and CMOs. Most of the founders are White men with varying degrees of educational experience.

Table 7.1. A Sample of the New School Managers

Name	EMO	CMO	Foundation	Charter
Jack Clegg	Nobel Learning			
Chris Whittle	Edison Schools			
Don Shalvey		Aspire Public Charter Schools	Supported by the Broad Foundation, New Schools Venture Fund	
Steve Barr		Green Dot Public Schools	Supported by the Broad Foundation	
Bill Gates			Bill and Melinda Gates Foundation	
Don Fisher		Supports KIPP	Fisher Family Foundation	
David Feinberg/ Jonathan Levin		KIIP Academies	Supported by the Broad, Walton Family, and Fisher Family Foundations	KIPP Academies

Wade Dyke/Octavio Visideo	Chancellor-Beacon Academies			Options for Youth
John Hall				
J. C. Huizenga	National Heritage Academies			
David Brennan	White Hat Management			
Eli Broad		Supporter of KIPP, Green Dot, and Aspire. Also supports the California Charter Schools Association, the New Schools Venture Fund, Pacific Charter School Development, and Children's Scholarship Fund	Broad Foundation	
John Walton (Deceased)		School Futures Research Foundation	Walton Family Foundation	

continued on next page

Table 7.1. (*continued*)

Name	EMO	CMO	Foundation	Charter
William Bennett	k–12, Inc.		Supported by the U.S. Department of Education	k–12, Inc.
Michael Connely	Mosaica, Inc.			
Steven Klinsky	Victory Schools			
John Gage	Charter Schools USA			

It should be noted that the organizations they represent have different orientations, goals, and purposes. In aggregating them, I do not suggest that they would necessarily identify with one another institutionally. Indeed, some CMO founders are likely to identify more strongly with public school leaders than with leaders of for-profit EMOs.

Political Strategy

Educational management organizations and CMO founders often are politically connected to state or local policy makers, university faculty, and elites from the private sector. These networks enable them to successfully apply for charters, secure community support for their schools, and acquire critical public and private funding. While charter school laws vary from state to state, most forbid for-profit entities from being granted charters. Instead, EMOs will usually form a nonprofit arm, or work with an existing nonprofit organization that will then contract with the EMO to run the school. There is evidence that EMOs in general, are not securing management contracts in a competitive bidding process, but rather using political connections and direct outreach to charter schools and school district officials to market their schools. For profit management of charters has been facilitated by the cooperation of some state politicians.[27]

In Massachusetts, a conservative think tank, the Pioneer Institute, actively promoted charter schools. Its former director played a key role in charter legislation, and its executive director served as acting under secretary of education. In addition to raising money for charter schools, "Pioneer also distributes a how-to manual, *The Massachusetts Charter School Handbook*, and sponsors seminars bringing together entrepreneurs selling curriculum packages, management systems, and assessment and evaluation programs in addition to companies that supply these services."[28]

In Massachusetts, then, the lines between the members of the political structure and the members of the for-profit management companies are blurry. The ambiguity of charter school legislation indicates a support for franchises to proliferate. There is not much competition for contracts to operate charters. "Rather, contractual partnerships are formed in spirit prior to applying for charters rather than afterwards with an eye towards finding the highest quality service for the lowest costs."[29]

An Ohio investigation showed that John Brennan, a controversial operator of for-profit charter schools, was able to acquire his schools through his political connections.[30] He donated over one million dollars to the Republican Party, as well as $89,000 to former Ohio Governor

Voinovich's campaign in 1990. In return, he was appointed to chair a commission that would create a voucher program in Ohio. His schools would have directly benefited from the program he created.

Brennan, however, turned his attention to charter schools. He had started a private school with his daughter, in 1993, that he wanted to convert to a charter in order to get state funding. But the law forbade such conversions for any private schools started before 1997. To circumvent this, Brennan claimed that he was dissolving his school. The new school, operating in the same building, was approved. He was able to do the same with four other schools. Brennan continued to have access to the new governor, Governor Taft, and was able to get legislation passed that enabled him to accept children from across school boundaries. His company, White Hat Management, operates multiple charter schools in Ohio. His chain of schools is bigger than three-fourths of the school districts in Ohio. Although Brennan may have used his political connections for his own market empowerment, he did not share the wealth. His schools paid teachers just $19,000 a year.[31]

Edison Schools, the largest for-profit EMO, also benefited from its political connections in Pennsylvania to then Governor Tom Ridge. Over community protest, the state awarded Edison contracts in Chester and Philadelphia to run their troubled schools—in Chester Upland, all of the schools, and in Philadelphia, twenty schools. Initially, although CEO Chris Whittle promised that Edison could run the schools better for less money, the schools contracted out in Philadelphia have been given more money than other schools with mixed results. Still, much of the protest over the contracts was due to the perception that Edison Schools had an inside track to Harrisburg and that the company had become an ally of the Republicans in the state capital.

The path many EMO founders follow in Florida is to first form a nonprofit to write and get the charter authorized, and then to contract with itself to run the school. But political connections have also proved important to EMO founders. For example, John Hage, a close advisor to Jeb Bush, helped the Florida governor enact charter schools legislation. He knew nothing of the reform when he began his work, having come from a business and political background, but he saw the opportunity to manage schools, and began a for-profit EMO, Charter Schools USA. "It was a classic business opportunity," he said, "lots of demand and very little supply."[32] In 2005, one third of Florida charter students were in for-profit charter schools. Some developers have teamed with companies to start schools in new upscale housing tracts. Hage created the nonprofit Polk Charter Foundation, and then applied for seven charters, whose applications it copyrighted. The proprietary nature of EMOs, in terms of curriculum and charter applications, is a hallmark of the new school managers, though as I will discuss in a moment, their curricula tend to be prepackaged programs created by developers who are often connected to the school choice and standards movements.

CMO founders are similarly connected. Two Teach For America alumnae, David Levin and Mike Feinberg, founded the Knowledge is Power Program (KIPP), charter schools. Their schools have grown from two in the Bronx, New York, and Houston, Texas, in large part due to the financial connections they established through Teach For America, The Fisher Family Foundation, and The Broad Foundation. Though Levin and Feinberg taught for a few years, they are now superintendents over a multistate school system. Their schools are regarded as successful models for teaching low-income children of color, and the men have come to be seen as experts on minority education, testifying before Congress, and speaking at the Republican National Convention.

Teach For America (TFA), an alternative teaching program founded in 1990 by Wendy Kopp, places inexperienced but talented college graduates into urban and rural school districts experiencing teacher shortages. Corps members commit to teach for two years, and most leave teaching after their stint is over. Teach For America alumnae also play a key role in the expansion of school choice and the development of EMOs and CMOs. As mentioned earlier, KIPP founders Levin and Feinberg are alumnae of the program. Many of the teachers in KIPP schools are former TFA corps members. In addition, Kopp's husband, Richard Barth, has been an executive in several EMOs and CMOs. Teach For America corps members are also in key leadership positions at the Broad Foundation, which is an influential donor to school choice, and holds school choice and market-based competition as the key for school improvement. In addition, TFA runs a job placement page for its alumnae on its Web site—on which EMOs and CMOs post heavily. Finally, TFA and school choice organizations receive funding from the same sources (see table 7.2). Thus, there seems to be a direct and indirect pipeline between TFA and the private management sector.

In addition to the TFA network, EMOs and CMOs have their own national advocacy organization, the Education Industry Leadership Board. Its mission "is to promote public understanding of the education industry and its commitment to advancing opportunities for lifelong learning in the global education economy," and to foster the development of a "vibrant and expanding education marketplace."[33] Of course, without financial resources, expanding the marketplace would be more of a challenge. For CMOs and EMOs, however, public and private funding is abundant.

Table 7.2. School choice planning & research community supporters

Corporations, CMOs & EMOs	Foundations	Think Tanks	Policy Makers	Universities & Researchers	USDOE	Donors
Aspire	Fordham Foundation	Heritage	Jeb Bush	University of Washington Center on Reinventing Public Education	NCLB	Broad Foundation
Green Dot	Broad Foundation	Cato	George Bush	Harvard University Program on Education Policy and Governance	Public School Choice Program	Bill and Melinda Gates Foundation
KIPP	Bradley Foundation	Manhattan Institute	Margaret Spellings	Jay Greene	Faith-Based Education	Theodore Forstmann
K12-connect	Walton Family	Center for Education Reform	Lisa Graham Keegan	Paul Peterson	U.S.D.O.E. Office of Innovation & Improvement	Sarah Scaife Foundation
Edison Schools	Bill and Melinda Gates Family Foundation	Hoover	Cory Booker	Caroline Hoxby		Walton Family Foundation

Leap Frog Learning	Childrens' Scholarship	Pacific Research Institute	Michael Bloomberg	Frederick Hess	Don & Delores Fisher
ETS	New Schools Venture Fund	Institute for Justice	Tom Ridge	Institute for the Transformation of Learning at Marquette University	Richaed & Betsy De Vos
k12, Inc.	KIPP Foundation/Pisces Foundation	American Enterprise Institute	Reed Hastings	Hoover Institute at Stanford University	Whitney Tilson
White Hat Management	Core Knowledge Foundation	Milton D. and Rose Friedman Foundation		Joe Nathan	Lynde and Harry F. Bradley Foundation

Funding and Political Networks

A key requirement for the new school managers is public and private funding and the support of elites in universities, business, and the media. Economists of education have long debated the degree to which money matters in education, and conservatives tend to want less public money spent on education while liberals prefer more. The new school mangers are ecumenical in their approach, and seek out public and private funds. Central to the expansion of EMOs and CMOs has been the support of particular foundations that support school choice, including the Broad Foundation, The Walton Family Foundation, the Pisces Foundation, and the Bill and Melinda Gates Foundation. Table 7.2 shows the expansiveness of this funding network.[34]

In 2004, the Walton Family Foundation gave a combined total of forty-six million dollars to school choice sources. These included advocacy groups, individual charter schools, and scholarship funds. Total giving for the foundation in 2004 was $117,020,891. Therefore, nearly half of the foundation's impressive resources went to support and advance school choice. The foundation supports what it calls systemic reform in education (K12) through its charter school and school choice initiatives and a third area it terms "school improvement."[35] The charter school initiative's goal is "To advance the charter school movement by targeting states and communities where market share of quality schools may be established."[36] These geographical areas include four states: Arkansas, California, Colorado, and New Mexico. In addition, specific urban areas are targets: Broward County, Florida; Chicago, Illinois; Detroit, Michigan; Fulton County, Georgia; Indianapolis, Indiana; Milwaukee, Wisconsin; Minneapolis and St. Paul, Minnesota; New York City districts 4 and 5, Ohio cities, Phoenix, Arizona, and Washington, DC.[37] The foundation has given money to individual charter schools as well as CMOs such as KIPP, and EMOs such as Leadership Public Schools, Inc.

The Broad Foundation is also a key supporter of school choice reforms. Started in Los Angeles, California, in 1999, by Eli and Edythe Broad, the foundation's mission is to "improve urban public education through better governance, management, and labor relations."[38] While the foundation invests in multiple initiatives related to these three areas, charters and competition are prominent among them. The combination of the funding areas—recruiting business professionals into school and school district leadership, award urban school districts with an annual prize for improved performance and management, and restructure labor unions while also encouraging school choice and competition—perhaps encapsulates the agenda and strategy of the new school managers best.

The Broad Center, the gateway for recruiting business executives to work in school districts, has an all-male executive board, none of which have experience in public education. While Broad does not seek to dismantle public education, he does want to reshape it according to business practices. The foundation has supported CMOS such as KIPP, Green Dot Public Schools, and Aspire Public Schools and several charter school associations and charter school real estate development organizations, as well as Teach For America.

The Pisces Foundation, which was started by Gap founders Donald and Delores Fisher, is a major donor to KIPP schools. The Fishers donated fifteen million dollars to establish the KIPP Foundation to train and recruit principals. Much like the Broad Foundation's approach, this program is housed at the University of California at Berkeley Haas School of Business, not the School of Education. KIPP's advisory board is also all male, including William Bennett who runs his own virtual charter school company, k12, Inc. When I toured a Bronx KIPP school, in 2002, that served roughly one hundred twenty students, the communications director shared that the school relied on roughly one and a half million dollars a year in private donations to sustain itself, in addition to the almost ten thousand per student it received in public funds. In total, the Fishers and Pisces Foundation have given KIPP thirty-four and a half million dollars. Pisces has also been a supporter of another CMO, Leadership Public Schools, which runs a chain of Bay Area, California high schools. This relatively new CMO began in 2000, and one of its administrators is the product of the Broad Foundation Urban Residency, further connecting funders and leaders of the school choice movement. As another piece of the network of new school managers, the Pisces Foundation is the largest private donor to Teach For America. Anjua Master, managing director, commented, "We don't select charter locations as much as we seek to locate effective leaders. Most important to us is the leader. We invest in people first."[39]

Another investor in school choice is the New Schools Venture Fund. One of the founders of this Silicon Valley organization is Kim Smith, who was a founding member of Teach for America. New Schools Venture Fund has given Leadership Public Schools five million dollars to support its expansion, as well as several other EMOs and CMOs. New Schools Venture Fund represents itself as the new philanthropy; agnostic about for-profit or nonprofit approaches to education, and regards its funding as investments, some of which provide a monetary return on their investment, and some of which do not. Silicon Valley venture capitalists, as well as the Bill and Melinda Gates Foundation, have financed much of the organizations efforts to increase new school models, especially charter school management organizations.

The support of these donors is not just financial, though the monetary support has been critical to the development of EMOs and CMOs. The donors also provide legitimacy to the leaders, and access to other social networks in government and business that can further advance the missions of the CMOs and EMOs. Thus, the financiers of the new school managers greatly assist with the restructuring of public education leadership and reform. Moreover, private funding drastically alters the ways in which public school funding is conceptualized.[40]

Ideology and Pedagogy

Bolstered with a mixture of public and private financing, most EMO and CMO founders share a common set of beliefs around the power of corporate-styled management. That is, the structures of the school systems they have created are remarkably similar regardless of the profit orientation. The CMO, Green Dot Public Schools, founded by Steve Barr, for example, says that its model includes world class management practices, and that "the best management practices of the private sector are applied, maximizing the dollars spent in the classroom."[41] All the founders identify themselves as either the superintendent, chief education officer, or chief executive officer. They all have boards of directors or advisory boards, whose members come primarily from the corporate sector, but also represent politicians and university faculty. These boards are also predominantly men. Though some educators serve, they are definitely in the minority.

The philosophies of the organizations read similarly as well. They emphasize high standards, standardization, and discipline. For example, for-profit Victory Schools, founded by Steven Klinsky, is based upon the belief that all children can learn. According to Victory's website, "Students are required to wear student uniforms and adhere to a behavior management plan that fosters social development and maturity at the earliest ages."[42] KIPP students, Edison Schools students, and Leadership Public School students are required to wear uniforms, and contracts stipulate behavioral norms. In some EMO-run schools, such as White Hat Management, prepackaged curricula are used.

Like many EMOs, the curriculum at Victory is proprietary, and includes Direct Instruction, Core Knowledge, Creative Thematic Enrichment, Balanced Literacy/Balanced Math, and Hands-On Science & Technology. Edison Schools also has a proprietary curriculum, and teachers' contracts require them to relinquish the rights to any innovation they develop while teaching at an Edison School.

Many CMO and EMO-run charters reflect a belief in selectivity of students. This is the case at Charter Schools USA. According to a report, a teacher at one of the Florida schools, Teddi Ackerman, said, "We have ways of asking people not to come back. We really operate like a private school."[43] Perhaps the most extreme example of the belief in student and parent selectivity is the KIPP schools, where parents, students, and teachers are required to sign contracts indicating their willingness to devote themselves to significant hours at the school (7:30 a.m.–5:00 p.m.), hours of homework, and meaningful involvement. Teachers also make themselves available by telephone until 10:00 p.m. to their students and parents. Students and their parents also agree to Saturday schooling. KIPP boasts of high achievement scores for its students, and helps to place middle school graduates into elite private high schools.

Given the rhetoric of some of the school choice advocates and new school managers, who argue that the availability of school choice is a civil rights imperative, the selectivity of students is a paradox. The Philanthropy Roundtable, a funder's group, issued a statement agreeing to core charter school principles, the first of which is "Moral and Civil Rights" (see table 7.1). The agreement states:

> Education is a cornerstone of equal opportunity. Equity requires that all parents, regardless of residence, race, wealth, or heritage, be able to choose among diverse, high-quality, publicly-financed options for their children. It is a moral imperative to provide equal access to high-quality education for all children.

What is interesting is the way in which established notions of educational equity are challenged by such a proclamation. Efforts to desegregate public schooling, equalize and redistribute state funding of schooling, reshape the curriculum to be both high-quality and representative of the diversity of students, and efforts to diversify the leadership and teaching force are not items of focus for the new school managers who tend to favor choice as a proxy for equity.[44] The new school managers network of university researchers, wealthy donors, CMO and EMO operators, and government officials are in the process of reshaping leadership in ways as dramatic as the administrative progressives discussed by Tyack did in the last century. Whereas, prior reformers placed the expertise over schooling in the hands of an educated elite that helped to establish graduate schools of education, the new school managers locate expertise in the business community, and its leaders tend to be White men. While the current policy and research community is focused on student achievement and its relationship to school choice, the questions this development of new school leaders raises must also be asked and explored by researchers.

Discussion and Implications

A fundamental question remains unanswered by this descriptive analysis of the new urban school leadership: namely, is the emergence of the new school managers a good or bad development? Rather than taking a definitive normative stance, the findings from this paper raise questions and implications that call for further research; research that must comprise theoretical examinations as well as empirical study. I point to five areas where implications and questions are especially abundant.

1. *Sustainability:* While policy makers, especially state legislators, play an important role in legalizing public-private hybrid schooling, the new school managers rely especially heavily on philanthropy to advance their organizations. It is unclear how long philanthropists will support this sector, and how much money they will be willing to contribute in the future. It is also unclear how the agendas of the philanthropists influence teaching and learning since schools are dependent on their money for survival. From a broader perspective, the influx of private money could decrease the pressure on state legislators to fund schools adequately, which raises concerns for traditional public schools that do not have access to private funding. In other words, the philanthropy could diminish the viability of other public schools—even unwittingly.

2. *Democracy:* A second issue needing closer examination is the relationship between the new school managers and our broader democracy and democratic processes. While the ways in which the public is able to engage in traditional public educational governance is clearly flawed, there exists at least an expectation that public officials respond and involve the public in decision-making. The private sector, from which many of the new school managers come, possesses no such mandate. For example, with virtually no public deliberation and debate, the new school managers and their supporters have drastically expanded school choice policy. The restructuring of the public schools in New Orleans is a key example of this. Ultimately, researchers and theorists must query whether the public sphere expands or constricts in relation to the growth of this new schooling sector.

3. *Community*: It might be difficult to remember, but an original goal of charter school advocates was to encourage local, grassroots organizations and teachers to start schools that would meet the needs of the students and families within a given community. How does the community-based school survive and flourish amidst market-driven schools and advocates? Another aspect of community that must be further explored is what happens to parental and community voice within schools managed by EMOs and CMOs.

4. *Equity*: Although the current policy framework tends to define equity in terms of outputs—performance on standardized tests, under the new school managers, we must consider the issue of educational inputs. Do EMO and CMO-run schools have fewer, similar, or greater resources than traditional public schools? Within the EMO/CMO sector, is there stratification? Another aspect of who has access—how do admissions and discipline policies work on the ground? Are all students accepted, and are disciplinary sanctions meted out fairly? Is there due process for students? These broader equity considerations tend to get lost in the politically charged debates over the meaning of the most recent achievement study.

5. *Diversity*: A final issue requiring further exploration is that of student and community diversity. A key under-examined area is the way in which many EMOs and CMOs brand and market themselves as service providers to Black and Latino students. Since EMOs and CMOs are founding the schools, in many ways they require that the school's racial compositions be homogenous since their marketing and branding presents the companies as such. In this regard, the relationship between segregated schools and the new school managers needs examination. In addition, more attention is needed as to how curricula about race, gender, and other multicultural issues are implemented within the schools—if at all—is needed.

Conclusion: Toward a New Empirical Agenda

Progressive researchers, advocates, and educational researchers have been critical of the private management of public services; concerned that what is at stake is an evisceration of the public sphere and commitment to equity. These critics have tended to query the segregative and stratifying effects of choice schools on the racial and ethnic student population. As school choice has expanded, there have been at least two generations of accompanying research. The first generation of school choice research comprised theoretical examinations of the likely stratification effects of widespread choice given the rational choice that individuals choose out of self-interest, and that privileged parents and schools would seek to maintain their status by excluding disadvantaged students.[45] Second generation research has been empirical, focusing on how issues of race and equity have played out in charter schools and voucher plans, though much of this work is contested because many choice plans have targeted poor students of color. Moreover, researchers have been surprised to find that in some contexts, students of color are overrepresented in choice schools and EMOs and CMOs seem to serve these populations in very high numbers. This has led researchers to ask new questions about the quality of education within these schools in terms of school design, facilities, expenditures versus revenues because many EMOs keep monies not spent, teacher experience and certification, and curricular offerings.[46] This third generation of school choice research also investigates the ways in which the individuals advocating for choice are positioning themselves in school reform (see Fuller 2003).

Setting aside questions regarding the philosophical implications of privatizing public school management (which should remain a focus of research and debate), this paper contributes to this third-generation of school choice research. Its findings raise questions about the impact that choice and privatization will have on the racial and ethnic diversity of school leaders in the choice and public school sectors. It also examines who the new school leaders are in terms of their racial, social class, and gender backgrounds and also their political ideology and pedagogy. By this I mean the set of assumptions and beliefs they hold as individuals and/or as a group regarding the educational needs, capacities, value, aspirations, and societal role of the mostly Black and Latino students their companies serve and on whose education they profit, much like the early architects described by Watkins.

This third generation of school choice research stands to benefit from an examination of existing literature on the pedagogies of teachers and leaders of color. It becomes important to compare and contrast leaders and teachers of color's educational philosophies and support networks with the new, predominantly White male urban school leaders.

Researchers have explored these issues in the context of African American and Latino teachers and leaders using ethnographic and qualitative methodologies to capture the distinct pedagogical orientations of successful practioners of color.[47] Among the characteristics discussed by scholars are educators who: believe in children's learning capacities regardless of background; care about students while valuing and placing culture in the curriculum; offer students the opportunity to develop critical thinking through rich pedagogy; and continuously make connections between school and community. Decidedly missing from their analyses are arguments that school choice is an essential requirement for this kind of teaching.

This chapter lays the groundwork for understanding new school managers—the mostly White men who have harnessed the market to start schools, for-profit EMOs, and CMOs—and defined themselves as leaders in the education of African American and Latino children. New school choice scholarship, in addition to asking questions about new educational markets, can attend to intersectionality, the ways in which race, class, gender and other categories interact with leadership, through this line of inquiry. This analysis follows Watkins by exploring "the body of ideas that undergird social, economic, racial and educational beliefs" about the education of poor children and children of color, "by examining the views, politics, and practices of the White architects that fund(ed), create(d), and refine(d) it."[48] Finally, this preliminary analysis considers the implications of private interests making public policy.[49]

Contemporary school choice scholarship can attend to issues of intersectionality—the ways in which race, class, gender, and other social categories interact with the new urban school leadership—through this line of inquiry.

Notes for Chapter 7

1. David Tyack, *The One Best System: A History of American Urban Education* (Cambridge, MA: Harvard University Press, 1974).

2. Thomas Byrne Edsall and Mary D. Edsall, *Chain Reaction: The Impact of Race, Rights and Taxes on American Politics* (New York: W. W. Norton, 1992); Jeffrey L. Pressman and Aaron Wildavsky, *Implementation: How Great Expectations in Washington Are Dashed in Oakland* (Berkeley: University of California Press, 1974).

3. John Chubb, "Lessons in School Reform from the Edison Project," in *New Schools for a New Century: The Redesign of Urban Education*, ed. Joseph P. Viteretti and Diane Ravitch, 86–122 (New Haven, CT: Yale University Press, 1997); David Osborne and Ted Gaebler, *Reinventing Government: How the Entrepreneurial Spirit is Transforming the Public Sector* (New York: Plume, 1992).

4. William H. Watkins, *The White Architects of Black Education* (New York: Teachers College Press, 2001).

5. Ibid., 4.

6. Arnetha F. Ball, "Empowering Pedagogies that Enhance the Learning of Multicultural Students," *Teachers College Record* 102, no. 6 (2002): 1006–34;

Michele Foster, *Black Teachers on Teaching* (New York: The New Press, 1997); Gloria Ladson-Billings, *The Dreamkeepers: Successful Teachers of African American Children* (San Francisco: Jossey-Bass, 1995); Christine E. Sleeter, *Empowerment through Multicultural Education* (Albany: State University of New York, 1991).

    7. John E. Chubb and Terry M. Moe, *Politics, Markets, and America's Schools* (Washington, DC: Brookings Institution, 1990); E. D. Hirsch, *Cultural Literacy: What Every American Needs to Know* (New York: Houghton Mifflin, 1987).

    8. The Thomas P. Fordham Foundation and The Broad Foundation, *Better Leaders for Better Schools: A Manifesto* (2003).

    9. Chris Whittle, *Crash Course: Imagining a Better Future for Public Education* (New York: Riverhead Books, 2005).

    10. Michael Engel, *The Struggle for Control of Public Education: Market Ideology vs. Democratic Values* (Philadelphia: Temple University Press, 2000); Betsy Levin, "Race and School Choice," in *School Choice and Social Controversy*, ed. Stephen D. Sugarman & Frank R. Kemerer, 266–99 (Washington, DC: Brookings Institution Press, 1999); W. Snider, "Conservatives' Civil-rights Agenda Puts Spotlight on Choice," *Education Week*, October 11, 1989; Jodi Wilgoren, "Young Blacks Turn to School Vouchers as Civil Rights Issue," *New York Times*, October 9, 2000, http://www.nytimes.com/2000/10/09/national/09/VOUC.html (accessed October 9, 2000).

    11. Gary Miron and Christopher Nelson, *What's Public about Charter Schools? Lessons Learned about Choice and Accountability* (Thousand Oaks, CA: Corwin Press, 2002).

    12. David N. Plank, David Arsen, and Gary Sykes, "Charter Schools and Private Profits," *The School Administrator* 57 (May 2000): 12–18; Craig E. Richards, Rima Shore, and Max Sawicky, *Risky Business: Private Management of Public Schools* (Washington, DC: Economic Policy Institute, 1996); United States General Accounting Office, *Private Management of Public Schools: Early Experiences in Four School Districts* (No. GAO/HEHS-96-3) (Washington, DC: United States General Accounting Office, 1996).

    13. Andrew L. Barlow, *Between Fear and Hope: Globalization and Race in the United States* (Lanham, MD: Rowman & Littlefield, 2003); Mark Walsh, "Hoping to Raise Profile, School 'Industry' Forms Trade Group," *Education Week*, May 2, 2001, 9.

    14. Thomas A. Fiore, Thomas R. Curtin, and Charles H. Hammer, *Public and Private School Principals in the United States: A Statistical Profile, 1987–88 to 1993–94* (2006), http://nces.ed.gov/pubs/ppsp/94755-2.asp (accessed January 30, 2006); National Center for Education Statistics, *Issue Brief: Where Do Minority Principals Work?* (No. IB-2-96) (Washington, DC: U.S. Department of Education, 1996).

    15. Beverly A. Tillman and Lessie L. Cochran, "Desegregating Urban School Administration: A Pursuit of Equity for Black Women Superintendents," *Education and Urban Society* 33, no. 1 (2000): 44–59.

    16. Khaula Murtadha and Daud Malik Watts, "Linking the Struggle of Education and Social Justice: Historical Perspectives of African American Leadership in Schools," *Education Administration Quarterly* 41, no. 4 (2005): 591–608.

    17. Tillman and Cochran, "Desegregating."

18. Dan A. Lewis and Kathryn Nakagawa, *Race and Educational Reform in the American Metropolis: A Study of School Decentralization* (Albany: State University of New York Press, 1995); Khaula Murtadha-Watts, "Cleaning Up and Maintenance in the Wake of an Urban School Administration Tempest," *Urban Education* 35, no. 5 (2000): 603–15.

19. Joseph Murphy, *The Privatization of Schooling: Problems and Possibilities* (Thousand Oaks, CA: Corwin Press, 1996).

20. Edward Wyatt, "New York Faces a Fight to Persuade Parents that 5 Schools Should Privatize," *New York Times*, January 30, 2001.

21. Paul T. Hill, Lawrence C. Pierce, and James W. Guthrie, *Reinventing Public Education: How Contracting Can Transform America's Schools* (Chicago: University of Chicago Press, 1997).

22. Michael R. Sandler, *The Emerging Educational Industry: The First Decade* (Washington, DC: Education Industry Leadership Board, 2002).

23. Alex Molnar, Glen Wilson, and Daniel Allen, *Profiles of For-profit Education Management Companies: Sixth-annual Report 2003–2004* (Tempe, AZ: Education Policy Studies, 2004).

24. F. Howard Nelson, Rachel Drown, Ed Muir, and Nancy Van Meter, "Public Money and Privatization in K–12 Education," in *Education Finance in the New Millennium: AEFA 2001 Yearbook*, ed. Stephen Chaikind and William Fowler, 173–90 (Larchmont, NY: Eye on Education, 2001).

25. Ibid., 176.

26. Jerry Horn and Gary Miron, *An Evaluation of the Michigan Charter School Initiative: Performance, Accountability, and Impact* (Kalamazoo: The Evaluation Center, Western Michigan University, 2000).

27. Lauren Morando Rhim, "Franchising Public Education: An Analysis of Charter Schools and Private Education Management Companies" (paper presented at the annual meeting of the American Education Research Association, San Diego, CA, 1998); Lauren Morando Rhim, "School Privatization Theory and Practice: A Case Study of a Privately Managed Public School" (paper presented at the annual meeting of the American Education Research Association, Montreal, QC, April 19–23, 1999).

28. Phyllis Vine, "To Market, To Market . . . The School Business Sells Kids Short," *Nation*, September 8–15, 1997, 11–17.

29. Rhim, "Franchising."

30. Doug Oplinger and Dennis J. Willard, "In Education, Money Talks" (1999), http://www.ohio.com/bj (accessed February 13, 2000).

31. Doug Oplinger and Dennis J. Willard, "Parents Have Freedom of Choice, but not Freedom of Information" (1999), http://www.ohio.com/bj/projects/whose_choice/docs/020546.htm (accessed February 13, 2000).

32. Kent Fischer, "Public School Inc.," *St. Petersburg Times*, September 15, 2002, http://www.sptimes.com/2002/09/15/State/Public_School_Inc.shtml (accessed January 5, 2003).

33. http://eilb.org.

34. Model adapted from Fowler 2002, 179.

35. http://www.wfhome.com/program_focus.htm.

36. Ibid.

37. Ibid.

38. http://www.broadfoundation.org.

39. M. T. Hartney, "A Powerhouse Charter-Funder Aims for the Next Level" (2004), http://www.philanthropyroundtable.org/magazines/2004/Sep-tOct/Powerhouse.htm (accessed January 11, 2005).

40. Janelle Scott and Jennifer Jellison Holme, "Public Schools, Private Resources: The Role of Social Networks in California Charter School Reform," in *Where Charter School Policy Fails: The Problems of Accountability and Equity*, ed. Amy Stuart Wells, 102–28 (New York: Teachers College Press, 2002).

41. http://www.greendot.org/schoolmodel/index.html.

42. http://www.victoryschools.org.

43. Fischer, "Public School Inc."

44. Amy Stuart Wells, Janelle T. Scott, Alejandra Lopez, and Jennifer Jellison Holme, "Charter School Reform and the Shifting Meaning of Educational Equity: Greater Voice and Greater Inequality?" in *Bringing Equity Back: Research for a New Era in American Educational Policy*, ed. Janice Petrovich and Amy Stuart Wells (New York: Teachers College Press, 2005).

45. See, for example, Bruce Fuller, Richard F. Elmore, with Gary Orfield, eds., *Who Chooses? Who Loses? Culture, Insititutions, and the Unequal Effects of School Choice* (New York: Teachers College Press, 1996).

46. See Fuller 2003.

47. Lisa D. Delpit, "The Silenced Dialogue: Power and Pedagogy in Educating Other People's Children," *Harvard Educational Review* 58, no. 3 (1988): 280–98; Ernestine K. Enomoto, "Probing Educational Management as Gendered: An Examination Through Model and Metaphor," *Teachers College Record* 102, no. 2 (2000): 375–97; Mike Rose, *Possible Lives* (Boston: Houghton Mifflin Company, 1995).

48. Watkins, *White Architects*, 1–2.

49. Ibid., 4.

Chapter 8

Where Does the Power Lie Now?

Devolution, Choice and Democracy in Schooling

Liz Gordon

School choice has proven to be a powerful rallying cry for reform. In societies driven by consumerist values, choice tends to be perceived as a good in itself. However, a number of studies have shown how the interpolation of discourses of school choice into even relatively benign school settings can disrupt existing relationships and systems.[1] In less benign settings, it is not surprising that proposals for reform have often been met with enthusiasm,[2] especially the notion that the power to educate can be delivered into the hands of communities and parents through choice.

This paper examines the claim that choice, in its many guises, can improve the educational outcomes of all children, or most children, or some children. The arguments outlined here rest heavily on the findings of research in a range of countries, because the school choice movement is not confined to one country, or even one group of countries. It is a global phenomenon. It develops and recurs in various guises, from whole system reform in New Zealand,[3] to Federal,[4] State[5] and local/charter[6] reform in the United States, to choice and specialization in England and Wales,[7] issues of public and private choice in Canada[8] and Australia.[9] Some nations have adopted forms of vouchers with the stated aim to facilitate choice.[10]

A study of the school choice literature can be quite perplexing. Different researchers have undertaken analyses of the same schemes, often using the same data, and arrived at quite different findings. Most famously in the Milwaukee voucher program,[11] but also in a range of other studies, similar data has lead to different conclusions. The overwhelming conclusion of the literature must be that, as currently implemented, there are no substantive, demonstrable, sustained, measurable benefits in adopting any school choice system. The fact that there are few studies showing overall benefits (and those that do show benefits to be very marginal) has not, however, prevented policy makers from instituting and supporting choice reforms. School choice is based on political exigencies, not empirical evidence; it is about power.

The concept of power itself is a highly theorized, highly contested concept. My main theoretical referents are threefold. First is Bourdieu's theory, which explains how power is structured in and through social relations and everyday life through the transformation of habitus into cultural and economic capital. Second, I am interested in Gramsci's theory of competing interests fought out on a terrain structured by existing power relations, and the concept of hegemony as expressing the always partial and contested victory of the dominant groups. Finally, there is Foucault, and his emphasis on how power relations are played out between people and groups of people, and the related technologies of power:

> what characterises the power we are analysing is that it brings into play relations between individuals (or between groups) . . . if we speak of the power of laws, institutions and ideologies, if we speak of structures or mechanisms of power, it is only insofar as we suppose that certain persons exercise power over others.[12]

For the purposes of this paper, I have found Foucault's emphasis on the characteristics of power relations between individuals and institutions particularly useful in providing a framework for examining elements of choice.

It is not difficult to justify an analysis of school choice based on power. More often than not, such policies are presented as empowering to individuals and groups: students, families, individual schools and communities. Sometimes the policy intention is clearly to reduce the perceived power of other groups—teachers or teacher unions, school administrators or others.

The aim of this paper is to reexamine the findings of international school choice research—or at least part of this large and diverse literature, and to consider how power relations work within the various elements of individual choices, school and regional systems and at the legislative and national levels. The scope of this paper is ambitious and, because of this, specific elements are not necessarily given the attention they deserve. The paper is comparative in the sense that school choice is an international phenomenon. However, far more detailed comparisons and analysis of the various levels of power relations within and between countries are possible than have been able to be achieved here, and should be pursued in other studies.

School Choice and Power Relations

What is power? The social theories of interest to me all reject the notion that power is something that resides merely in the political sphere. Power can and does reside in that sphere, and we might call that the professional and lawfully structured exercise of power. Decisions made in the political sphere have the authority of the state, but are often made at significant social distance from their intended targets. Thus, while political power has significant potency, its effects may often be diluted in practice, and may even have unintended consequences and perverse effects.

Of much more immediacy is the power that derives from social intercourse structured by our history, habits, and relative (perceived) position in society. Bourdieu's work is of crucial importance in demonstrating how social existence is transformed into relations of power, while Gramsci's work examines how the institutions of civil society structure the terrain and shape power relations.

Foucault suggests that a number of points must be established when attempting to analyse power relations, and he borrows freely from other theorists in constructing his typology.[13] The five forms he identifies are: (1) the system of differentiations; (2) the types of objectives pursued; (3) instrumental modes; (4) forms of institutionalization; and (5) the degrees of rationalization. These five levels of the exercise of power provide a useful framework for examining particular phenomena, for examining how power plays out in specific situations, however defined. Foucault warns that the study of power cannot be reduced to the study of particular institutions,[14] but can be found in and through their study.

The first level, the system of differentiations, refers to the differences of status and privilege that structure interactions at every level. These include class, gender, ethnicity, linguistic competence, know-how and economic differences among others. This is similar to Bourdieu's concept of habitus. Foucault notes that "every relationship of power puts into operation differences that are, at the same time, its conditions and its results."[15] These differentiations refer, in the schooling sector, to the evident knowledge that the institutions of schooling systems are never a neutral meritocracy, but always structured by the predispositions of its populating groups.

The second form of power relation is the type of objectives expressed by participants. Such power may relate to the reproduction of privilege, occupational status, statutory requirements, or other factors. If the system of differentiations demonstrates that people have differing status and ability to be heard, the type of objectives shows that different groups and individuals require different outcomes.

The third form of power refers to the ways in which it is exercised: whether by force, persuasion, economic disparities, rules, coercion, or other forms, which may be more or less overt, manifest, and subject to enforcement. Here it is important to recognize that compulsion does not only arise from coercion, but also from a selection among alternatives or unthinking obedience, or a range of other factors. In fact, Foucault rejects the notion that force is power in any useful sense; power is the ability to get others to comply or act without force.

The fourth form of power relation is the institutions that surround and act on persons in society. These institutional forms encompass formal state institutions through to the institutions of civil society. It is within these that the habitus of individuals becomes transformed into forms of cultural capital, in which certain individuals, through their habits and understandings, are advantaged while others are not.

The fifth form of power relation is what Foucault calls the degrees of rationalization. Power is not just formed through the existence of institutional forms, but through their adaptation—through the interactions they facilitate—to life: "The exercise of power is not . . . an institutional given: it is something that is elaborated, transformed, organized; it endows itself with processes that are more or less adjusted to the situation."[16]

It is by no means easy to understand power in schooling systems, but this framework provides some useful tools for analyzing school choice systems.

Individuals and Choice

Systems of school choice can be contrasted to systems of state allocation in terms of one key dimension that has multiple effects: that parents, caregivers, children—someone—must choose a school: more than one option is offered. For example, in New Zealand there is a system of universal mandatory choice, what Wylie calls the voucherless voucher.[17] There is no general requirement that a person attend their local school or any particular school. In practice, however, there are many barriers to choice. In many rural areas, schools are a long way apart and transport systems very sparse. In many urban areas, popular schools are soon full so that choice becomes impracticable. For many children with disabilities, choices are effectively, but not legally, limited.

Many systems in other countries have partial choice. Parents may choose certain types of school under certain conditions. The American response to calls for choice, apart from the very limited programs of vouchers and privatization, has revolved around magnet schools and charter schools. This means that a child can either go to their local school, or choose another on some other basis. The British response has focused on generating differences between schools, through the development of specialisms,[18] and trust and technology schools.[19] Many European countries such as France,[20] Germany[21] and Finland[22] maintain low levels of school choice and, in the case of Germany, high levels of selectivity, or tracking, at high school level. At the level of individual choices, there are several interrelated issues dealt with in the literature. Two aspects will be examined here: who is choosing, and on what basis are choices made?

Individual choices are driven primarily by the first and second of Foucault's sources of power: the system of differentiations and the type of objectives held by choosers. There is now significant literature which demonstrates that school choice systems in effect increase segregation between population types. Choice takes place within systems that have historically been differentiated in numerous ways. Over time, links grow up between the social characteristics of neighborhoods and the schools within them. In the United States, there are also enormous regional funding discrepancies, the savage inequalities that condemn the poorest areas to have the worst-resourced schools.[23] But in New Zealand, a unified funding system actually provides significant additional resources to the poorest schools, and yet the social hierarchy of rich schools, poor schools applies equally, even if the gaps in provision are somewhat smaller.[24]

In practice, this means that wealthy families can send their children to the local school with no dissonance between their social aspirations, their location and their right to attend. As educationally advantaged families cluster in such areas, aspirant families also seek places in the same schools. This means that these schools fill very quickly, which, ironically, both further enhances their reputation and puts them out of reach of families. How this is dealt with in public systems is considered in the next section.

The key to this analysis, however, is that there is little or nothing about the educational characteristics of the school that matters in the market. Whereas the educational marketplace was intended to reward good schools, it in fact rewards desirable school communities. From the earliest New Zealand research on the educational market, it has been clear that choices are made primarily on the basis of social characteristics.[25] There have been numerous studies that demonstrate how power relations dictate school choice. In Britain, studies have shown how knowledge gleaned from social networks outweighs and nullifies official knowledge in making school choices; it is not what is being said, but who says it, that matters.[26] The power of middle-class choice extends beyond individual families and affects choices for others, too.[27] Diane Reay's study of women who head single parent families noted that some ruled themselves out of the market: a common view was that school choice was not for working-class mothers and their children.[28]

The first element of power here, then, is that the middle classes, by their habits and actions, have the ability to shape the educational landscape. While social networks appear to be making choices about which schools are best by their actions, they are simultaneously defining the hierarchy of desirability. One disturbing aspect to emerge from this research is the apparent cavalier fashion with which this power of yea or nay is dispensed. Jennifer Holme describes how middle-class families are prepared to uproot themselves and buy expensive houses in the right area, in order to ensure their children attend the best high schools. Her study showed that this choice is made largely on the basis of networks and reputation; most families never visit the schools they are rejecting, nor the schools they are buying into, before making the move:

> Status, in fact, dominated every aspect of these parents' choices. They not only implicitly trusted the information given to them by other high-status parents, but also read a great deal into these parents' own school choices. As such, the parents in this study assumed that those schools serving the children of high status parents—whether neighborhood school or private schools—were superior to those serving the children of lower-status parents. Thus, for the parents in this study, the assumed quality of the schools was directly associated with the status of the families they served.[29]

Many other research papers echo these findings. A significant element is the nexus of race and class. While school choice has been frequently touted as the cure for racial segregation, research findings demonstrate, on the one hand, that racial segregation increases in choice systems,[30] and, on the other hand, that some people of color choose to move into racially distinctive schools.[31] The implication for democracy of increased racial fragmentation and school segregation has yet to be analysed.[32] Although the main focus of the work on ethnic separation is American, research in other choice systems has also reported similar trends.[33] While some argue that the challenge of school choice is to ensure that segregation, such as that described in the research, does not occur,[34] the clear message is that dominant class groupings make and break educational reputations and determine the distribution of educational space and prestige. To ignore these trends, or see them as a correctable policy blip, misses the point.

So where are poor people of color and the educationally disadvantaged in choice systems? Why do they appear not to be able to take advantage of choice of schools? The points made above provide one response to this: that the dominant class groupings make educational success by virtue of their own choices, however poorly conceived they may be. Dominant class groupings also have more resources than others,[35] for example the ability to work flexible hours and to be able to transport children across town to school. The other side of this story is that nondominant groupings make school reputations too, but often negatively.

In looking at power relations, it is also worth noting that nondominant groups often do not want their children to go to the dominant groups' schools, even where they may identify those schools as being the best. This signals a complex form of power, wherein, at a cultural level, alternate hierarchies are constructed that resist or counter dominant social relations.[36] The more common form is where nondominant families desire the products of education, but see themselves and their children marginalized in the race to acquire these.[37] If it is true that dominant groups carry educational power and prestige with them, then a belief by nondominant groups in their subordinate status in choice systems, as a group, is necessarily correct.

The Apparatus of Schooling and Choice

This section draws attention mainly to the third and fourth forms of power articulated by Foucault. In this context they are closely linked with one another. The third form of power relates to the mechanisms of control: how power is exercised. In school choice systems, power is actively devolved from national and regional systems to local and individual choices, although within this distinction there are myriad different forms of schooling system. The fourth form of power relates to state agencies. The fact of public education and its gatekeeping role, the disposition of organizations of schooling in societies, the redefinition of childhood and success that it entails, its links to the economic apparatus, the status hierarchies it involves and so on all contribute to specific forms of power relations. In terms of school reform, we need to examine what has changed, and how it has changed, as manifestations of altered power relations. A key question is: If schools are now controlled by parent power, why aren't they more different from one another in diverse societies?[38]

The phenomenon of increased homogeneity around conservative schooling forms was first noted by Geoff Whitty and his colleagues.[39] The principle can be expressed as follows: when exposed to market competition, schools tend towards a conservative portrayal of themselves, stressing uniformity (and uniforms), discipline, and academic subjects. In New Zealand, fifteen years of school reform has led to virtually no innovation, and a significant increase in the discourses of uniformity and discipline. In England, too, schools are remade into a parody of the public (private) school. Reforms in the United States are more interesting because of the ability of communities to start their own charter schools, cater to specific and often alienated groups, and thus bypass the problems of middle-class definition described above:

> Increasingly, educational reformers view charter schools as a way to provide a more effective education to students who are ill-served by the public school system as it is currently structured. Support for charter schools comes from a wide array of groups, including conservatives who also support taxpayer-financed vouchers; business leaders ... African American and Hispanic civic groups; community leaders; and parents searching for ways to reform public education without totally destroying or abandoning it.[40]

There is some evidence of diversity in charter schools. Shopfront schools, longer school days, bilingual programs and similar options appear to focus closely on community needs.[41] At state and school district level, charter schools are often used as a basis to bring in antiunion agendas and partial privatization, including the contracting out of schooling to private companies such as Edison.[42]

The pro-choice literature portrays marketized and privatized schools as more responsive and innovative than public schools. Not only does this assume these schools will be innovative, it assumes that public schools are not. Chris Lubienski's work demonstrates that there is nothing particularly special, innovative, or responsive about charter schools compared to the public school system.[43] Lubienski's meta-analysis uncovers a sustained pattern of organizational change coupled with pedagogical and curricula conformity in charter schools.[44] This finding has significant implications for policy in the United States and beyond.

It is evident from the research that certain forms of schooling cast a long shadow. While schools appear free to set up in forms that reflect community need (and many new schools in both the United States and England specifically cater to the needs of education-poor communities), their tendency to adopt traditional forms must reflect a power exigency.

As well, there are numerous ways in which new schools and existing systems have been shaped by power exigencies from above, such as the need to define and demonstrate success, or to operate within a particular environment. In the United States, the funding for charter schools is particularly sparse and, unless schools are able to access significant, ongoing funding from other sources,[45] the need to fund set-up costs as well as teaching and learning systems can be prohibitive. In England, the government has found that the start-up costs of new technology and trust schools has been high, and that business and community agencies have been reluctant to invest funds in schools. Other social and economic barriers also exist.

In many countries and regions, school choice has meant changes in the governance of schools. Perhaps the most radical of these reforms was in New Zealand, where the 1989 reforms devolved school governance to elected boards of trustees, made up largely of parents. The same reforms swept away the regional bodies that governed most schools at the time, labeling them unnecessary bureaucracies. The loss of capacity that occurred at the time proved disastrous, and New Zealand legislation has been in reregulation mode since around 1998, albeit within an unaltered governance system. An OECD official memorably called boards of trustees self perpetuating oligarchies.[46] The reason for their reproductive power is quite evident from the framework used here. The parental power to choose was incorporated into the very system of education. Boards of schools in poor areas dealt with the hardest problems and biggest challenges with the least human resources to do the work.

In England and Wales, there have been ongoing attempts to shift governance away from Local Educational Authority (LEA) to individual schools. The current reform proposals have been heavily criticized as unfair, inconsistent, and poor value for money.[47] The extension of the trust schools policy would see schools become independently run, and would include a range of governance models including significant privatization. A number of American firms, led by Edison, see the reforms as an opportunity to take over the running of some British schools.

In the United States, governance operates most significantly at the level of the district. School districts serve populations that range from homogenous to extremely diverse, and are subject to political influence, takeover, and external attack.[48] One of the most interesting case studies concerns Boulder, Colorado. A campaign initially launched by one woman eventually shifted a content and reasonably effective school district towards a system of choice and increasing differentiation.[49]

How power is exercised, its disciplines, scope, and nature, is directly dependent on its locus of control. The removal or reform of regional schooling bodies, especially if they are to be replaced at the school level, allows for more direct or indirect control from above, through regulation or legislation, and also transforms a schooling system into a series of individual enterprises. A reduction in regional governance also affects institutional supports for schools, significantly weakening those close to the school, while strengthening central steering mechanisms.

The final issue discussed in this section relates directly to the relations and rules of power: the system of admissions to school. In New Zealand, the educational free market of the early 1990s led to a range of significant problems, such as children inexplicably left out of schools or people living next door to a school barred from attending. As the market took hold, the wealthiest schools became increasingly popular, and places in these schools more contested, middle class parents found their access to the best schools becoming more problematic. There was a perceived, and, in some cases actual shift in decision-making power from parents to schools.

A system of school choice inevitably produces more or less popular schools. The question of how to regulate entry is thus at the heart of the system, although there is evidence that often little attention is given to this aspect.[50] Systems that guarantee entry to local people and use neutral systems to allocate places will have quite different outcomes to systems that allow schools to choose. There is significant evidence that, where schools can "cream skim," they will do so.[51]

Local and regional structures and practices are themselves framed by national or subnational legislation, regulation, funding, control, and influence. The school choice movement accompanies rhetoric that school systems are failing, and education levels need to improve—and is often presented as the solution to these problems. In the United States, such rhetoric is clear within No Child Left Behind, the choice and specialization policy documents of the UK government, and in the recent legislation increasing school accountability for planning and reporting student achievement in New Zealand. Where does the power lie, then, when governments start articulating and demanding improvements to schooling for disadvantaged groups?

National and Federal Systems: Public and Private

This final section examines the role of government in legislating for systems of education. It is the most difficult part of this paper because it involves the interaction of all five elements of Foucault's distinctions—to an extent the first four produce the fifth. Elements of social and economic status, the ability to express objectives and be heard, the modes of the exercise of power, and the institutional forms, all pattern national responses and effects through the elaboration, transformation and organization of the social world. What makes such responses very complex is that they can be formed by contradictory and conflicting goals, and again they may have unintended consequences and effects.

The No Child Left Behind Act (2001) presents as legislation that is concerned with improving student achievement, particularly for certain categories of at risk child. The law has four basic planks: (1) the requirement for accountability through testing, linked to remedial action; (2) increased freedom to spend federal grants according to local needs; (3) a shift to programs and practices based on rigorous scientific research; and (4) a rule that children who attend failing schools (as defined) may be transferred to a better-performing school, with transport costs met by the school district, and remedial services offered to children who stay at such schools.

The literature addresses all these elements and a range of other concerns, such as the effects on children with disabilities.[52] The main effect of the legislation is to hold schools and teachers accountable for student achievement. As many authors point out, this forces teachers into narrow test-based pedagogies.[53] A fascinating paper, Arce, et al., examines the winners in the testing game. They are the testing publishers, the testing companies, and the private companies that offer tutoring and other remedial services. From this perspective, the law essentially opens the door for a large shift in funds from the public education sector into the hands of private corporations:

> Through No Child Left Behind, the Bush Administration has legitimized the role of private corporations in public education. This heavy-handed involvement is determined by corporate CEOs and board members who decide what is worthy of

teaching and learning, and who should have access to opportunities. Unfortunately, while corporations profit from public
education, many schools and their communities are being
underserved educationally, socially, and economically.[54]

The remedies offered by No Child Left Behind are choice and
privatization, further incursions of the private into public education,
and the adoption of scientific methods that can never embrace and
transform the profoundly social processes that underpin education and,
thus, the privileging of particular relations of power. By misrepresent-
ing the causes of educational failure at the school level, No Child Left
Behind ensures that, while test scores will rise, educational opportunity
will not improve.[55]

The second approach of interest here argues that schools should
become more different from one another. This approach forms the centre of current government reform efforts in England and Wales. The
main argument is that widening access to choice "will enable access to
good schools and drive up standards."[56] While this is the old notion
that competition improves standards, the policy is contradictory in that
the flagship specialist schools are also intended to co-operate with and
provide networks with other local schools, in order to share expertise.
This sends contradictory messages to schools.[57]

The recent audit commission report points out a number of flaws in
the specialist schools scheme.[58] These flaws include: that the admissions
scheme offers insufficient checks and balances necessary to secure equity
of access and treatment of parents and children; that choice, rather than a
realistic preference, is not possible; that assumptions are made that spare
places are the result of poor performance; that a system of choice needs
spare capacity, which is not available in key areas; and that a reduction
in local authority power improve accountability.

The key feature of the policy from an analysis of power is that
it is driven by heavily competing goals. To begin with, the reification
of choice as the main driver of school quality privileges the choosers.
Underpinning that is the subsidiary role to use specialisms as a lever to
improve quality in all schools. Not only does this assume that educational
failure is solely the product of inexpert schools and teachers, West and
Bell point out that these schools were found through inspection to be
weakest on their community relations and networking roles.[59]

A significant aspect of the ongoing reforms in the United Kingdom
involve the development of public private partnerships in education.
Companies have expressed interest in setting up trusts to run schools.
Why would private businesses be interested in running schools, and

what value would they add to the education process? Where does the power lie? The striking thing about this policy is, that even if it worked according to its stated intentions, the main gains would accrue to the educationally advantaged, and only crumbs would trickle down to the have-nots in the form of a small overall improvement in the schooling system. Far more likely, as various critics have pointed out, is the development of a two-tier system involving fewer opportunities for those who need them most.

Finally, there is the notion that public education is bad and the private sector is good. Most of the reform processes we have seen—choice, vouchers, charter schools and so on—are based at heart on the primacy of the private. The power relations here are simple. Those that work in the public schooling system are seen as unmotivated, lazy, driven by the wrong incentives and ineffective, with no motivation to change their behavior. It is argued that the private sector could deliver education better, cheaper, and more effectively.[60] This model disempowers teachers, by treating them as mere drones responding only to external incentives. It ignores the role of education in communities, and the role of communities in schooling. It ignores the profoundly social causes of educational success and failure. Despite many attempts to prove it, there is no research evidence that, all things being equal, private is better than public. After twenty years of vouchers in Chile, the call is for more educational reform and more access to the still inaccessible—more change. In the end, the promise that choice empowers, improves, and transforms is a hollow one; everything may be changed, and yet nothing changes. The power relations that govern education are embedded in the social systems of our society, and only change at that level can 'reform' school outcomes.

Conclusion

The main reason given for school choice is to empower families to choose the school that best meets their needs, thereby encouraging "non-chosen" schools to improve. It rests on specific assumptions derived from the economic sphere, and not only shares some problems of consumer choice (not all consumers have equal resources to choose), it also fails to take in account at all the deep cultural and historical discourses of power that shape schooling.

Thus it is not surprising that school choice has not worked. While it may have improved the schooling experience of some specific individuals, the system improvements promised by choice have failed to occur.

The first section of this paper examined how power is exercised at an individual level. The research notes that the exercise of choice and the modes of choosing barely differ from prechoice systems. Those who have always been able to exercise their first choice continue to do so. What choice does, because it requires competition, is make top end schools increasingly responsive to top-end parents, to ensure their market dominance is maintained. Such responses may have much more to do with ensuring that disruptive or diverse elements are removed from the classroom, than improving educational outcomes. There is a dangerous tendency here for schools to increasingly serve homogenous communities.

What of schools and systems? How has school choice affected them? The research is clear that more devolved, autonomous, or privatized forms of schooling do not bring about innovative practices. Such schools, freed from the bureaucratic burden that reformers claim prevents good schooling, tend to immediately reproduce existing school formats, often in their most conservative guise. There is no sustained evidence that new categories of schools improve performance. There are individual exceptions, involving both innovative practice and opening up opportunities for disenfranchised youth. But there always have been alternative routes for some. Schools such as charter schools and UK specialist schools may have more power, but operate under significant constraints. As in New Zealand, the stripping away of regional support systems has placed new burdens on schools.

New Zealand has a radical system of governance based on parental power. This model actually encourages conservative forms. With boards elected every three years from among parents, there is little opportunity for expertise to build up. Therefore, the onus falls heavily onto school principals to determine policies and practices within national guidelines. The shift in empowerment towards communities, brought about by local governance, is at least equaled by the increased pressures of compliance to external regulations, funding shortfalls, and, in poor schools, deep set social and community issues.

What was devolved in New Zealand in the 1990s was the power of over-subscribed schools to select students. The right of schools to choose their own intakes is a heavily contested area, largely because the power to select the right students complements the power of the middle class chooser. The lesson from New Zealand is that free market choosing is disastrous and inefficient public policy. Now, schools must ballot spare places. In the United Kingdom, the proposed policy to allow selection on some kind of academic merit inevitably raises the specter of social segregation.

Does NCLB in the United States, and reforms in the United Kingdom empower disadvantaged students by improving education and driving up achievement? No, and neither, it appears, are they intended to do so. Behind NCLB is a discourse of discipline focused on the poorest communities and their schools. If these schools do not achieve the unachievable, they will be closed. Poor communities will lose schools, and the resulting message will be: decent schooling does not occur in poor communities. This, of course, was the message of desegregation in the 1950s, and is the message now. The profound social gaps in educational achievement in the United States attest to the failure of bussing as the apex of education policy. No Child Left Behind will not empower poor communities.

The concept of power, based on a scheme outlined by Foucault that tries to come to terms with the complexity of the discursive and multilayered practice of education, provides an approach to assessing the multiple levels at which school choice operates. This analysis both builds on and confirms the overwhelming research finding that school choice does not shift educational power towards the disenfranchised. The political rhetoric that choice reforms increase the power of children, families or communities is not reflected in research findings.

Notes for Chapter 8

1. Linda Miller-Kahn and Mary Lee Smith, "School Choice Policies in the Political Spectacle," *Education Policy Analysis Archives* 9, no. 50 (2001).

2. Michael Apple, "Strategic Alliance or Hegemonic Strategy? Conservatism Among the Dispossesed," *London Review of Education* 1, no. 1 (2003): 47–60.

3. John Codd, "Educational Reform, Accountability and the Culture of Distrust," *New Zealand Journal of Educational Studies* 34, no. 1 (1999): 45–53; Hugh Lauder, David Hughes, Sietske Waslander, Martin Thrupp, Jim McGlinn, S. Newton, and Ann Dupuis *The Creation of Market Competition in New Zealand: An Empirical Analysis of a New Zealand Secondary School Market 1990–1993* (1994).

4. John Leland Berg, "No Child Should Be Left Behind. Working to Fix What Is Broken in Public Schools," *Teacher Education and Practice* 13, no. 2 (1997): 46–60; Lance D. Fusarelli, "The Potential Impact of the No Child Left Behind Act on Equity and Diversity in American Education," *Educational Policy* 18, no. 1 (2004): 71–94.

5. Gregory Camilli and Katrina Bulkley, "Critique of 'An Evaluation of the Florida A-Plus Accountability Program,'" *Education Policy Analysis Archives* 9, no. 7 (2001); Haggai Kupermintz, "Effects of Vouchers: Another Look at the Florida Data," *Education Policy Analysis Archives* 9, no. 8 (2001).

6. Beatrice S. Fennimore, "'Brown' and the Failure of Civic Responsibility," *Teachers College Record* 107, no. 9 (2005): 1905–32; Kathleen Ferraiolo, Frederick Hess, Robert Maranto, and Scott Milliman, "Teachers' Attitudes and the Success of School Choice," *Policy Studies Journal* 32, no. 2 (2004): 209–24; Lance D. Fusarelli,

"Charter Schools: Implications for Teachers and Administrators," *Clearing House* 76, no. 1 (2002): 20–25; Christopher Lubienski, "Innovation in Education Markets: Theory and Evidence on the Impact of Competition and Choice in Charter Schools," *American Educational Research Journal* 40, no. 2 (2003): 395–443.

7. Nick Adnett and Peter Davies, "Schooling Reforms in England: From Quasi-markets to Competition?" *Journal of Education Policy* 18, no. 4 (2003): 393–406; Anne West and Kate Bell, "Specialist Schools: An Exploration of Competition and Cooperation," *Educational Studies* 29, no. 2/3 (2003): 273–89.

8. Lynn Bosetti, "Determinants of School Choice: Understanding How Parents Choose Elementary Schools in Alberta," *Journal of Education Policy* 19, no. 4 (2004): 387–405; Scott Davies, Janice Aurini, and Linda Quirke, "New Markets for Private Education in Canada," *Education Canada* 42, no. 3 (2002): 36–38.

9. Simon Marginson, "Education and the Trend to Markets," *Australian Journal of Education* 43, no. 3 (1999): 229–39; Thomas A. O'Donoghue, "Issues in Primary and Secondary Education in Australia: Past, Present, Future," *International Journal of Educational Reform* 9, no. 1 (2000): 50–58.

10. Martin Carnoy, "National Voucher Plans in Chile and Sweden: Did Privatization Reforms Make for Better Education?" *Comparative Education Review* 42, no. 3 (1998): 309–37; Lisbeth Lundahl, "Sweden: Decentralization, Deregulation, Quasi-markets—and Then What?" *Journal of Education Policy* 17, no. 6 (2002): 687–97; David N. Plank and Gary L. Sykes, eds., *Choosing Choice: School Choice in International Perspectives* (New York: Teachers College Press, 2003); Helen Raham, "A Tale of Two Education Systems: Policy Lessons from Sweden," *Policy Options* (October 2003): 63–67.

11. Paul E. Peterson, Jay P. Greene, and Chad Noyes, "School Choice in Milwaukee," *Public Interest* 125 (1996): 38–56; John F. Witte, "The Milwaukee Voucher Experiment," *Educational Evaluation and Policy Analysis* 20, no. 4 (1998): 229–51; John F. Witte, "The Milwaukee Voucher Experiment: The Good, the Bad, and the Ugly," *Phi Delta Kappan* 81, no. 1 (1999): 59.

12. Michel Foucault, *Power*, trans. Robert Hurley and others, ed. James D. Faubion (New York: New Press, 2000), 336.

13. Ibid., 344–45.

14. Ibid., 345.

15. Ibid., 344.

16. Ibid.

17. Cathy Wylie, "Is the Land of the Flightless Bird the Home of the Voucherless Voucher?" *New Zealand Journal of Educational Studies* 34, no. 1 (1999): 99–109.

18. West and Bell, "Specialist Schools."

19. Geoff Whitty and Tony Edwards, "School Choice Policies in England and the United States: An Exploration of Their Origins and Significance," *Comparative Education* 34, no. 2 (1998): 211–27.

20. Marie Duru-Bellat, "Social Inequalities in French Secondary Schools: From Figures to Theories," *British Journal of Sociology of Education* 17, no. 3 (1996): 341–50.

21. Christian Dustmann, "Parental Background, Secondary School Track Choice, and Wages," *Oxford Economic Papers—New Series* 56, no. 2 (2004): 209–30.

22. Piia Seppanen, "Patterns of 'Public-School Markets' in the Finnish Comprehensive School from a Comparative Perspective," *Journal of Education Policy* 18, no. 5 (2003): 513–31.

23. Jonathan Kozol, *Savage Inequalities: Children in America's Schools* (New York: Harper Perennial, 1991).

24. Liz Gordon, "School Choice and the Social Market in New Zealand: Educational Reform in an Era of Increasing Inequality," *International Studies in Sociology of Education* 13, no. 1 (2003): 17–34.

25. Lauder et al., *The Creation of Market Competition in New Zealand.*

26. Stephen J. Ball and Carol Vincent, "'I Heard It on the Grapevine': 'Hot' Knowledge and School Choice," *British Journal of Sociology of Education* 19, no. 3 (1998): 377–400.

27. Diane Reay and Stephen J. Ball, "'Spoilt for Choice': The Working Classes and Educational Markets," *Oxford Review of Education* 23, no. 1 (1997): 89–101; Diane Reay and Stephen J. Ball, "'Making Their Minds Up': Family Dynamics of School Choice," *British Educational Research Journal* 24, no. 4 (1998): 431–48.

28. Diane Reay, "Contextualising Choice: Social Power and Parental Involvement," *British Educational Research Journal* 22, no. 5 (1996): 581–96.

29. Jennifer Jellison Holme, "Buying Homes, Buying Schools: School Choice and the Social Construction of School Quality," *Harvard Educational Review* 72, no. 2 (2002): 177–205.

30. Kenneth R. Howe, Margaret Eisenhart, and Damian Betebenner, "The Price of Public School Choice," *Educational Leadership* 59, no. 7 (2002): 20–24; Salvatore Saporito, "Private Choices, Public Consequences: Magnet School Choice and Segregation by Race and Poverty," *Social Problems* 50, no. 2 (2003): 181–203.

31. Lawson Bush, "Access, School Choice, and Independent Black Institutions—A Historical Perspective," *Journal of Black Studies* 34, no. 3 (2004): 386–401; Kathryn Herr, "Private Power and Privileged Education: De/constructing Institutionalized Racism," *International Journal of Inclusive Education* 3, no. 2 (1999): 111–29.

32. Weiher and Tedin, "Does Choice Lead to Racially Distinctive Schools?"

33. Sjoerd Karsten, "Neoliberal Education Reform in the Netherlands," *Comparative Education* 35, no. 3 (1999): 303–17.

34. Charles Glenn, "The Challenge of Diversity and Choice," *Educational Horizons* 83, no. 2 (2005): 101–9.

35. Michael Apple, "Comparing Neo-Liberal Projects and Inequality in Education," *Comparative Education* 37, no. 4 (2001): 409–23.

36. Paul Willis, *Learning to Labour: How Working Class Kids Get Working Class Jobs* (Farnborough: Saxon House, 1977).

37. Stephen J. Ball and Sharon Gewirtz, "Education Markets, School Competition, and Parental Choice in the UK: A Report of Research Findings," *International Journal of Educational Reform* 5, no. 2 (1996): 152–58; Diane Reay

and Helen Lucey, "Children, School Choice and Social Differences," *Educational Studies* 26, no. 1 (2000): 83–100.

38. Michael Apple, *Education and Power*, 2nd ed. (London: Routledge, 1995).

39. Geoff Whitty, Sally Power, and David Halpin, *Devolution and Choice in Education: The School, the State, and the Market* (Buckingham: Open University Press, 1997).

40. Fusarelli, "Charter Schools."

41. Bush, "Access, School Choice, and Independent Black Institutions"; Milo Cutter, "City Academy," *Phi Delta Kappan* 78, no. 1 (1996): 26; Mike Kennedy, "Charter Schools: Threat or Boon to Public Schools?" *American School & University* 75, no. 4 (2002): 18–26; Eric Premack, "Charter Schools: California's Education Reform 'Power Tool,' " *Phi Delta Kappan* 78, no. 1 (1996): 60; William Windler, "Colorado's Charter Schools: A Spark for Change and a Catalyst for Reform," *Phi Delta* Kappan 78, no. 1 (1996): 66.

42. Ira Bloom, "The New Parental Rights Challenge to School Control: Has the Supreme Court Mandated School Choice?" *Journal of Law & Education* 32, no. 2 (2003): 139–83; Katrina Bulkley and Jennifer Fisler, "A Decade of Charter Schools: From Theory to Practice," *Educational Policy* 17, no. 3 (2003): 317–42; Felicity Fletcher-Campbell, *The Edison Schools Initiative: An Evaluation of the Evidence* (2001); Bruce Fuller, Elizabeth Burr, Luis Huerta, Susan Puryear, and Edward Wexler, "School Choice: Abundant Hopes, Scarce Evidence of Results," (Berkeley: Policy Analysis for California Education: 1999); Natalie Lacireno-Paquet, Thomas T. Holyoke, Michele Moser, and Jeffrey R. Henig, "Creaming versus Cropping: Charter School Enrollment Practices in Response to Market Incentives," *Educational Evaluation and Policy Analysts* 24, no. 2 (2002): 145–58.

43. Ann C. Lewis, "A Modest Proposal for Urban Schools," *Phi Delta Kappan* 78, no. 1 (1996): 5; Christopher Lubienski, "Innovation in Education Markets"; Christopher Lubienski, "Public Schools in Marketized Environments: Shifting Incentives and Unintended Consequences of Competition-Based Educational Reforms," *American Journal of Education* 111, no. 4 (2005): 464.

44. Chrisopher Lubienski, "Innovation in Education Markets," 413.

45. Cutter, "City Academy."

46. Donald Hirsch, "The Other School Choice: How Oversubscribed Schools Select Their Students" (paper presented in a public lecture at London Institute of Education, May 1995).

47. Audit Commission, *Report on "Higher Standards, Better Schools for All: More Choice for Parents and Pupils"* (London: Audit Commission, 2006).

48. Thomas L. Alsbury, "Superintendent and School Board Member Turnover: Political versus Apolitical Turnover as a Critical Variable in the Application of the Dissatisfaction Theory," *Educational Administration Quarterly* 39, no. 5 (2003): 667; Katrina Bulkley, "Charter School Authorizers: A New Governance Mechanism?" *Educational Policy* 13, no. 5 (1999): 674; Abe Feuerstein, "Elections, Voting, and Democracy in Local School District Governance," *Educational Policy* 16, no. 1 (2002): 15; John Fitz and Bryan Beers, "Education Management Organisations and the Privatisation of Public Education: A Cross-National Comparison

of the USA and Britain," *Comparative Education* 38, no. 2 (2002): 137; Chris Pipho, "The Changing Governance Scene," *Phi Delta Kappan* 77, no. 1 (1995): 6; Janice Shamon, "Massachusetts Charter Schools: When Reform Goes Wrong," *Radical Teacher* 49 (1996): 17.

49. Kenneth R. Howe and Catherine Ashcraft, "Deliberative Democratic Evaluation: Successes and Limitations of an Evaluation of School Choice," *Teachers College Record* (2005): 2275–98; Howe, Eisenhart, and Betebenner, "The Price of Public School Choice"; Miller-Kahn and Smith, "School Choice Policies."

50. Liz Gordon and Diane Pearce, "School Zoning since 1990: A Christchurch Study," unpublished manuscript, 2005; Saporito, "Private Choices, Public Consequences"; Anne West and Audrey Hind, *Secondary School Admissions in England: Exploring the Extent of Overt and Covert Selection* (Research and Information on State Education Trust, 2003), http://www.risetrust.org.uk/admissions.html; Anne West, Audrey Hind, and Hazel Pennell, *Secondary Schools in London: Admisison Criteria and Cream Skimming* (London: Centre for Educational Research, London School of Economic and Political Science, 2003); Anne West, Audrey Hind, and Hazel Pennell, "School Admissions and 'Selection' in Comprehensive Schools: Policy and Practice," *Oxford Review of Education* 30, no. 3 (2004): 347–69; Anne West, Hazel Pennell, and Audrey Hind, "Secondary School Admissions—Selection by Stealth," *Education Journal* 70 (2003): 2003–5.

51. West, Hind, and Pennell, *Secondary Schools in London*.

52. Shanon S. Taylor, "Special Education and Private Schools—Principals' Points of View," *Remedial and Special Education* (2005): 281–96; H. Rutherford Turnbull III, "Individuals with Disabilities Education Act Reauthorization: Accountability and Personal Responsibility," *Remedial and Special Education* 26, no. 6 (2005): 320; Mitchell L. Yell, Erik Drasgow, and K. Alisa Lowrey, "No Child Left Behind and Students with Autism Spectrum Disorders," *Focus on Autism and Other Developmental Disabilities* 20, no. 3 (2005): 130.

53. Fusarelli, "Potential Impact," 71; Douglas N. Harris and Carolyn D. Herrington, "Accountability, Standards, and the Growing Achievement Gap: Lessons from the Past Half-Century," *American Journal of Education* 112, no. 2 (2006): 209; David Karen, "No Child Left Behind? Sociology Ignored!" *Sociology of Education* 78, no. 2 (2005): 165; Dan Laitsch, "NCLB Meets School Realities: Lessons from the Field," *Teachers College Record* 180, no. 1 (2006): 103; James E. Ryan, "The Perverse Incentives of the No Child Left Behind Act," *New York University Law Review* 79, no. 3 (2004): 932.

54. Josephine Arce, Debra Luna, All Borjian, and Marguerite Conrad, "No Child Left Behind: Who Wins? Who Loses?" *Social Justice* 32, no. 2 (2005): 56, 64.

55. Roslyn Arlin Mickelson and Stephanie Southworth, "When Opting Out Is Not a Choice: Implications for NCLB's Transfer Option from Charlotte, North Carolina," *Equity & Excellence in Education* 38, no. 3 (2005): 249–63; Lisa Snell, "No Child Left Behind: The Illusion of School Choice," *Current* 467 (2004): 16.

56. Audit Commission, "Report on 'Higher Standards.' "

57. West and Bell, "Specialist Schools."

58. Audit Commission, "Report on 'Higher Standards.' "

59. West and Bell, "Specialist Schools."

60. Milton Friedman, *Capitalism and Freedom* (Chicago: Univeristy of Chicago Press, 1962); Eric A. Hanushek, "The Failure of Input-Based Schooling Policies," *The Economic Journal* 113, no. 485 (2003): F64.

Chapter 9

Parental Choice

The Liberty Principle in Education Finance in Postapartheid South Africa

Bekisizwe S. Ndimande

Introduction and Historical Context

Parental choice is a fairly new phenomenon among Black communities in South Africa.[1,2] Choice has historically been state-determined, that is, parents were instructed where to send their children to school based primarily on race and on urban and rural homeland division of Black South Africans. Even after 1994, the new and democratically-elected government gave very little direction to schools or school districts as to school choice for purposes of deracializing White and Black schools; for example, there was no bussing as in the United States, and there was a strong rezoning policy that would force the issue of Black students accessing White schools. In theory and according to the law, parents could choose to send their children to any school regardless of race. In practice, White schools determined who gained access to their schools through self-created policies based on high tuition fees, exclusive language policies, and self-defined catchment areas from which students would be chosen. Together, these strategies effectively excluded the Black poor, even though it provided access to small numbers of Black middle-class parents in the mainly English-medium White schools. "Choice" was, therefore, overwhelmingly determined by social class among Black township families.

Parental choice is also associated with the concept of liberty in education, which I borrow from Rolle and Houck, who argue that when we utilize the concept of liberty in education, we are "concerned with how an individual's freedom to choose without coercion is affected by policy decisions as well as the number and quality of educational options."[3] Rolle and Houck were commenting on the negative learning outcomes in choice programs in the United States.[4] For my purpose, I use the concept of liberty in education to illustrate how the freedom of poor Black parents to choose better schools is affected mainly by the imposition of the self-imposed policies by wealthy schools, which make it difficult for Black children to access public schools with better educational resources.

The historical context of educational struggles in South Africa is crucial in this analysis. Ever since the beginning of formal education, in what was known as slave schools in the Cape Colony under Dutch colonial rule in the seventeenth century,[5] the education of Blacks did not offer any prospect of improving social life. Later, in the early 19th century, the apartheid government intensified educational inequalities by legislating an unambiguous policy of segregation, and grossly underfunding the education of Black communities.[6] Inequality of access and underfunding for Blacks was further reinforced by the establishment of eighteen separate departments of education which served different parts of the racially driven education system based on the government's racial policies of segregation.

The early 1990s was a watershed in the political landscape of South Africa. Because of the mounting pressure of resistance to apartheid and Bantu education, the government was forced to reevaluate some of its racial policies on education. The first response occurred in 1990, when the government engaged in quasireform initiatives to deracialize some White public schools that were running half empty. This became known as the Model C schools.[7] However, major policy changes, with various progressive intentions in education, were soon to follow in postapartheid South Africa. Yet, with all these policy changes, education inequities, especially in access and school funding, did not radically disappear. Inadequate funding in township schools,[8] mismanagement of funds in government departments of education,[9] and inefficiency and bureaucracy in school funding distribution,[10] posed as major hindrances to equity in educational funding between poor and wealthy public schools.

The purpose of this chapter is to demonstrate how the liberty principle operates in South Africans schools to constrain choice along race and class lines, effectively marginalizing the Black poor from participating in well-resourced public schools, based partly on ability to pay and partly on school-level initiatives that reinforce the race and class character of schooling in this young democracy. I focus on three specific areas: First, I present the reasons why most Black public schools are still trapped in financial crisis amid government mantras such as equal access to public education, compulsory education for all students, and so forth.[11] I contend that there is something wrong when township schools are dysfunctional because of mismanagement of funds and a government bureaucracy which essentially reproduces inadequate funding opportunities. It is not only the negative legacy of apartheid, but also the failure of postapartheid administration to effectively allocate greater financial capacity to poor and Black public schools, thereby giving Black parents greater possibilities for real choice in decisions about schools. In this chapter, I show that funding inequalities have created fundamental financial disparities between schools in the townships and schools in the suburban areas.

Second, I present the voices of Black parents who transferred their children from underresourced township schools to wealthy, formerly White-only schools in suburban areas. These parents relate their personal experiences and frustrations regarding the high costs of school fees and general financial requirements in these well-resourced suburban public schools. Using Bourdieu's analysis of social class and socioeconomic status,[12] I contend that poor, Black parents have every right to send their children to any public school in the nation, if they think this will help improve their material conditions.[13]

Third, I argue that it is unjustified for public schools with better facilities to impose high tuition,[14] knowing well that some parents will not be able to afford the high financial costs and I emphasize that this results in the systematic exclusion of children whose parents cannot afford schools with better educational resources. In addition, I contend that it is not only through school fees that White schools consciously exclude Black students, they also use other manipulative policies, such as blurry zoning policies,[15] to marginalize already marginalized communities. Agreeing with Jansen, who argues that such blurry demarcations consciously exclude poor neighborhoods and thus reproduce social inequalities, I conclude by arguing that crucial issues regarding educational finance and access to education are highly racialized. The politics of who gets access to funding and funding information, such as the eligibility of school fee waivers—which poor parents rarely access—becomes crucial. I posit that the underlying crisis about school funding, access, and the distribution of educational resources, is embedded within the larger neoliberal agenda of privatizing the public sphere and the neoconservative's attack on multiculturalism and diversity.[16] This neoliberal and neoconservative agenda can systematically exclude the Other.[17]

A Promise for Better Educational Resources

Under apartheid, the education of Blacks was grossly underfunded. This was in accordance with the apartheid ideology of White supremacy and the suppression of Black populations. Abundance of educational resources and school finance were channelled to White public schools. Table 9.1 below shows the funding disparities in schools that served different racial communities.

As a result, school finance was characterized by staggering funding disparities between schools that served different racial communities.[19] The reader will note from table 9.1, for example, that funding for a White student between the years 1983 and 1984 was a whopping R1533 more than that allocated to a Black student.

However, the postapartheid era began with various democratic changes, including initiatives to provide equal and quality education for all citizens. In addition, the postapartheid administration promised effective funding of all public schools—including those in the township. In its compelling preamble, the South African Schools Act states the following:

> WHEREAS the achievement of democracy in South Africa has consigned to history the past system of education which was based on racial inequality and segregation; and WHEREAS this country requires a new national system for schools which will redress past injustices in educational provision, provide an education of progressive high quality for all learners. . . . WHEREAS it is necessary to set uniform norms and standards for the education of learners at schools and the

Table 9.1. Per capita expenditure on education in apartheid South Africa[18]

Year	African	Coloured	Indian	White
1953–1954	17	40	40	128
1969–1970	17	73	81	282
1975–1976	42	140	190	591
1977–1978	54	185	276	657
1980–1981	139	253	513	913
1982–1983	146	498	711	1211
1983–1984	169	639	1112	1702

*All numbers in South African Rand.

organization, governance and funding of schools throughout the Republic of South Africa.[20]

Ending school segregation and channelling funding to all public schools was a necessary and correct thing to do, especially given the important role education plays in building democracy in a nation. Put simply, the postapartheid government realized a pressing need to deracialize education and provide resources to all schools in order to further the goals of a nonracist society.[21]

Education policy changes did not, however, guarantee an unproblematic transition from apartheid education to integrated schools.[22] In other words, despite changes in education policy and curriculum reform, the postapartheid school system contends with other dilemmas. For instance, changes did not easily improve the troubling shortage of education resources in township schools. These schools remain poorly equipped in both human and financial resources.[23] Given the financial privileges they enjoyed in the past, White schools possess better-equipped libraries, science laboratories, computer facilities, better prepared teachers, and all other kinds of educational resources. In Vally and Dalamba's account:

> The 'African' township and ex-homeland schools (catering for the overwhelming majority of learners in South Africa) remain almost wholly racially exclusive and underresourced. The latter is partially a result of a legacy of apartheid but also because of the inability of these communities to significantly supplement state subsidies.[24]

I do not wish to equate the underfunding situation in Black schools in apartheid to that in postapartheid era. Underfunding of Black schools under apartheid was a conscientious decision by the state to meet the development plans of apartheid.[25] Yet, in postapartheid, this happens through a combination of factors, including mismanagement of resources, government bureaucracy, inefficiency, and rightist impulses, et cetera. Regardless of the reasons, however, the reality is that Black public schools in postapartheid South Africa are still not comparable in terms of the financial resources privileged, formerly White-only schools continue to enjoy.

Lack of funding in Black schools is puzzling because education receives the highest budget, in all provinces, compared to other public services such as health care, housing, and welfare.[26] As Jansen illustrates, there is no doubt that a positive growth in the total government expenditure for public education seems to trigger positive growth in education investment in general. "South Africa," Jansen states, "has clearly and consistently made significant investments in school education since 1994 with a 'pro-poor' bias in expenditure both at the level of provinces, schools and individual learners."[27] This is absolutely good news for equity in education. Unfortunately though, while there appears to be sufficient budget for poor schools, there is also an overwhelming evidence of mismanagement such as illegal payments to contractors, transfers of funds to entities without monitoring the resources, overspending on substitute teachers, and other forms of waste in education resources.[28]

Indeed, the funding of schools and resource allocation is complex and often contradictory. Indeed, the funding of schools and resource allocation is complex and contradictory. There are situations when money is available, but the bureaucratic machinery of the state does not get the money to where it is needed most and urgently. In 2001, a substantial amount of money made available for improving the country's most disadvantaged public schools remained unspent by the end of that fiscal year.[29] MacFarlane reports, in the *Mail & Guardian*, that the Thuba Makote Rural Building Project spent only R1.5 million of R45 million allocated to spend in one fiscal year. This report shows that most of the money gets trapped in the bureaucracy of the treasury and the department of education because officials have, in some instances, been unable to work out a clear plan of how to spend the money. It is also the case, argues Sayed, that the government hasn't figured out yet how to deal with bureaucracy—especially when it involves funding.[30] "The new government," contends Sayed, "had not captured control of the important state apparatuses, including the education bureaucracy."[31]

I do not wish to be simplistic and naïve about these bureaucratic tendencies as if they are objective and happen in a sociopolitical vacuum. Rather, I want to argue that while on the surface, underspending may appear as a simple bureaucratic and inefficiency matter, it is also political. Our government subscribes to neoliberal ideologies, the World Bank (WB), the International Monetary Fund (IMF), and programs such as Growth, Employment, and Redistribution (GEAR), as its economic policy.[32] This underspending in public institutions is consistent with the broader neoliberal ideology that opposes the development of public institutions as a waste of money, instead favoring the privatization and marketization of institutions and utilities.

There is an abundance of literature on this phenomenon, with evidence that social inequalities are reproduced by neoliberal market oriented programs.[33] Apple captures this situation eloquently when he argues that, for neoliberalism, "Public institutions such as schools are 'black holes' into which money is poured—and then seemingly disappears—but which do not provide anywhere near adequate results."[34] I return to neoliberal and neoconservative ideologies and financing of institutions in the concluding part of this chapter.

It should be of concern to educational researchers and policymakers that, even with education receiving the highest budget in national spending and the redistribution of resources in favor of poor schools, these schools still do not receive adequate funding. It should also be worrisome that this funding situation, in particular, has damaged these schools. Again, it should be worrisome that policies, such as free schooling and no fee schools, are unrealistic given the poor state of Black schools and the dependency on even minimal school fees. Nor do these policies enable township parents to access well-resourced schools, which in practice, continue to limit the numbers of Black students through an array of mechanisms, including nontuitions cost of participation—for example, school uniforms.[35]

In the next section, I show the hurdles encountered by Black parents when they try to escape poor township schools, especially working-class Black parents. As Black parents share their experiences, it is not hard to tell that these parents face challenging experiences on two fronts. On the one hand, township schools are poor and dysfunctional, on the other hand, even when Black parents try to transfer their children to well-resourced schools, financial gatekeeping in wealthy schools pose another challenge.

At this point, I turn to the accounts of Black parents who are directly affected by poor school resources and have been trying the best they can to access better education for their children. I want to center parents' voices in an effort to illustrate the dilemmas they face as a result of inequitable distribution of resources. These parents have adopted certain socioeconomic strategies to help them respond.

Conversion Strategies and Exodus of Black Children

The grim situation created by the underfunding of public schools in Black townships has forced some Black parents to engage in what I call parental choice for a better school.[36] Research shows that most Black parents who live in the townships have increasingly transferred their children from poorly-funded township schools to better-resourced schools in the suburban areas—and the number continues to increase.[37] By 1997, for instance, the number of Black students enrolled in formerly White-only schools had grown to an average of 27 percent in the Gauteng province alone.[38] Evidently, Black parents have appropriated the choice policy because it is perceived as an alternative to underresourced, impoverished, and dysfunctional township public schools. It is not uncommon, especially for poor people, to use different kinds of strategies and mechanisms that can provide them with some kind of agency to withstand challenging situations.

Pierre Bourdieu's insights on reconversion strategies help us think about these issues from different and nuanced perspectives. According to Bourdieu, strategies which individuals and families employ, with a view to safeguard or improve their position in social space, are reflected in transformations, which modify both the volume of the different class fractions and the structure of their assets.[39] Central to Bourdieu's argument is the reconversion of economic capital into what he calls cultural capital.[40] Unlike economic capital, cultural capital is assumed to be reliable to maintain and safeguard [high] social status positions for most of the family members in the future. In other words, through cultural capital, the family's social class tradition passes from parent to child and then to their children. Working-class, low-income, and marginalized families may want to accumulate a viable cultural capital in order to improve their economic capital and elevate their social class status. While Bourdieu is talking about class, oppression in South Africa is mainly based on race. Black parents, in general, want to use these strategies to get themselves out of the poverty inflicted by apartheid. Take, for instance, a comment made by a Black parent, who is proud of the accomplishments of her sons in a formerly White-only school:

> My sons attended these schools and we paid a lot [of money], but I don't regret. My first-born son was educated at Advanced State School . . . [i]t is an expensive school. It costs R30,000.00 [for both] per annum. But you know what? He got a 'B' in French and now he speaks fluent French, as if it is his mother tongue. He is currently working for Data Centric Company in Lowland because of the skills he acquired from these formerly white-only schools.[41]

It is precisely for this reason that most Black families may want to utilize the reconversion strategies—mainly high qualifications in education—because these have potential for class mobility, especially for people who have been marginalized. Put simply, Bourdieu argues that reconversion strategies may provide economically disadvantaged people with an opportunity to improve their subject position(s) in relation to their material conditions. This is, indeed, an influential social field of power, which Black parents can utilize, to strategically access possibilities for a better future for their children, or, cultural capital can be utilized as a site for mobilization against hegemonic institutions.

Parents' Voices

In this paper my data are based on a study I conducted in the Gauteng province to explore the ideological beliefs and common sense that inform the school choices of Black South African parents.[42] In 2003, I conducted focus group interviews with 122 Black parents in three different sites in the Gauteng region. I sampled parents who chose to send their children to formerly White-only schools and those who did not choose to do so. For the purpose of this chapter, I focus on the former. Since my major focus is to evaluate the articulation of common sense of Black parents around desegregated schools, I show protocol related to funding and school access only. The following four questions were asked:

1. Why did you choose to send your child to a formerly White-only school in the suburb rather than a township school?

2. What do you see as good qualities of formerly White-only schools in the suburbs?

3. Sending your child to a formerly White-only school must cost you a lot of money.

4. What does it cost you (transportation and tuition)? Why are you prepared to make such a sacrifice?

To the first question, about why they chose to transfer their children from township schools to suburban schools, most parents responded that they chose to do so because formerly White-only schools have better educational facilities and resources than most Black schools in the townships. They said that they were mainly driven by the resource factor, in other words, the availability of resources in formerly White-only schools. Below are some of the excerpts that articulate parents' reasons why they choose to send their children to formerly White-only schools and their funding experiences in these schools:

> There are no facilities in our black schools. I discovered that [formerly][43] white schools have all the resources, for example, natural science experiment materials. In our [black] schools, when you speak of a glass beaker, you have to draw it on

the board because there aren't any materials for experiments. Children won't be able to see the real one. But in [formerly] white schools, they do have these materials. In short, I took my children there for better facilities.[44]

I think [formerly] white schools are better than township schools. They have facilities. At our [township] schools, we don't have these facilities. [Formerly] white schools have computers—-this generation of children will eventually use computers worldwide. Therefore, it is important for our children to get such knowledge.[45]

Overwhelmingly, these parents said the abundance of resources available in formerly White-only schools was the major reason why they transferred their children from poor schools to formerly White-only schools in the suburban areas. Similarly, when asked what they view as good things about formerly White-only schools, their responses came down to the question of better resources and viable funding in those schools:[46]

[A]nother thing is that these schools [formerly white-only school] have libraries—a very good thing. That is the reason all children there are able to read the language. Another thing about the facilities—I think our government has to prioritize efforts to provide facilities in the township too. The government has to build libraries in township schools too. The government has to build science labs as well. Science is not only theoretical; it has to be learned practically as well [meaning, experiments]. For me, these are some of the reasons that I send my children to a school.[47]

They have a better education than the township schools because they were fully funded by the government during apartheid. They have far more resources than township schools. While the school funding is the same now because we are now all equal, this doesn't consider the deficit incurred under apartheid in township schools. Therefore, suburban schools continue to have a better educational advantage over township schools.[48]

Let me also problematize another striking phenomenon I came across in my conversations with the parents. Given parents' accounts, it is obviously clear that township schools lack educational resources. What is puzzling is that, even when they try to access public schools with resources, they encounter different kinds of challenges. Parents mention that they are required to come up with exorbitant amounts to pay for school fees and transportation. When asked how much they pay for school fees and whether or not the amount they pay is affordable, parents shared these experiences:

> [I pay] R600.00 for school fees, compare to here in the township where I used to pay R60.00 only for my daughter. I have to pay for transportation as well. It comes up to almost R900.00 per annum. If they could improve education in the township I would stop sending my child over to [formerly] white schools. Look, I also have a son who goes to Msithini [secondary school—referring to a poor school in a township] currently.[49] He is good too."[50]

> [I pay] R170.00 and R150.00 per month (unintelligible). It is a heavy amount. I had to cut back other things from my household just to pay for this. But I do it for my children so they get a good education.[51]

> [Each] year they raise the school fees. This is how they try to keep us [black families] out . . . To me this is a kind of exclusion. It takes us back to the apartheid era because most poor parents won't be able to afford this money; inevitably they [our children] will eventually be excluded.[52]

Listening to these testimonies, two puzzling scenarios regarding school funding and access come to mind. On the one hand, township schools are not funded adequately, and on the other hand, the cost of education in public schools with resources is too expensive for these parents to afford. To understand this situation in nuanced terms, I examine it within the broader sociopolitical context that influences social policy and politics in postapartheid South Africa. This context is also influenced by international politics. South Africa is, no doubt, not immune to international politics because some of our current public policies are founded on international experiences.[53]

The Politics of School Finance and Access

Michael Apple argues that throughout the world we have witnessed a rightist movement—the hegemonic bloc—that has not only opposed social democratic values, but has also committed to a different agenda—the conservative restoration agenda—which often defines social politics in a retrogressive manner.[54] The hegemonic bloc has two major groups that have dominated the debates: the neoliberal and the neoconservatives.[55] According to Apple, these groups have engaged in a project that tries to create new politics of official knowledge, especially regarding school policies. For example, neoconservatism, in formerly White-only schools, has manifested in two distinct practices—namely the tendency to deny information about eligibility for school fee waivers and efforts to institute measures that exclude Black students, including unreasonable zoning demarcations around these wealthy schools. Considering that most parents I interviewed cited high tuition rate as one of the major obstacles for them to access formerly White-only schools, I went on to interview a government official who works for a provincial department of education about this situation:

Question: What kind of financial assistance is available for poor parents who cannot afford the school fees in suburban schools?

Response: The issue of school fees, from a policy point of view—parents can be exempted from paying school fees. They can be exempted partially or receive 100 percent exemption depending on their financial background and situation. But these schools do not disclose that information to [Black] parents.[56]

Question: Do you mean to say that poor parents do not get access to this information?

Response: That's exactly what I mean. And another thing is that Black parents do not know that school fees are not mandatory. They [formerly White-only schools] are not supposed to charge school fees. The school fee is part of the fund that the school gets from the government. Let me explain: The government subsidizes the school. Government formulates a budget and determines the allocation of money based on the school's needs. The schools take a certain percentage from the provincial department of education—that would constitute approximately 60–80 percent of their budget. Once they get this amount, they start looking at fundraising possibilities. The school may be looking at 15 percent from fundraising. This 15 percent has to be divided by 80 percent of learners in the school. This is where they could determine the amount of necessary school fees. All these things constitute what I call school funds, but the school would not disseminate this important information to [Black] parents.[57]

This is a sobering testimony. By all account, it reveals racialized practices at some formerly White-only schools that have consequential effects on Black children. Indeed, some parents in this study have expressed apprehension about how formerly White-only schools impose high school fees as a mechanism to systematically exclude their children. Concealing this pertinent information about fee exemption should raise an alarm to everyone concerned about education reform and equal educational opportunities. As the interview with the government official shows, this is a race as well as a class issue. School choice, and who gets access to which resources or information, ought to be seen within the context of the widening gap between rich and poor. The escalating unemployment rate in South Africa is alarming.[58] My interviewee did not specify who gets this information from these schools. However, with the current socioeconomic conditions, it is arguable that the concealment of information about school fee waivers affects some groups more than others.

Research shows that wealthy parents are mostly likely to have school connections and thus access to school information because of their cultural capital.[59] These are the parents who also have connections to people (even outside school) who can share hidden information. Indeed, there are instances when cultural capital seems to be stronger than economic capital. Overall, this situation has created heavy handed gatekeeping in wealthy public schools, and has led to stratified access. In Samoff's observation, while the differentiator is money rather than race, since money often correlates with and is distributed according to race, racial distinctions have reemerged.[60]

Based on my interviews, I argue that formerly White-only schools have revealed elements of neoconservatism in the manner in which they relate to Black parents whose children attend their school. In one interview, a parent lamented discrimination at parents meetings by linguistic exclusion. In this case, a White school principal refused to conduct the meeting in English, a language better comprehended by most Black parents as opposed to Afrikaans.[61] In some instances, parents meetings were segregated.[62] This gets suspicious when parent meetings are segregated because it is hard to tell if the agenda, including dissemination of such information as school fee exemption, is the same for both Black and White meetings. This is an odd sort of irony when schools are said to be desegregated, yet parents meetings are called in a segregated fashion.

The zoning lines drawn by these wealthy schools leave much to be desired. It is true that the democratically elected government gave very little direction to schools and school districts for purposes of deracializing White and Black schools. Soudien, et al., states that the demarcation of boundaries was left to local governments.[63] In such situations, some schools manipulated the zoning policy. Jansen argues that privileged schools have racialized the school zoning policy and have used it to retain their privilege while exacerbating social and educational inequalities:

> Throughout our country [South Africa], the more privileged schools make conscious decisions to deny entry to children who fall outside their "zones"—often marking these cut-off points arbitrarily but also consciously so that those from poor and Black communities do not overwhelm the school. Some schools such as Westville in KwaZulu Natal have been able to remain virtually all White, through their manipulation of these geographical cut-off points to access.[64]

Attitudes and deliberate attempts to exclude certain individuals or groups are by and large informed by racist nativist[65] ideology. Jansen; Vally and Dalamba; and Ndimande all point to White school repudiating social policies or measures that intend to promote equal opportunities, in this case, equal educational opportunities.[66] Such attitudes are connected to what Apple characterizes as a neoconservative sense of loss that has resulted in fear of the Other:

> Behind much of the neo-conservative positions is a clear sense of loss—a loss of faith, of imagined communities, of a nearly pastoral vision of like-minded people who share norms and values and in which the "Western tradition" reigned supreme ... of purity and danger, in which what was imagined to exist is sacred and "pollution" is feared above all else. We/they binary oppositions dominate the discourse and the culture of the "Other" is to be feared.[67]

Numerous scholars remind us that school reforms that utilize parental choice are modeled after neoliberal policy agendas that typically reward few individuals and exclude the Other.[68] The South African situation is no different. Most poor parents do not have access to well-funded schools because of the nature of these school reforms. As I alluded earlier in this chapter, South Africa adopted a neoliberal economic policy—Growth, Employment, and Redistribution (GEAR) programme. GEAR is a structural adjustment policy which "recommended the complete privatisation of non-essential state-owned corporations and the partial privatisation of others. It called for wage restraints by organised labour ... [T]he entire strategy depended heavily on new investment, particularly from foreign sources, pouring into South Africa."[69] This is a questionable economic strategy in a nation that has adopted democratic principles.[70] In some African countries in particular, the World Bank and IMF supported programs have been criticized for being profit oriented, while neglecting poor communities and ignoring the goal of egalitarian state.[71]

Neoliberalism believes that privatization of the public sphere and the belief in markets will solve every social problem; all we need is to have faith in the invisible hand of the market and its order, and things will turn out well for everybody.[72] The assumption is that private companies will generate capital for the country and increase employment opportunities, thus improving the economy. Yet this does not seem to be the case. As Bond, Gumede, and Pillay[73] contend, this actually decreases state expenditure on the public sector and is contrary to the fundamental principles of democracy. Neoliberal programmes tend to oppose a welfare state. Take, for example, basic utilities such as water, which are being privatised in South Africa.[74] How can poor parents afford school fees in these trying economic times largely caused by neoliberalism?

Conclusion

Although the postapartheid era began with multiple promises for a better education, race continues to play a constitutive role in educational access for poor children in the townships. While research shows that there has been an increased effort to fund Black schools—the pro poor bias expenditure—the bottom line is that there are fundamental financial problems in poor schools. The problems seem to be related to mismanagement and bureaucracy, yet the broader analysis shows that problems of access and funding are much more complex. Even when Black and poor parents try to escape poor schools in the townships, privileged, formerly White-only schools use tactics that allow these schools to remain exclusively White. As we know from the compelling testimonies of Black parents, clearly the liberty principle in education has been affected by these negative policies.

In a marketized democracy, it is easy to talk about liberty to choose when the rhetoric of market and choice is encouraged. Yet, research shows that there is no liberty in market and choice when the playing field is uneven. The market will not solve every social problem because participation in choice requires resources—tuition and money for transportation—for parents to participate. In addition, it requires cultural capital—which generally comes with wealth—to access well-resourced schools. Ability to pay fees and the ability to access information becomes difficult for

Black parents. Money is not the only thing that excludes Blacks from privileged, formerly White-only schools. The treatment of their children in these schools—around issues of language, race, and general negative attitudes[75]—altogether destroys the concept of choice.

Funding of all public schools, especially poor public schools marginalized by apartheid, should take priority. The mismanagement of resources and government bureaucracy could end if we all work toward social equality. It is simply not enough for the Constitution to say that schools will be funded equally, when, in fact, some schools were already privileged by apartheid laws. I support Sonia Nieto's insight that, in order to create better education for all students, we should eliminate what she calls resource gaps in our public schools.[76] Nieto maintains that we should provide students with all the resources necessary to reach their full potential. Indeed, as Nieto argues, working toward democracy also means adopting conscious decisions to end social poverty by opening the doors of learning to all students, a mantra that was dominant in the 1980s during the People's Education Movement in South Africa. Increased funding of poor schools, with efficient mechanisms to distribute resources, elimination of racism and acculturation in privileged, formerly White-only schools, could help end parental choice dilemmas, and transferring students from poor schools to wealthy schools, because all neighbourhoods would have adequate resources and maintain the positive cultural understanding needed to live and function together. Even where there are legitimate reasons for parents to engage in choice, let there be no student who is denied access to a school of their choice simply because they could not afford it or did not know about school fee waivers. Let all our public schools receive funding equity and wealthy schools provide access to its resources for the liberty principle in education to truly liberate all students.

Notes for Chapter 9

1. An earlier version of this piece appears in *Perspectives in Education* 24, no. 2 (2006): 143–56.

2. I am deeply indebted to Jonathan Jansen and Kristen Buras who provided thoughtful, and at times provocative, comments on this essay. Anne Rene Elsbree and Jessica Karstetter also provided comments on various parts of the essay. I am also grateful to Walter Feinberg and Christopher Lubienski who invited me to the School Choice Conference at the University of Illinois at Urbana-Champaign. The serious discussions which emerged at this conference helped me realize vexing issues in my own analysis on school choice and education policy.

3. Anthony Rolle and Eric A. Houk, "Introduction to the Peabody Journal of Education's Special Issue on the Future of School Finance Research," *Peabody Journal of Education* 79, no. 3 (2004): 2.

4. Rolle and Houk's comments were directed to Patrick J. McEwan's findings that school "choice" in the United States produced unequal student learning outcomes. See Patrick J. McEwan, "The Potential Impact of Vouchers," *Peabody Journal of Education*, 79, no. 3 (2004): 57–80.

5. Frank Molteno, "The Historical Foundations of the Schooling of Black South Africans," in *Apartheid and Education: The Education of Black South Africans*, ed. Peter Kallaway, 00–00 (Johannesburg: Ravan Press, 1984).

6. See Peter Kallaway, *Apartheid and Education: The Education of Black South Africans*, (Johannesburg: Ravan, 1984); Peter Kallaway, *The History of Education under Apartheid 1948–1994: "The Doors of Learning and Culture Shall Be Opened* (Cape Town: Maskew Miller Longman, 2002); Pam Christie, *The Right to Learn: The Struggle for Education in South Africa.* (Braamfontein, Johannesburg: Ravan Press, 1985).

7. There were other major changes in educational policy simultaneously taking place, which were precipitated by the mass mobilization of Black students and community activists. The People's Education Movement of the mid 1980s and early 1990s is an example. See Shireen Motala and Salim Vally, "People's Education: For peoples' Power to Tirisano," in *The History of Education under Apartheid 1948—1994: "The Doors of Learning and Culture Shall Be Opened*, ed. Peter Kallaway (Cape Town: Maskew Miller Longman, 2002); Mokubung Nkomo, "Introduction" in *Pedagogy of Domination: Toward a Democratic Education in South Africa* (Trenton, NJ: Africa World Press, 1990), 1–15.

8. Salim Vally and Yolisa Dalamba, *Racism, "Racial Integration' and Desegregation in South African Public Secondary Schools* (Education Policy Unit, Johannesburg: University of the Witwatersrand, 1999); David MacFarlane, "South African Education's Marginalised Millions," *Mail & Guardian*, April 19, 2002, http://www.mg.co.za.

9. Jonathan D. Jansen, "Does Money Matter? Towards an Explanation for the Relationship between Spending and Performance in Education in South Africa" (paper, Institute for Justice and Reconciliation, Cape Town, 2005).

10. Yusef Sayed, "Post-apartheid Educational Transformation: Policy Concerns and Approaches," in *Implementing Education Policies: The South African Experience*, ed. Yusef Sayed and Jonathan D. Jansen, 00–00 (Cape Town: University of Cape Town Press, 2001).

11. These mantras are stated in the South African Schools Act of 1996 document and in the Constitution itself.

12. Pierre Bourdieu, *Distinction: A Social Critique of the Judgment of Taste* (Cambridge, MA: Harvard University Press, 1984).

13. Let me acknowledge Kristen Buras who reminded me that while Black parents do have every right to send their children to any public school in the nation, it is also important to make clear that they should not have to pursue options in the suburbs. These families have a right to well-funded schools in the immediate vicinity. Without this clarification, "choice" may appear as the answer rather than adequately funding the schools in all communities.

14. Bekisizwe S. Ndimande, "Cows and Goats No Longer Count as Inheritances: The Politics of School "Choice" in Post-apartheid South Africa" (PhD diss., University of Wisconsin-Madison, 2005).

15. Jonathan D. Jansen, "Access and Values in Education" (paper, Saamtrek Conference on values, education, and democracy in the 21st century, Kirtenbosch, Cape Town, 2001).

16. Michael W. Apple, *Educating the "Right" Way: Markets, Standards, God, and Inequalities* (New York: Routledge, 2001).

17. I borrow from Kevin Kumashiro, who defines "Other" as the term that refers to those groups that are traditionally marginalised, that is, the groups that are not normalized by the dominant discourse of that society. See Kevin K. Kumashiro, "Toward a Theory of Anti-oppressive education," *Review of Educational Research* 70, no. 1 (2000): 25–53.

18. Christie, *The Right to Learn*, 98. Data for the years between 1983 and 1984 were taken from Nkomo, *Pedagogy of Domination: Toward a Democratic Education in South Africa*, 317.

19. Christie, *The Right to Learn*; Nkomo, *Pedagogy of Domination*.

20. South African Schools Act, *Government Gazette of the Republic of South Africa* 377, no. 84 (November 15, 1996): 1.

21. I am mindful that the educational system is not a dependent variable influenced by the dynamics of the state. Wong and Apple note there are possibilities that the educational system will work in ways counter to the [democratic] intentions of the state. See Ting-Hong Wong and Michael W. Apple, "Rethinking the Education/State Formation Connection: The State, Cultural Struggles, and Changing the School," in *The State and the Politics of Knowledge*, ed. Michael W. Apple, 00–00 (New York: Routledge, 2003).

22. Jonathan D. Jansen, "Why Outcomes-based Education Will Fail: An Elaboration," in *Changing Curriculum*, ed. Jonathan D. Jansen and Pam Christie, 00–00 (Kenwyn, South Africa: Juta, 1999); Jonathan D. Jansen, "Race and education after ten years," *Perspectives in Education* 22, no. 4 (2004): 117–28; Joel Samoff, " 'Education for All' in Africa but Education Systems That Serve Few Well," *Perspectives in Education* 19, no. 1 (2001): 5–28; Sayed, "Post-apartheid Educational Transformation"; C. Soudien, H. Jacklin and U. Hoadley, "Policy Values: Problematising Equity and Redress in Education," in *Implementing Education Policies: The South African Experience*, ed. Yusef Sayed and Jonathan D. Jansen, 00–00 (Cape Town: University of Cape Town Press, 2001).

23. Vally and Dalamba, *Racism, "Racial Integration" and Desegregation*.

24. Ibid., 17.

25. Christie, *The Right to Learn*.

26. Jansen, "Does Money Matter?"

27. Ibid., 6.

28. Jonathan D. Jansen's "Does Money Matter?" is absolutely crucial for those interested in government spending on public education and other social functions.

29. MacFarlane, "South African Education's Marginalised Millions."

30. Sayed, "Post-apartheid Educational Transformation."

31. Ibid., 251.

32. Patrick Bond, "From Racial to Class Apartheid: South Africa's Frustrating Decade of Freedom," *Monthly Review* 55, no. 10 (2004): 45–59; William Mervin Gumede, *Thabo Mbeki and the Battle for the Soul of the ANC* (Cape Town: Zebra Press, 2005); Devan Pillay, "Between the Market and a Hard Place," *Sunday Times*, October 6, 2002.

33. See, for example, Apple, *Educating the "Right" Way*; Stephen J. Ball, Richard Bowe, and Sharon Gewirtz, "Market Forces and the Parental Choice: Self-interest and Competitive Advantage in Education," in *Educational Reform and Its Consequences*, ed. Sally Tomlinson (London: IPPR/Rivers Oram Press, 1994); Bond, "From Racial to Class Apartheid"; Noam Chomsky, *Profit over People: Neoliberalism and Global Order* (New York: Seven Stories Press, 1999); Barbara Garson, *Johannesburg and New Jersey Water*, http://www.nyenvirolaw.org/pdf/Garson-newjerseyand johannesburgwater.pdf (accessed December 2002); Hugh Lauder and David Hughes, *Trading in Futures: Why Markets in Education Don't Work* (Philadelphia: Open University Press, 1999); Geoff Whitty, Sally Power and David Halpin, *Devolution and Choice in Education* (Philadelphia: Open University Press, 1998).

34. Apple, *Educating the "Right" Way*, 38.

35. I would like to acknowledge Jonathan Jansen for reminding me of the often forgotten nontuition cost of participation in these schools, other than just transportation.

36. I am certainly not making an argument that parental "choice" is a positive undertaking and am certainly not its proponent either. Rather, I believe that "choice" in education has long-term negative effects on marginalized communities. See, for example, Michael W. Apple and Thomas C. Pedroni, "Conservative Alliance Building and African American Support of Vouchers: The End of *Brown*'s Promise or a New Beginning?" *Teachers College Record* 107, no. 9 (2005): 2068–105; Ball, Bowe, and Gewirtz, "Market Forces and the Parental Choice"; Lauder and Hughes, *Trading in Futures*; Christopher Lubienski, "The Politics of Parental Choice: Theory and Evidence on Quality Information" (paper, School Choice Policies and Outcomes Around the Globe, University of Illinois at Urbana-Champaign, Champaign, IL, March 31–April 1, 2006); Whitty, Power, and Halpin, *Devolution and Choice*; and others, who have provided thoughtful arguments and empirical evidence regarding how school choice is framed along individualistic and consumer perspective, which negate any thought around the broader socioeconomic and political issues that affect education.

37. Vally and Dalamba, *Racism, "Racial Integration" and Desegregation*.

38. Ibid., 17.

39. Bourdieu, *Distinction*, 134.

40. In a Bourdieuan sense, cultural capital is the production of class privilege where power is transmitted largely within families through economic property. Further, it is ways of understanding and acting on the world that acts forms of cultural capital that can be and are employed to protect and enhance one's status in a social field of power.

41. Transcript, CD, April 8, 2003. The name of the school and the location of the data company are all pseudonyms.

42. For a detailed discussion of Black parents who transfer their children from poor township public schools to better-resourced formerly White-only schools in the suburban areas. See Ndimande, "Cows and Goats No Longer Count as Inheritances."

43. It was striking to notice that throughout the interviews, parents did not use the phrase "formerly" when referring to formerly White-only schools in the suburban areas. Using such language is not a simple misunderstanding of the new changes (that schools have been desegregated). Rather, this may suggest a profound way to show the unequal socioeconomic landscapes regarding who has access to what kinds of schools. It may also imply that although they send their children to these schools, Black parents do not see themselves as co-owners because of the attitude and the manner in which these schools relate to them.

44. Transcript, KM FG, June 5, 2003.

45. Transcript, DE, March 17, 2003.

46. Some readers may argue that the first and second questions are similar, but they are not. Asking what is good or bad about something is not equivalent to asking why you choose or do not choose something. Of course, there may be overlapping answers to these.

47. Transcript GH 1, April 1, 2003.

48. Transcript AB, March 20, 2003.

49. This is a pseudonym.

50. Transcript, KL, March 8, 2003.

51. Transcript, LM, March 27, 2003.

52. Transcript, AB, March 20, 2003.

53. See, for instance, the argument invoked by Jansen regarding the role played by overseas consultants in developing options for the financing of public education in postapartheid South Africa. (Jonathan D. Jensen, "Political Symbolism as a Policy Craft: Explaining Non-reform in South African Education after Apartheid," *Journal of Education Policy* 17, no. 2 (2002): 199–215.)

54. Apple, *Educating the "Right" Way.*

55. Ibid.

56. Transcript, KL_GO, March 8, 2003.

57. Ibid.

58. According to Statistics South Africa, the official unemployment rate was 26.2 percent in September 2004. Statistics South Africa further shows the "expanded definition of unemployment," meaning discouraged workseekers, which have pushed the number to 41 percent in September 2004. Given the demographic representation of the nation, this number reflects high percentage of Black people without employment.

59. Stephen J. Ball, *Class Strategies and Educational Market: The Middle Classes and Social Advantage* (London: Routledge, 2003); Lauder and Hughes, *Trading in Futures;* Whitty, Power, and Halpin, *Devolution and Choice.*

60. Although I understand Samoff's overall point, the claim still seems questionable. The difference is not solely money. We should not too easily collapse class and race. I show elsewhere (Ndimande, "Cows and Goats No Longer Count as Inheritances") that even when Black students pay all the required

fee and gain access, racial divisions still prevail. See also Vally and Dalamba, *Racism, "Racial Integration" and Desegregation*; and Jansen, "Race and Education after Ten Years."

61. Ndimande, "Cows and Goats No Longer Count as Inheritances."

62. Ibid.

63. Although I must hasten to mention that Soudien, et al. were referring to public schools in the Western Cape, the trend seems to be the same throughout the nation's provinces.

64. Jansen, "Access and Values in Education," 2.

65. The term "nativism" is associated with the immigration policy in the United States, whereby native born, White, English speaking groups hold the belief that the borders should be tightly monitored through immigration laws so that the "Other" may not be allowed to enter. In essence, nativism is tied to the struggles of who can claim the right to land or the right to resources and wealth of the land. It is embedded in the politics of socioeconomic and political domination of one group over others. Thus most of the views about land, wealth, and resources held by nativists tend to be racist. Unlike in the United States, immigration laws were not invoked to monitor land in South Africa, although the Group Areas Act served that purpose. The nativism of the British and the Afrikaners toward the Indigenous peoples was declared mainly through the 1913 and 1936 Land Acts, in which all the White groups claimed the right to the land to a degree that indigenous groups were stripped off of their ancestral land.

66. Jansen, "Race and Education after Ten Years"; Vally and Dalamba, *Race, "Racial Integration" and Desegregation*; Ndimande, "Cows and Goats No Longer Count as Inheritances."

67. Apple, *Educating the "Right" Way*, 48.

68. Apple, *Educating the "Right" Way*; Ball, Bowe, and Gewirtz, "Market Forces and the Parental Choice"; David Gillborn and Deborah Youdell, *Rationing Education: Policy, Practice, Reform and Equity* (Philadelphia: Open University Press, 2000); Whitty, Power, and Halpin, *Devolution and Choice*.

69. Gumede, *Thabo Mbeki*, 90.

70. Pushing toward a market oriented economic program benefits corporate interest (Chomsky, *Profit over People*) and has consequential effects on social programs that are intended to help the majority of the people, not just a few who have the privilege to participate in the markets. My argument here is that even when there are no budget cuts, neoliberal driven policies can (re)produce negative effects because of their opposition to democratic principles. See for example, McChesney who argues that neoliberalism across the world is opposed to participatory democracy and helps create a society with individuals who feel demoralized and socially powerless. (R. W. McChesney, Introduction to Noam Chomsky, *Profit over People*, 7–16.)

71. Brock-Utne provides an analysis of World Bank and IMF driven structural adjustments in various countries of Africa, documenting how these adjustments have brought increasing poverty in these countries. See Birgit Brock-Utne, *Whose Education for All?: The Recolonization of the African Mind* (New York: Falmer Press, 2000.)

72. Ball, Bowe, and Gewirtz, "Market Forces and the Parental Choice."

73. Bond, "From Racial to Class Apartheid"; Gumede, *Thabo Mbeki*; Pillay, "Between the Market and a Hard Place."

74. Garson, *Johannesburg and New Jersey Water*.

75 Ndimande, "Cows and Goats No Longer Count as Inheritances"; Vally and Dalamba, *Racism, "Racial Integration" and Desegration*.

76. Sonia Nieto, "Creating New Visions for Teacher Education: Educating for Solidarity, Courage, and Heart" (paper, American Association of Colleges for Teacher Education [AACTE], San Diego, CA, January 30, 2006).

Chapter 10

The Dialectic of Parent Rights and Societal Obligation

Constraining Educational Choice

Walter Feinberg

Introduction

While the idea of school choice and vouchers originated in the 1960s and 1970s with the writing of Milton Friedman, and Coons & Sugarman,[1] the policy itself developed in part as a response to an increase in government involvement in education. During the 1960s and the 1970s the federal government became increasingly active on behalf of minority and historically oppressed groups. Desegregation and school busing orders to achieve racial integration, as well as the mandated mainstreaming of children with disabilities, were added to court-ordered abolition of school prayer. These policies generated considerable backlash and in part the appeal of choice can be explained as a part of this backlash.

Yet, behind the emotional appeal is a much deeper philosophical principle that has yet to be raised to the surface of the debate and adequately defended against other, competing principles. The principle I have in mind is the claim that parents have a right to educate their own children in the manner they see fit and that the state must serve largely to facilitate parents' educational aims. Given this principle, school choice appeals to many different kinds of parents: religious parents who want their children to learn to be pious and love God; ambitious parents who want their children to excel academically or at sports, minority parents who want their children to appreciate their own cultural heritage; and parents whose children are confined to an

219

unsatisfactory neighborhood school. By satisfying this principle, choice can satisfy every one of these parents and, by exercising their own right to choose, each of these parents, in turn, is recognizing the right of all other parents to do the same for their child. Choice then, may be seen as a principled response to policies like bussing, forced integration, and the rejection of prayer. To its supporters school choice places the critical decision of where and how to educate children back into the hands of parents, where it belongs.

However, a parent's interest is not the only interest that counts. For example, Brighouse is a proponent of choice, not only and perhaps not even primarily, because he accepts a parent's right to educate their own child, but also because he believes it is possible to arrange choice in a way that can advance equality.[2] Since choice policy is not only about the right to educate one's child, but also about the claim on public resources and tax dollars to support that right, the larger social concern makes sense. Hence the claim, of parents for the right to educate their children as they see fit, must compete with the claim of society that each of its members has a stake in the education of other people's children. I call this conflict and its possible resolution the dialectic of parental rights and social responsibility.

The stakes in this dance between individual rights and social obligation are magnified when society is asked to foot the bill, but its significance is not dependent on the question of who pays the bill. A society's continued existence depends on the reproduction of basic skills, attitudes and understandings from one generation to the next.[3] In addition, children have a stake in their own future independent of the stake of their parents. In this essay, I explore each of these stakes more closely, the principles that support them, and then I evaluate different choice policies. I argue that choice can best meet these two demands when it operates within a background of taxation that takes into account differences in the ability of parents to educationally advantage their children, and that provides incentives for that advantage to be shared.

Retail versus Wholesale Choice

We need to differentiate between choice on both the retail level and wholesale level. On the retail level, choice refers to the options available to individual children as a result of a serious mismatch between child and school. When exercised on the retail level, choice is not an option that is widely publicized, and it is not generally available for students who are having some minor adjustment difficulty. It is undertaken as a result of negotiation between the school and the parent. The school is not punished if it is exercised, and choice is undertaken with the stability of the school, as well as the well-being of the child in mind. It is retail because it is available, but not widely used. On the wholesale level, choice is promoted as a national policy designed to further a national agenda. It is triggered by an automatic mechanism, such as the average scores on a standardized test or the income of parents. The school is not a partner in the negotiation, and it likely is undertaken to penalize the school for student performance and without concern for school stability. Retail choice is familiar to many people committed to public education, and it makes considerable sense. It is not available just on a whim, and the fact that it is available only at the margins communicates to students the importance of commitment and persistence. Wholesale choice takes away the role of the school in the negotiation and, should it become too easy, may actually diminish the child's sense of responsibility for her own work, commitment to the school, and to other students.

It is important to note this difference. On the wholesale level, choice makes intuitive sense because it borrows sentiments connected to choice on the retail level. However, on the one hand, there is a big difference between a program that allows dissatisfied students to exit one school and enter another after reasonable means to correct the problem have been made. On the other hand, having a government policy that supports choice on a system level, actually encourages students to exit schools when they are dissatisfied or fail. Most people understand that there can be a bad match between a school or a teacher and a student that would support choice as an exception to the general policy. However, many of these same people would find wholesale choice puzzling because of the resources involved, the tone it sets, and the instability it introduces. Hence, choice on the wholesale level should involve considerably more deliberation than choice on the retail level. It is important to keep this distinction in mind when exploring the basic principles at play in wholesale choice schemes because what is justified on the retail level may need different kinds of justifications on the wholesale level.

In the following section I explore the implications of the principle of a parent's right to educate her own child, and show how that right is limited by two other principles, the obligation of society to provide a level playing field, and the right of a child to autonomy, or an open future. These three principles can be played out in different ways, and autonomy can attach itself to either a public or a private education—and both can deny it as well. Private schools can insist on shaping students towards a certain set of religious or ideological beliefs, and public schools can encourage conformity and discourage creativity. There are differences, however, which are discussed in a more general way in the final section of this chapter.

Why Does a Parent Have a Right to Educate Her Own Child?

The right of a parent to educate his or her own child has not been universally recognized. Plato thought it bred selfishness, and Marx thought it contributed to capitalist greed. Some forms of education, the Israeli kibbutz for example, have attempted to minimize parental involvement in education and to make the education of each and every child a communal affair, under the principle that every child is the child of everyone. Even John Rawls, the principle philosopher of contemporary liberalism, argues that a child's talents are matters of accident and how they are to be developed has communal implications.[4] While Rawls does not reject a parent's right to educate their children and develop their child's talents, he argues that the development of such talents should be constrained by both the principles of justice and the needs of the least advantaged person. In societies like our own, committed to equality, but in which resources for education such as the best schools, teachers, et cetera are limited, and providing the best for one means providing less for others, there is obviously a need to justify, on some societal basis, the intergenerational advantage that one parent provides for her own child at the disadvantage of other children.

The two principles are thus in tension. If my means allow me to educate my children in the very best schools, while you are restricted to educating yours in a minimally adequate one, then I satisfy my right and your child is denied equality. Similarly, if the state insists on equality, then my right to educate my child to the best of my ability will be frustrated. Of course, from one side, it is easy to dismiss the other as greedy and insensitive to a larger social responsibility—the other as intrusive and dictatorial. Yet, in truth, both of these positions make sense from a social and individual point of view. There are many reasons society wants me to educate my child to the best of my ability, and there are also many reasons for society to want for your child equal opportunity to advance. However, satisfying one means denying the satisfaction of the other.

The strongest argument for allowing me to educate my own children occurs where I am investing my own funds and asking nothing from society at large. Using society's resources in the form of public funds complicates matters, but the social benefits are still the same. I invest in my own child's education and society benefits. If my child becomes a wonderful poet, a fabulous musician, a teacher, or even a doctor or a lawyer, she will develop a skill that will benefit many. The social benefits of my private investment are bountiful. Few object when these benefits are simply an indirect result of living in a certain kind of home. Michael Jordan's child will have an advantage over mine (even given equal talent) when it comes to playing basketball and Yo-Yo Ma's child will have a big advantage in playing the cello. Few would object to these advantages as they are transmitted within families. They enrich the lives of us all.

Moreover, even outside of a single family, other children can profit from my investment. When education takes place in a communal setting—a school and a classroom—any advantage I provide for my child is likely to be provided for other children as well. Michael Jordan is likely to insist on a school hiring a good coach and Yo-Yo Ma's is not likely to tolerate a school with an inadequate music program. If I am willing to buy a more expensive house in a better school district where my property tax will pay the salaries of good teachers, other children in that school will benefit. My sacrifice is even greater if, in order to get into a better educational district, I must pay higher school taxes. These taxes contribute to hiring better teaches who then instruct many more children than my own. The higher salaries may also draw more people into education and thus contribute to a more skilled teaching force for everyone. Finally, the value that I place on education is likely to be contagious, and other parents may, as a result, come to value education more, forming a synergy that raises the quality of education even higher. Thus it is that society reaps the benefits of the investment I make in my child's education. Clearly, my child also benefits and because my child benefits, I too am happy. However, my happiness should not detract from the benefits society receives from my investment. In addition to the social benefits that my investment yields, there is an equally important one that benefits every parent.

Most every parent wants to do the best by her children, and by affirming my right to do so, I am also affirming the right of every other parent to do the same. By asserting my right, I contribute to a fortification against the state interfering with the rights of all parents. This is the deepest argument for choice, much deeper than the questionable view that parents always know what is best for their children—a claim disputed in many cases by children who regret their parent's choices for them. Individual parents have a big stake in protecting my right to provide the best education possible for my own child, not because I will always know what is best, but because in protecting my right their own is protected as well.

Granted, to the extent that you and your children are not like me, it is likely that you will not fully benefit from my child's wonderful education. To the extent that you are different from me—you speak a different language, have a dialect I must strain to understand, do not mow your lawn on the same schedule that I mow mine, go to a different church, wear different kinds of clothes, listen to louder music—it is likely that I will not want to live near you and will not be interested in having your children attend school with my children. And, if I am successful in excluding your children from my children's school, then your children will not benefit very much from the extra investment that I am making in my children's education. In fact, in so far as I can outbid you and the likes of you for better teachers, newer buildings, more up to date texts and more able coaches, my investment will detract from your children's education.

Moreover, to the extent that my investment is successful, my children will come to like people who are like me (and them) and not like you (and yours). That is, they will like people who speak the same language in the same way, go to the same church, wear similar cloths, listen to the same music at about the same volume and mow the lawn with the same regularity. Hence my children and the children of parents like me form a we, a community of people with similar values and similar tastes, and the skills developed as a result of their education will form the cultural and intellectual capital of that community. You may benefit on the margins, as for example when one of our lawyers defends you in an accident case, or one of our doctors repairs you after an accident, but your benefits are marginal. You are the defendant, the patient, we are the lawyers, the doctors. If you are lucky you may pay our fees only once, but we will continue to collect the fees of you and your kind forever. And what about our children? Well, just as my father had a special right to advantage me so I have a special right to advantage my children and my children will have a special right to advantage theirs. You must realize of course that you have that same right, even if your means to carry it out are not the same. And so, my children will find themselves incorporated into my community while yours will be incorporated into your community. What is fair is fair.

Social Obligation from the Standpoint of the Advantaged Parent: A Question of Fairness

Sadly, what is fair in my mind may not be so fair in yours and some people find the lottery of the womb, to use Warren Buffett's term,[5] unreasonable. In your mind, my children did nothing to deserve their advantages and your children did nothing to merit their disadvantages.

Indeed, you may even be thinking that the fact that my children are involved in a network of skills disadvantages your children even more. You may think that their "undeserved" privilege makes it more difficult for your children to realize their talents as writers, poets, painters, to say nothing of doctors and lawyers. And, if I were in your position (which I am not) I might even think the same thing. However, I probably cannot count on correcting your way of thinking and hence must find ways to accommodate it.

I know enough social science to understand that when, in the aggregate, people like you have life chances that are radically different than those of people like me and, when you cannot see any rhyme or reason to these differences, when you do not believe that they are serving your ends, you may begin to despair. And, when you feel also that there is no hope for your children or your children's children, hopelessness may travel across generations and turn into rage. And, if you or your children come to believe that the fault lies *not* in yourselves nor in your stars but in a wall of undeserved privilege that I have and you do not, the very stability that sustains us all is threatened.

Because I do not want this threat to materialize, I may begin to rethink my position in one or more possible ways. I may fear the resentment and social destabilization that might arise from your despair and your child's hopelessness, and may begin to question the right of my children to undeserved privilege; Or, I may just feel that it is harmful for children to grow up with excessive privilege. Or, I may understand that my competence as a doctor, lawyer, et cetera, depends on the competence and trust of a long line of people from the janitors who clean the building and dispose of the waste, to the pharmacist who serves as a check on my possible mistakes. In this I come to understand that my work depends on their education. I may also realize that in advancing my less competent children over your more competent ones, I am placing my own future health and well being in danger. And, I may also begin to question the link that provides a special and ever lasting tie of blood, say rather than talent or character to one set of children and not others. In any event, the fact that I want to advantage my children need not blind me to the concern that you have to do the same for yours. The above is somewhat of an ideal of course and in reality this insight may need some encouragement. Nevertheless, my realization that you are not completely powerless provides a kernel of recognition and is the beginning of equality. When I realize that I must depend on you and yours for security and comfort, then I recognize that the education of your children is important to me. (Today this is called human capital.)

Fairness from the Standpoint of the Educationally Disadvantaged

The chain is seen differently from the other side. The parent of the educationally disadvantaged love their children as much as those of the educationally advantaged love theirs, and, whatever the logic may be, they find it hard to understand how a society, where opportunity depends so much on education, can allow the children of the advantaged to inherit educational privilege from their parents at the expense of the education of the disadvantaged. To them, the person who splits hairs over a right and a privilege is a wealthy parent or a philosopher, one of those logic choppers who profess neutrality.

The parents of the educationally disadvantaged see few good reasons why wealthy children should inherit undeserved advantages. Because they begin from a position of perpetual disadvantage, their impulse for equality is stronger than their willingness to grant an unfettered right to rich, as well as to poor to provide the best education possible for their children, because their right is already fettered. They may even reason that unconstrained advantage not only diminishes opportunities for their children, it harms the advantaged child, contributing to insensitivity, selfishness, isolation, and poor character. This is what Freire likely meant when he claimed that the oppressed must liberate the oppressor.

Educational advantages can trickle down as the advantaging parent argued, but the price is high. Children of the poor, who are sick in just the right way, can receive medical attention from the services of educationally advantaged physicians but the treatment of hunger, malnutrition, loss of heat in the winter, or dehydration from loss of air conditioning in the summer, is not normally treated or covered in the diagnostic manual. Hence, for the parent of the educationally disadvantaged, the obligation of society to level the playing field takes precedent over the right to advantage one's own child. Given their present condition, a principle of equality must be acknowledged first, in order to properly constrain an undisciplined desire to provide the very best education for one's own child at the cost of the education of other children.

The Social Interest Defined

The social interest in our (your and my) children's education is to be found in those positions where there is not a direct concern regarding which of our children is educationally advantaged and which is disadvantaged, but rather in how our children ultimately use their educational advantage. These socially interested positions are not just some abstract neutral fiction. They are the positions of real people—people who will need doctors, lawyers, legislators, as well as a generally safe and civil environment. They are we at our most needy and they are we at our most interdependent. The interests here range from a concern for an appropriate level of stability, one that allows others to make plans with reasonable expectations that they will be carried out, to advancing the quality of social life from basic services such as health care, to the moral quality of life, such as the treatment of strangers and those who are different than we are; to the excitement of sports, and the grace, insight, and beauty of art.

Society, as such, benefits when an investment in the education of a child contributes to social stability and to moral and creative progress. It does not benefit to the extent that the education of one group serves to block the development of the talent of another or when stability is severely disrupted. Its interest differs from the minimal interest in the education of the less advantaged that characterized the concern of the more advantaged for their own security and competence. Society has an interest in its own development and hence it has a strong interest in promoting the development of all its members regardless of their initial advantage.

Society clearly is served when private wealth is used to serve this interest, but social efficiency and justice is served best when social wealth is directed unevenly toward those children who cannot be provided with the benefits of private wealth. For example, the public cost of teaching the child of a college professor to read will be less than that of teaching the child of an immigrant laborer to read simply because of the material available in the home environment. Yet the social benefits can be the same. Hence from a social efficiency as well as a social justice point of view there is a social advantage in equity directed policies.

Social Interests, Limited Markets and Choice

The social interest in education is expressed in even the most conservative proposals for choice by the fact that education is singled out as its own market. Parents are not provided money to spend in any way they like. They are directed to spend it on something that passes for an educational experience and, more specifically, something like a school. This is an important, yet, overlooked fact about choice policies. The fact that choice stipulates the kind of market in which a parent can spend public funds—an educational market—is an expression of a social interest.

Some choice proposals only half-heartedly recognize this interest[6] and are willing to give up accountability to market factors alone. If enough parents do not choose a school, then under this view, the school will go under and all interests will be served. A social interest is recognized but monitored only through private preferences. The problem is even more visible in the case of religious schools, many of which, as Reich suggests,[7] may well serve common social goals, but nevertheless, where social accountability is restricted because of concerns about religious freedom. The fact that society has a special interest in education also means that it has an interest in what schools do and in what ends they serve. At the very least, in a highly technological society, one where change is a general rule and where older forms of life are always under considerable pressure from newer ones, including new inventions—technological and moral—society has a considerable interest in the development of reflective and critical thinking skills and consensus building abilities. In other words it has an interest in the development of autonomy.

The Child's Interest in Autonomy

Children share this interest in the development of their own autonomy, and in their own future as open-ended. Because parents may sometimes serve to close off that interest, either because they view the child narcissistically as an extension of themselves or because they have limited understanding of alternative forms of life, a child has an interest in limiting her parent's right to control her education. In other words, while she has a strong interest in maintaining the love, care, and nurturance of her parents, she also has a strong interest in limiting their control of her own education and finding additional sources of guidance, inspiration and growth.

The Private School Conundrum

Each one of these interests, that of the advantaged and the disadvantaged parent, that of society and that of the child, all speak to both the right of a parent to select their child's own education and the need to limit and constrain that right toward both equality and autonomy. Most choice policies address only the first part of this dialectic, although a few[8] have attempted to insert rules that would tame choice in the direction of equality. All of these attempts run into the problem of private schools, or the fact that in most liberal western societies wealthy parents can escape from public education entirely by paying for a high priced private education for their children. The penalty for doing so is slight, no greater, than the taxes paid by childless people to maintain a public education system.

A private system also has the negative impact of reducing the inclination of parents to adequately support the public schools. And because a private school can escape most of the requirements of public education, deciding who to accept, who to reject, who to keep, who to expel, and what kind of religious or ethnic groups to preference in the hiring of teachers and the selection of students, it has the likely effect of reducing the effectiveness of the public school system. This need not be the case, as some of the essays in this volume suggest[9] is true, but without further constraints, it is not something that the public can rely on.

A choice policy that accepts private schools can move in one of two directions, but there are costs to each. It can move in the direction of parents' rights and eliminate any means test allowing all parents to send their children to whatever school they choose with the state providing public funds but setting minimal standards and no accountability. To move in this direction advantages the already advantaged providing them with an additional state provided educational bonus. To move in the other direction by exerting a lot of state control on schools—limiting who they can accept, and reject, who they can keep and expel, requiring ethnic and social class integration, monitoring classrooms, requiring certain levels of achievement, establishing universal hiring standards and moving teachers around according to need, et cetera—provides incentives for advantaged parents to abandon the public school system altogether, or to move to homogeneous districts. In this situation, while the public school segment and choice moves in the direction of equality, the private system becomes a larger piece of the whole, and when public and private schools are taken together, the result is that inequality increases.

The availability of private schools creates an additional problem for equity minded reformers. Most public schools in the United States are funded primarily through local property taxes and this means there are considerable discrepancies between funds provided for children in wealthy and in poor districts. One proposed solution to this inequity is to shift the source of funding from the local to the state level, substituting income tax funds for property tax support. The argument is that state funding would then be provided to schools on an equal basis.

The argument makes sense if equality is the only value at stake, and it might also make sense if private schools were not an option. However, there are other values that need to be considered. One of them is the value derived from high-quality public schools. Under this proposal, the loss of public funds must be accompanied by a serious reduction in local control, and an increased incentive for those who can afford it to send their children to private schools. As the children of these parents leave public schools, these schools loose their major supporters. As these parents increase their spending on private schools, they are less willing to be taxed for public education, and the quality of public education will likely decline. California has served as a test case for this in the recent past where, when it switched funding from the local to the state level, the quality of schools declined from one of the highest in the nation to one of the lowest. Hence, centralized funding alone is an inadequate solution.

The critical question for educational policy is how to treat this dialectic of parental right and social obligation so as to maintain both parents' rights to educate their own children and society's obligation to even the playing field and provide a reasonable level of equality. The existence of private schools, reasonably justified both on grounds of parents' rights as well as a concern over undue pressures for conformity or nonautonomy,[10] means that policy innovation must work under the constraints that they provide. Moreover, the public has a stake, and can benefit from the investment of private individuals in the education of their own children. Hence, private schools are defensible from the standpoint of the public good as well as from the standpoint of parental rights, and opportunities for autonomy in some instances (in the form of non conformity). Nevertheless they create problems for equality and for any choice policy that intends to advance equality. And, they can in other instances create problems for autonomy (in the form of rigid, ideologically driven private or religious schools).

Choice and the Tide against Equality

Some argue that choice will tilt the scale in favor of equality because parental choice and the possibility of selecting a better school for one's child will provide poorer parents with the same opportunities that middle-class and wealthier parents receive when they decide to change from one neighborhood or district to another for the sake of a better school. While the essays in this volume have not refuted that argument, they have shown that markets alone are unlikely to fulfill its promise and that many additional mechanisms will need to be in place before a significant tilt toward equality is possible.

Indeed, in the United States, it is important to see just how the definition of equality has been changed by the kind of debate that is carried on to measure the success of choice. For example, the debate in Milwaukee is about whether children in underfunded choice schools do better than children in underfunded nonchoice schools. It is not how these children compare to those in the wealthier suburbs. Indeed, if choice has accomplished one unambiguous thing, it has been to change the focus of the debate and to accept the view that inner-city schools are inner-city schools, and that achievement there means something different than it does elsewhere. Given the tone of the debate in the 1960s, 1970s, and 1980s, this is a remarkable, even if questionable, advance for a conservative agenda.

A dose of reality is in order here. With welfare on the rocks, health care and mental health care underfunded, single mothers required to be in the work force, and public housing on the decline, it is unlikely that poorer families will have the time or the resources to scout out the best school for their child, and, if they manage to do this, it is even less likely that they will have the time or the resources to transport their children far away from their neighborhood.[11] And, as we have seen, for parents without time and resources, preferences are not often formed independently without mediation. That the school should have a role in shaping a parent's idea about what is best for her child, as Bell shows they do,[12] should not be taken as some sinister plot to deprive poor children of their educational entitlement. However, school teachers and administrators are concerned with the climate of an entire school, not just the well being of one child, and that influences their call about what is best for any individual child. Children, whose parents have the time and the means to reshape a school's judgment, are, in the terms of the market, better positioned to enable their child to take advantage of the products marketed. The problem here is neither with parent child or teacher. It is with the assumption that preference formation is a neutral factor and that preferences are all equal. Some believe that religious and private schools can take up the slack, but it is questionable whether they can be effective once they are more than marginal institutions. Even as marginal institutions, their effectiveness, when compared to public schools, is in question.[13] As it stands, research on the effectiveness of choice is unclear.

The fact that the effectiveness of choice is uncertain in the present situation, where all choosers are voluntary and can be expected to have a focused interest in their children's education, is not promising. Under a full-scale choice program, the vast majority of choosers will be compelled to choose, and are not likely to have the same time, resources, or understanding of educational quality as those relatively few voluntary choosers who are active today. This is not to say that choice should be rejected, but that quality requires more than markets and choice should be a marginal part of a nation's educational policy. It can serve some children caught in an impossible situation, but it should not be seen as a cure for a problem that lies well outside of the control of individual schools and teachers, and well into the area of housing, health care, job creation, and preschool care.

Clearly, there are empirical claims imbedded in my argument, for example, choice will not have a significant impact on reducing the achievement gap or on poverty rates, and that these claims could prove wrong. However, assuming that choice has been oversold, does that mean it should not be adopted? One answer is that, even if it does not decrease the achievement gap or contribute to reduce poverty, choice should be given serious consideration because it satisfies the first principle—that parents have a right to educate their own children. However, the full answer depends on a number of factors. For example, in the context of a private, tuition-based pay educational segment, where wealthier parents can opt-out of public schools, a system that stresses strong equality would likely alienate more of these parents, leaving the public system worse off then it would be if ways were found to keep their children in the tax supported public schools.

Until recent court orders allowing tax funds to pay tuition at private and religious schools,[14] compromise allowed parents to opt-out of the public school system, but required that they, or the private school, in the form of tuition or grants, provide the financial means to do so.[15] The fact that these parents, like childless people, were still required to pay taxes to support public schools means that there was a tilt toward a common, tax-supported public education. The advantage of the earlier approach was that it allowed public scrutiny over the content and quality of education for the vast majority of students; public standards for hiring teachers; and public accountability for accepting or rejecting students. However, wealthy parents could opt-out of the system entirely by selecting private schools and somewhat less wealthy parents could choose to live in relatively exclusive areas where the schools had some of the characteristics of private schools, for example, income segregation.

The problem then is to find a choice policy that can allow private investment to advance the public good, as religious and private schools can do, while encouraging substantial equality by raising the educational standards of those whose performance falls below an acceptable level as a result of income inequality. Substantial equality requires that goals for individual students be established relatively independent of parental income, time or superior educational knowledge.[16] The goal is not to eliminate inequality, but to add to the resources of the less well-off in ways that diminish the significance of income disparity in terms of guidance, goal setting, and quality of instruction. Parents would not be discouraged from providing enriched education for their children in the form of travel, smaller classes, et cetera, but they could not do so independent of the situation of those less educationally advantage. For example, Bell and others in this volume show social class makes a big difference in the way educational preferences are shaped and children's educational potentials and needs defined.[17] A move toward substantial equality would require that as wealthier parents improve the quality of education for their children, some fraction of that improvement will be diverted to provide more independent guidance for the less advantaged schools.

A reasonable resolution to the problems that choice on the wholesale level raises needs to address the social, political, and economic context in which choice policies are being advanced. On one level, this context must examine the way inequality, and especially poverty, is addressed in general, and must include housing, health care, and other factors that make parenting under conditions of poverty traumatic for parent and child. An educational policy that focuses on academic achievement alone can be counterproductive, forcing schools that are addressing issues of poverty, such as parenting, education, health care, nutrition, and education, be classified as failures if children fail to measure up to some externally imposed standard of test performance. However, a reasonable resolution needs to address the educational context, and especially the fact that public education is operating within the context of increasing growth in private and religious schools, and that many of these schools are unregulated and unsupervised.

The Dialectic of Parental Rights and Social Obligation Reconstructed

A reasonable resolution must avoid two extremes, first, the extremes of leaning too much towards parent rights and short changing equality, and second, the extremes of leaning too close to equality and short changing parental rights. One way to strike a reasonable balance is to rethink two critical features of American education. The first is local support of schools, and the second is the distinction between private and public schools.

Local control has been strongly criticized by those whose primary concern is to reduce inequalities.[18] The argument is that local control provides choice but only to those who can afford to move out of one district and into another.[19] For a few very exclusive districts, this observation is absolutely true, but for many it is an exaggeration—granted one helpful in making a needed moral point—neglecting highly motivated families who will rent, or buy less adequate housing, to provide a high quality education for their children.

Still, the exaggeration is true enough to correctly highlight the disturbing fact that choice is vastly unequal for many school children and their parents. It also questions the fairness of having a child's future depend on the income or the motivation of her parents. One obvious resolution could be to rethink school districts and form them independent of housing costs. This solution, however, runs the risk, much like the income tax alternative to the property tax, of provoking an exodus from public schools, and along with it, the cultural and intellectual capital that educationally informed parents could provide for other children in the schools that their children attend. If this loss includes commitment to educational quality and the characteristics of good teaching, the loss is serious. To the extent that private school might be even more homogeneous than the locally controlled public one, the policy is self-defeating in terms of the public interest in equality. While both the income tax and redistricting can provide part of the solution, by themselves they are not sufficient. Schools need to be provided with incentives to work for equity.

One way to think about a reasonable response to the opposition of parental rights and social obligation is to rethink what it means for school to be called public and private and to develop policies that provide special advantages to those schools that approach the public end of the scale and assess costs to those that are nearer the private end. For example the concept of public schools is associated with such features as open access to children of all social, economic, racial, and religious groups, and a reasonable chance that any given child will attend that school. To the extent that neighborhood or choice schools limit enrollment to certain kinds of students, they are less public than other schools that do not. Similarly, public schools set minimum standards for the hiring of teachers, and only teachers who meet those standards will be considered for positions in those schools. To the extent that special characteristics such as religion, race, or social class are preferred, they must be justified on public grounds or for reasons acceptable to the community as a whole (as they are in situations where affirmative action is called for). Also, a public school is accountable for retaining students, and cannot arbitrarily expel students or create environments where certain kinds of students will feel so unwelcome that they will want to leave on their own. A public school must be accountable to a body of citizens that represent a reasonable crosssection of the community and preferably are either elected themselves or serve as the surrogate of an official who is elected. In addition, the curriculum of a public school will reflect public concerns in ways that promote or encourage a public good. Finally, a public school is one that promotes a reasonable level of autonomy by introducing students to forms of life that are different than those they are familiar with, and by developing skills of performance and deliberation that will enable them to make informed and reasonable choices about their own futures.

This list in not meant to be exhaustive, and there are obviously many gaps that need to be filled it. However, it is meant to be suggestive and to provide a way to think about public support for schools. To begin to think about what makes a school public and to do so in degrees rather than in absolutes might allow more nuanced thinking about how such schools could be supported. For example, given a school that falls far on the private side of the scale, the school might protect its exclusivity by requiring parents to pay a high tuition, but the government might require a marginal amount of those funds to be transferred to other areas and used to raise the level of education for schools that meet the standards set for a public school but that are under funded (according to some reasonable standard that takes into account the needs of the children they serve, and the real choices they have).

Moving somewhat closer to the public side of the scale, by allowing schools in exclusive neighborhoods, supported by property tax and governed by elected school boards, to tax citizens as high as they will allow, is to provide wider recognition to the principle that private investments in education can serve public goods, while stemming the exodus from these relatively public schools. Nevertheless, by taxing these districts a portion of what they spend on their own schools and using the funds to address educationally needy and more inclusive schools, the principle of equality is addressed. Hopefully, the educational gap is narrowed. Moreover, as the school becomes less exclusive, taxes would be reduced. Hence, there is an incentive to move the school toward the public side of the scale. This kind of scheme has the advantage of acknowledging that education is a public good and encouraging private citizens to contribute to that good by spending their own resources on education. It also provides serious recognition to the concern for equality and that the public good in liberal democratic societies requires an education system that encourages autonomy and the development of talent at all levels. When choice is contextualized in this way, it can satisfy the right of parents and the obligation of society to promote equality and a level playing field.

There is, of course, reason to approach any plan with considerable caution. This one is no exception. There are clearly experts in educational finance who would have sounder ideas about how to serve these two

236   *School Choice Policies and Outcomes*

principles, nevertheless, serve them we must, and I hope that this paper helps bring them in conversation with one another.

Notes for Chapter 10

1. Milton Friedman, "The Role of Government in Education," in *Economics and the Public Interest*, ed. Robert A. Solo (New Brunswick, NJ: Rutgers University Press, 1955); John E. Coons, William H. Clune III, and Stephen D. Sugarman, *Private Wealth and Public Education* (Cambridge, MA: Belknap Press of Harvard University Press, 1970).

2. Harry Brighouse, *School Choice and Social Justice* (Oxford: Oxford University Press, 2000).

3. John Dewey, *Democracy and Education* (New York: Macmillan, 1916).

4. John Rawls, *A Theory of Justice* (Cambridge, MA: Harvard University Press, 1971).

5. Warren Buffett, interviewed by Charlie Rose, *Charlie Rose*, originally aired July 10, 2006.

6. John E. Chubb and Terry M. Moe, *Politics, Markets, and America's Schools* (Washington, DC: Brookings Institution, 1990).

7. Rob Reich, "Common Schooling and Educational Choice as a Response to Pluralism," this volume.

8. Brighouse, *School Choice*; Samuel Bowles and Herbert Gintis, *Schooling in Capitalist America: Educational Reform and the Contradictions of Economic Life* (New York: Basic Books, 1976).

9. Reich, "Common Schooling."

10. John Stuart Mill, *On Liberty* (New York: Appleton-Century-Crofts Inc., 1947), 108.

11. Harry Brighouse, "School Choice and Educational Equality," this volume.

12. Courtney Bell, "Social Class Differences in School Choice: The Role of Preferences," this volume.

13. Christopher Lubienski and Sarah Theule Lubienski, *Charter, Private, Public Schools and Academic Achievement: New Evidence from NAEP Mathematics Data*, Occasional Paper No. 111 (New York: National Center for the Study of Privatization in Education, 2006).

14. *Zellman v. Simmons-Harris*, 536 U. S. 639 (2002).

15. *Pierce v. Society of Sisters*, 268 U. S. 354-35 (1925).

16. Harry Brighouse, *School Choice and Social Justice* (Oxford: Oxford University Press, 2000).

17. Courtney Bell, "Social Class Differences in School Choice."

18. Jonathan Kozol, *Savage Inequalities: Children in America's Schools* (New York: HarperPerennial, 1992).

19. Reich, "Common Schooling"; Brighouse, "School Choice and Educational Equality."

Contributors

Walter Feinberg (Co-editor) is the Charles Dunn Hardie Professor of Philosophy of Education at the University of Illinois. He works in the area of citizenship education and has written on the issue of Choice and Religion. His work has been published by the leading journals in philosophy of education as well as by Cambridge, Oxford, and Yale University Presses. He was recently the keynote speaker at the British Philosophy of Education Society 2004. He gave the John Dewey Lecture 2006 at the John Dewey Society annual meeting as well as the Freemann Butts Lecture at the American Educational Studies Association meeting in 2005.

Christopher Lubienski (Co-editor) is Associate Professor of Educational Organization at the University of Illinois, and has completed his post-doctoral studies in the Advanced Studies Fellowship Program at Brown University. His research focuses on the political economy of market-based education reform. His work on school choice has been published in the *American Educational Research Journal*, the *American Journal of Education*, the *Congressional Quarterly Researcher*, *Educational Policy*, *Equity and Excellence in Education*, *Phi Delta Kappan*, and *Teachers College Record*. He has previously been named as a post-doctoral fellow by the National Academy of Education.

Kathleen Knight Abowitz is Associate Professor of Educational Leadership at Miami University of Ohio, where she studies social foundations, philosophy of education, and educational ethics. Professor Abowitz earned her PhD in the philosophy of education from the University of Virginia in 1996. She has published articles on school choice in *The Clearing House, Educational Theory*, and *Kappa Delta Pi Record*. Her research interests include citizenship education and pedagogical issues in teaching the social foundations of education.

Courtney Ann Bell, Assistant Professor, the University of Connecticut, received her doctorate in Educational Policy from Michigan State

University in 2004, where she studied with some of the leading scholars investigating school choice. She was a Spencer Foundation Dissertation Fellow and was awarded the American Educational Research Association Dissertation of the Year award from Division L. Her work focuses on the relationships between policy and practice in school choice, teacher professional development, and teacher preparation for diverse learners. Bell has published several articles on educational reform, which appear in journals such as *Equity and Excellence in Education* and *The Urban Review*. Her recent projects include a national study of teacher learning and a state study of Connecticut's school choice programs.

Harry Brighouse is Professor of Philosophy and Affiliate Professor of Education Policy Studies at the University of Wisconsin, Madison. He formerly held the Chair in Philosophy of Education at the Institute of Education at the University of London. He is author of *School Choice and Social Justice*, perhaps the definitive philosophical work of school choice, and of *On Education*. His work ranges from political philosophy, through philosophy of education, to critical commentary on education policy. He is currently working on a book with Adam Swift about the place of the family in liberal theory, entitled *Family Values*.

Liz Gordon is Pro-Chancellor at Massey University, and the managing director at Network Research in Christchurch, New Zealand. She spent six years as a Member of Parliament in New Zealand between 1996 and 2002. Previously, Dr. Gordon was Lecturer and Senior Lecturer at, respectively, Massey University and the University of Canterbury, and a Visiting Fellow at the Institute of Education at the University of London. Her work in analyzing processes of educational reform in New Zealand has been of ongoing international importance. With Geoff Whitty, she cowrote a paper in 1997 on school reform and school choice, which has been widely cited since. She argues that there is a need for a large-scale international project to examine and compare school system reforms across a range of countries. She has worked with colleagues in the United States and other countries to develop a proposal for such a study.

Kenneth R. Howe is Professor in the Educational Foundations, Policy, and Practice program area, and director of the Education and the Public Interest Center at the University of Colorado at Boulder. Professor Howe specializes in education policy, professional ethics, and philosophy of education. He has conducted research on a variety of topics, ranging from the quantitative/qualitative debate to a philosophical examination of constructivism to a defense of multicultural education. His current research is focused on education policy analysis, particularly school choice. His books include the *Ethics of Special Education* (with Ofelia Miramontes), *Understanding Equal Education: Social Justice, Democracy and Schooling*, *Values in Evaluation and Social Research* (with Ernest House), and *Closing Methodological Divides: Toward Democratic Educational Research*. Professor Howe teaches courses in the social foundations of education, the philosophy of education, and philosophical issues in educational research.

Bekisizwe Ndimande is Assistant Professor of Curriculum & Instruction and African Studies at the University of Illinois at Urbana-Champaign. He received a PhD in Curriculum & Instruction from the University of Wisconsin in 2005. Dr. Ndimande's research interests include the politics of curriculum and examining the policies and practices in post-apartheid desegregated public schools and the implications of school choice for Black communities in South Africa. He is currently a Visiting Fellow in the Faculty of Education at the University of Pretoria.

Rob Reich is Assistant Professor of Political Science, Ethics in Society, and, by courtesy, Education at Stanford University. He is the author of *Bridging Liberalism and Multiculturalism in American Education* (University of Chicago Press, 2002) and coauthor of *Democracy at Risk: How Political Choices Undermine Citizen Participation and What We Can Do About It* (Brookings Institution Press, 2005). Currently, Reich's research focuses on the ideals of equality and adequacy in education policy and reform, as well as topics in ethics, public policy, and philanthropy. Prior to pursuing his doctorate, he was a sixth-grade teacher at Rusk Elementary School in Houston, Texas.

Janelle Scott is Assistant Professor in the Educational Leadership program at New York University's Steinhardt School of Culture, Education, and Human Development. A former urban elementary school teacher, Scott earned a PhD in Education Policy from the University of California at Los Angeles. Scott's research considers the politics of urban education with an emphasis on issues of race, class, and equity. Research areas include charter schools, educational privatization, and the impact of school choice reforms on high poverty communities of color. She is the editor of *School Choice and Diversity: What the Evidence Says* (Teachers College, 2005).

Index

accountability
  achievement, 4, 6, 64, 86, 88, 102,
    149, 187, 221, 229
  consumers, 227–228
  operating guidelines, 87
achievement research, 6, 12, 65, 108,
  187
admissions and enrollment, 53, 55,
  137–141, 169, 181, 186, 190, 199,
  208–210

bureaucracy, 15, 150–151, 154–155,
  168, 202

charter schools, 1, 8, 67–70, 106, 124,
  137, 151–153, 155–160, 181, 184
child's freedom and autonomy, 4–5,
  16, 28, 32, 35, 104, 220–221, 228
choice
  advocacy, 63–66, 109, 153, 166
  as political movement, 15, 100–101,
    153, 166, 221
  choosers and nonchoosers, 6, 8,
    107, 231
  individual freedom, 3, 4, 10–11, 15
  international comparisons, 49–50,
    100, 105, 122, 177–191, 197–210
  legal justification, 22, 25, 36–38
  residential choice, 22, 47–48, 223,
    233
  as civil right, 101, 153, 157, 169, 219
citizenship, 1, 25, 31–32
class, 13, 15, 121–145, 179, 182, 199,
  204–209, 232–233
Colorado school choice, 68–69

commodities, consumer goods, 42–43,
  50, 103, 110–111
common school, 5, 11, 21–38, 234–235
community, 8, 9, 15, 93, 171
competition, 5, 43, 108, 188
conservatism, 62–74, 101, 153, 184,
  207–209, 231
conservative foundations and other
  organizations, 11, 12, 63–66, 70,
  161–163
consumer information, 8, 12–13,
  44–45, 99–114, 121–145
cultural capital, 131–136, 178–179,
  204–207
curriculum and instruction, 88, 93,
  112, 127, 153, 168, 184–185, 187

democratic participation, 4, 5, 73, 155,
  170
disadvantaged families and students,
  10, 13, 49, 54, 63, 68, 79, 86,
  101–102, 129, 153, 184, 197–210,
  219, 224–226
diversity. *See* pluralism

educational management organization
  (EMO), 150–174
effectiveness, 5, 6, 44–45, 66, 101–102,
  108
  school ratings, 105, 111–113, 182
efficiency, 5, 6, 14, 43, 44, 52, 101–101,
  157, 202
environmentalism, 12, 80
equality, 11, 16, 17, 49–58, 74, 198–
  212, 220–233

equity, 7, 16, 65, 104, 171, 188, 221, 220–233
funding issues, 56, 87, 150, 157, 166, 170, 185, 198–212, 222–223, 229
gender
    school leadership, 14, 149–174

innovation, 1, 168–169, 181, 184, 190

liberalism, 21–28, 63–71

magnet school, 138–141, 181
market dynamics and theory, 2, 7, 13, 44, 46, 101–103, 220–221, 227–228
marketing schools, 107, 110–111

Ohio school choice, 79–95, 161–162
open-enrollment plans, 2, 55

parents
    child's autonomy interests, 4–5, 16, 28, 32, 35, 104, 220–221, 228
    expectations, 13–14, 121–145
    liberty interests and rights, 21–22, 30, 37–38, 44, 90, 101–104, 178, 197–212, 219–236
    parental participation and input, 5, 92, 93, 121–145, 155, 169, 185, 190
    parents as consumers, 2, 13, 99–114, 180, 203–209
    preferences, 13, 22, 30, 44, 103–104, 121–145, 205–206, 223–224
    resources, capital, 13–14, 126–131, 207–209, 231
    respect afforded to, 82, 87
pluralism, 4, 10–11, 21–38, 92, 171, 224
politics. *See* choice as political movement
poor. *See* disadvantaged

power, 14–15, 177–191
private schools, 16, 47, 86–87, 94, 106, 108, 128, 228–229, 232
producer advantages, 44, 46, 56, 112–114
profit motive, 1, 150, 161
public purposes of education, 5, 8, 11, 25, 29, 50, 104, 109, 171, 220–222, 226–229, 234–235

race
    parental preferences, 121–123, 183, 203–209, 219
    racial sorting, 2, 107, 122, 182, 197–212
    school leadership, 14, 149–173
rational choice, 101–103, 105–107, 121, 137
research
    methodology, 6, 67
    school effects, 57, 66, 67–72, 108, 177–178, 190

segregation, 12, 29, 49, 56, 67, 69, 72, 151, 181–183, 197–212, 219–220, 224
social capital, 8, 131–136, 150, 157, 161, 182, 209
social justice, 41–58, 79–95, 153, 211, 222–225
sorting, 7, 113, 169, 182, 186
South Africa, 197–212
special needs students, 53–54, 127, 156
sustainability, 12, 83, 88, 90

unions, 70–71, 178
US Department of Education, 66, 114, 187
vouchers, 1, 51–53, 72, 79, 82, 85–95, 152, 181

6447432R0

Made in the USA
Lexington, KY
20 August 2010